You Never Step into the Same Pulpit Twice

You Never Step into the Same Pulpit Twice

Preaching from a Perspective of Process Theology

RONALD J. ALLEN

CASCADE *Books* · Eugene, Oregon

YOU NEVER STEP INTO THE SAME PULPIT TWICE
Preaching from the Perspective of Process Theology

Cascade Books
An Imprint of Wipf and Stock Publishers
199 W. 8th Ave., Suite 3
Eugene, OR 97401

www.wipfandstock.com

PAPERBACK ISBN: 978–1-7252–5965–2
HARDCOVER ISBN: 978–1-7252–5966–9
EBOOK ISBN: 978–1-7252–5967–6

Cataloguing-in-Publication data:

Names: Allen, Ronald J. (Ronald James), 1949–, author.

Title: You never step into the same pulpit twice : preaching from the perspective of process theology / Ronald J. Allen.

Description: Eugene, OR: Cascade Books, 2022. | Includes bibliographical references.

Identifiers: ISBN 978–1-7252–5965–2 (paperback). | ISBN 978–1-7252–5966–9 (hardcover). | ISBN 978–1-7252–5967–6 (ebook).

Subjects: LSCH: Preaching. | Process theology. | Theology.

Classification: BV4211.2 A45 2022 (print). | BV4211.2 (ebook).

VERSION NUMBER 061722

Scripture quotations are taken from the New Revised Standard Version Bible, copyright 1989, Division of Christian Education of the National Council of the Churches of Christ in the United States of America. Used by permission. All rights reserved.

Figure 1: "Voices in the Circle of the Preaching Conversation."

Circle Computer Icons Black And White Shape Set. Clip Art is a completely free picture material, which can be downloaded and shared unlimitedly. https://www.seekpng.com/ipng/u2w7w7t4q8u2t4u2_circle-computer-icons-black-and-white-shape-set/ (accessed September 17, 2021).

For
Eleanor Loreane Allen
Lovingly Known as "Ms. Busy"
Always Asking Questions
Sparkling Brown Eyes
Happy Big Sister
Faster than 5G

Contents

Abbreviations

TORAH, PROPHETS, AND WRITINGS

Gen	Genesis
Exod	Exodus
Lev	Leviticus
Num	Numbers
Deut	Deuteronomy
Judg	Judges
Ruth	Ruth
1–2 Sam	1–2 Samuel
1–2 Kgs	1–2 Kings
1–2 Chr	1–2 Chronicles
Ezra	Ezra
Neh	Nehemiah
Job	Job
Ps/Pss	Psalms
Prov	Proverbs
Eccl	Ecclesiastes
Song	Song of Songs
Isa	Isaiah
Jer	Jeremiah
Lam	Lamentations
Ezek	Ezekiel
Dan	Daniel
Hos	Hosea
Joel	Joel
Amos	Amos
Obad	Obadiah
Jonah	Jonah
Mic	Mic

Hab	Habakkuk
Zeph	Zephaniah
Hag	Haggai
Zech	Zechariah
Mal	Malachi

GOSPELS AND LETTERS

Matt	Matthew
Mark	Mark
Luke	Luke
John	John
Acts	Acts
Rom	Romans
1–2 Cor	1–2 Corinthians
Gal	Galatians
Eph	Ephesians
Phil	Philippians
Col	Colossians
1–2 Thess	1–2 Thessalonians
1–2 Tim	1–2 Timothy
Titus	Titus
Phlm	Philemon
Heb	Hebrews
Jas	James
1–2 Pet	1–2 Peter
1–2–3 John	1–2–3 John
Rev	Revelation

Illustrations

Introduction

WHEN I BEGAN FORMAL theological study as an entering student in college in 1967, it was almost *verboten* to use the first-person singular pronoun "I" in academic writing. Preachers were discouraged from speaking in the first person, though once in a while a preacher could be excused for saying, "Pardon a personal reference . . ."

In keeping with cultural changes over the decades, the "I" has become more common. I speak a lot in the first-person singular in this book for two reasons. First is to take personal responsibility for what I say. It is easy for an author to hide behind passive grammatical constructions and indirect expressions. Second, every theologian's journey is influenced by autobiographical elements that provide context for understanding what has happened in that person's thinking. I hope the personal voice comes less from egocentrism and more from an interest in providing context as well as offering a story with which some others may identify.

A PERSONAL STORY

I am a fourth-generation member of the Christian Church (Disciples of Christ). I began kindergarten in 1955 and went straight through: high school (1967), university (1971), seminary (1974), and graduate school (1977). Personal testimonies have not been a significant part of Eurocentric Disciples life, but I begin this book with such a personal witness.

I began attending church the first Sunday of my life when my parents took me to the nursery of First Christian Church (Disciples of Christ), Poplar Bluff, Missouri, a county seat on the eastern edge of the Ozark Mountains. I was in worship and Bible School every Sunday morning, and in youth group and worship every Sunday evening. Christian Youth Fellowship was a center of my social life. I was immersed at the age of ten (an age of accountability). The Disciples break the bread and drink from the cup

1

every week: to this day, a week without receiving the loaf and the cup is a week without a compass.

Our family had two businesses—dentistry and law. My uncle was a circuit judge. The family assumed I would follow one of these paths. But I was hooked by the congregation of my youth in ways that would not let me go as I entered young adulthood. To use language I later learned from Bernard Meland, Christian community helped me feel something More in the universe that we call God.[1] I felt a great assurance week after week when we broke the bread and drank the cup together. I received a sense of a sustaining power for life. I came away with the sense that life itself could be "more" and that I had a mission to help it be so.

"I AM FROM MISSOURI. YOU HAVE TO SHOW ME"

But, at the same time, I could not get away from issues and questions that my engagement with Christian faith continued to raise. Some questions came from what I then perceived as tension between science and the Bible. The world came into being in seven days (Gen 1:1–2:4)? Not according to my science textbook. The sea opened and a large group walked across on dry ground while the sea drowned an army that was pursuing them (Exod 14:1—15:20)? That did not happen in Vietnam. An axe head floating on the water (2 Kgs 6:1–7)? Really? Someone came back from the dead? Not in Poplar Bluff.

My issues with the Bible were not confined to science. I loved Isaiah saying the time would come when we beat our swords into plowshares (Isa 2:4). But Joel sees beating plowshares into swords. (Joel 3:10). Now, which is it?

I later learned that other issues had to do with philosophy, theology, and ethics. How could we know what God is really like? Why does God do what God does—and why does God not do some things I thought God should do, such as end the war in Vietnam or grant civil rights to all people or feed the starving children whose haunting eyes looked out at us from the posters on the wall of the church building? How could God order the killing of the Canaanites? Why did our family friend suffer an excruciating death from cancer? If Jesus ascended, where did he go in a universe that our science teachers taught us is ever expanding? What can I count on God doing to make things better, and what do I have to do?

---

1. Meland, *Fallible Forms and Symbols*, ix, 43, 48–49, 174–75.

As we know so well today, social location plays into who we are. The motto of Missouri is the "Show Me State." According to legend, a Missourian in the congressional House of Representatives listened to a series of speeches and concluded, "Frothy eloquence neither convinces nor satisfies me. I am from Missouri. You have to show me."[2] In my soul, I am this kind of Missourian.

As I thought more and more about many of the standard religious views so popular in the Mid-South, I concluded I could not accept many of them. Furthermore, I was not alone. One day in the quiet of the kitchen my mother confessed to me, "I just can't believe a big fish swallowed a person and then burped him up on the shore." She could not believe a lot of things. Add to these personal elements the fact that our Disciples tradition often emphasizes the importance of the rational element in faith.

I have been ever grateful to God that our minister and our Bible School teacher, respectively Roger K. Guy and Robert L. Sutton, Sr., created safe spaces in the church to bring such questions into the open. They invited me to stop by the church building one day after school and said the elders had been talking about young people in the youth group who might consider going into the ministry, and I was one. They liked my open spirit and believed that God could use it to connect with other open spirits.

I did not say "Yes" at that moment, but I came to see that my "fit" with ministry was much better than with dentistry or law. I decided to give my life to a More whom I powerfully felt and through whom I experienced assurance, grace, and power but whom I did not fully understand and about whom I had questions and issues.[3]

THE MOVEMENT TO PROCESS CONCEPTUALITY GRADUALLY OCCURS

I wanted a faith. But I wanted a faith in which I could truly believe. I wanted a faith in which I could be confident. I wanted a faith that would be true to my experience, especially one that could make sense in light of what I believed about the world by way of science. I wanted a faith that would stand up to the toughest moral questions and that illuminated my deep intuition of Something in the universe that was bigger than the biggest things I could imagine.

2. Rossiter, "I'm from Missouri," 16.

3. Unlike many clergy, I have never had a direct, personal experience in which I felt God calling me to the ministry. Such call as I have had has been through the life of the community.

In the College of the Bible, Phillips University, Enid, Oklahoma, I read a little Whitehead for the first time in History of Philosophy but, frankly, I found it obscure. By contrast, in the Philosophy of Art course, Robert L. Simpson assigned Susanne K. Langer, *Philosophy in a New Key*, a book dedicated to Whitehead, "my great Teacher and Friend."[4] Langer illuminated not only my experience of art but my whole understanding of perception. Langer's work is not theologically oriented and could not resolve my theological issues, but it opened the doorway into the wider room of perceiving the world through a process lens.

At the College of the Bible and subsequently at Union Theological Seminary, New York, I made acquaintance with the theological families prominent in the late 1960s: evangelicalism, liberalism, neo-orthodoxy, existentialism, early liberation theologies, and process. Daniel Day Williams, who had recently published *The Spirit and the Forms of Love*, represented process at Union, but I was caught up studying the Bible from the standpoint of historical criticism, and protesting the war in Vietnam, and did not give the attention to theological matters that they deserved.[5] When pursuing graduate work at Drew University in preaching, and in Gospels and Letters, I was fortunate to work with Charles L. Rice who appreciated Langer and was oriented to Tillich, and with Neill Q. Hamilton who made the hermeneutical move from the first-century apocalyptic theology in the Gospels and Letters to contemporary theological appropriation in a way that resembles a process perspective.[6]

By the time I become cominister with my spouse, Linda McKiernan-Allen, at First Christian Church (Disciples of Christ), Grand Island, Nebraska (1977), I had enough process to be careful about what I said (and did not say). For example, in the opening prayer in worship, I would never pray, "Come, O God, and be present here today" because I interpreted that prayer as indicating that God might not be present. In my mind, God is always present everywhere and does not need to be "prayed into the worship space."

However, like too many ministers, I let myself get trapped into thinking theologically on the fly while preparing and preaching in multiple services each week, teaching two or three times, managing programs in

4. Langer, *Philosophy in a New Key*, iv.

5. Williams, *Spirit and Forms of Love*. At that time, I did not realize his *God's Grace and Man's Hope* was a signal work.

6. Hamilton, *Jesus for a No-God World*, 169–203. In conversation, Professor Hamilton indicated that process assumptions lie behind this hermeneutical proposal. At Drew, I returned to Langer as the basis for a dissertation: "Feeling and Form in Exegesis and Preaching."

the congregation, making pastoral calls, recruiting new members, keeping up with administrative details, and trying to make a witness in the wider community. I did my best to keep abreast with the scholarly literature in preaching and in Gospels and Letters so that my exegetical and homiletical perspectives enlarged. But my theological method remained only partially articulated.

I would not come to real clarity and confidence in theological perspective and method until I joined the faculty at Christian Theological Seminary in 1982 and engaged in daily theological conversation with colleagues up and down the row of faculty offices and with students in the classroom and in the cafeteria. I came to Whitehead this time through extensive conversation with Clark M. Williamson and J. Gerald Janzen, process thinkers who, respectively, taught systematic theology and Torah, Prophets, and Writings. Others added to the mix, including K. Brynolf Lyon, Marti Steussy, Michael Miller, Brian Grant, Charles Allen, and especially Helene Tallon Russell.Although a student at the time, Charles R. Blaisdell became a teacher for me.

"MY SOUL WAS RESTLESS, UNTIL I CAME TO REST IN PROCESS"

To adapt a phrase from Augustine, "My soul was restless, until I came to rest in process."[7] The notion of "coming to rest in process" sounds like a non sequitur. I was restless continuing to search for a reliable theological perspective. A reliable theological interpretation of life began to fill out as I encountered the fundamental idea that life is ever in the process of becoming. In addition, I received the vision of a God within life process who is not distant, unchanging, and all-powerful, but is ever becoming and ever offering possibilities for the good of the world. This God cannot do anything and everything. God cannot, for instance, end evil with a single stroke. But every possibility from God is for love, peace, justice, and abundance.

I felt I was floundering in the swift current of theology. But my colleagues threw me a lifebuoy made of process thought. This theology gives me a perspective within which to keep my head above water, a sense of the currents flowing through the river of life, and the theological perceptions and skills for navigating those currents so that the river can lift and carry me while I can avoid many of the rocks and whirlpools. Whitehead sought to set out "a coherent, logical, necessary system of general ideas in terms of

7. Adapted from Augustine, *Confessions* 1.1.

which every element of our experience can be interpreted."[8] I have found that hope fulfilled in living in light of the process vision.

Liberation theology began to get its feet just as I was beginning theological study. I have always resonated with its insistence on liberation, but aspects of liberation theology per se have always troubled me, especially its binary opposition of the oppressed and oppressor, and the ways in which it so often caricatures Jewish people, practices, and institutions as oppressive and from which Jesus came to liberate us. Process aims for liberation in a comprehensive sense, and it does so in a way that faces up to the repressive realities of life while seeking inclusive well-being through creative transformation into communities of mutual support. Process re-envisions relationships not only in the human community but all relationships in the cosmos.

I also respect the cry to "resist!" However, more than resistance is needed. Process offers a positive invitation towards communities of love, justice, peace, and abundance.

To be sure, I know process thought puts off many Christians. I have even heard Barthians and others refer to a few advocates of process theology as "flakes." Process does not provide the kind of fixed security and certitude that traditional forms of theology claim to offer. A student who subscribed to a traditional line of Christian thought asked, "What is the point in believing in the weeny God of process theology?" Moreover, the vocabulary of process philosophy—especially in the writings of Alfred North Whitehead—is obscure and difficult. Another student lamented, "Why should I have to learn a whole new language just to talk about God?" In conversation, a friend vividly said, "I would rather have a faith rooted in the Bible than in early twentieth-century English philosophy." This book is my answer to such questions and issues.

Per Whitehead above, I find in process a vision of God and the world that makes theological sense of the full range of experience—including life's most difficult moments and questions. It honors the best insights of the Bible and of wider Christian tradition. It respects others and believes that conversation with others can open fresh windows of possibility. At the same time, process is not imprisoned by ideas from Christian tradition that seem contradictory or that no longer seem true to experience. Process offers a hope in which I can truly believe. In the language of Clark M. Williamson, process offers an interpretation of life that is both deeply faithful and "intellectually and morally credible."[9]

---

8. Whitehead, *Process and Reality*, 3.

9. Williamson, "Preaching as Conversation," 72.

Moreover, I find that process theology is not only a trustworthy guide to theology and life, but it also offers engaging and faithful ways to preach.[10] Process theology generates perspectives on hermeneutics and preaching that are a welcome lens through which to engage the Bible and that offer preachers life-giving options for sermons. However, to this point in time, the field of preaching has generated only a few articles, chapters, and books that articulate process approaches to preaching. For instance, Norman Pittenger, a popular process theologian in an earlier generation, wrote two volumes that interpret preaching in a process spirit, though Pittenger keeps explicit process perspective largely in the background: *Proclaiming Christ Today* and *Preaching the Gospel*.[11] Embodying the relational nature of the process worldview, a community of scholars—William A. Beardless, John B. Cobb Jr., David J. Lull, Russel Pregeant, Theodore Weeden Sr., and Barry A. Woodbridge—jointly authored *Biblical Peaching on the Death of Jesus*, which interprets preaching through a process lens and then shows how that mode of preaching plays out in extended case studies of the death of Jesus in Scripture.[12] Marjorie Suchocki offers an explicit interpretation of the preaching event from a process perspective in *The Whispered Word*.[13] No one will ever match her eloquence on the subject of preaching. Clark M. Williamson and I identify implications of process for articulating models of God, systemic injustice, and biblical interpretation in *A Credible and Timely Word*.[14] We also examine preaching and other aspects of worship from a process point of view in *Adventures of the Spirit*.[15] Casey Sigmon draws extensively on process theology in her PhD dissertation at Vanderbilt University, "Engaging the Gadfly: A Process Homilecclesiology for a Digital Age," and in her recently published "Preaching from the Perspective of the Process Theological Family."[16] Despite the promise of process, the current monograph is the first fully developed exposition of a process homiletic in almost a generation.[17]

---

10. Each theological family generates approaches to preaching that are characteristic of that family. For a simplified overview of major historic and contemporary theological families and their distinctive perspectives on preaching, see R. J. Allen, *Thinking Theologically*. For more detailed consideration, see R. J. Allen, *Preaching the Manifold Grace*, 2 vols.

11. Pittenger, *Proclaiming Christ Today* and *Preaching the Gospel*.

12. Beardslee et al., *Biblical Preaching*.

13. Suchocki, *Whispered Word*.

14. Williamson and R. J. Allen, *Credible and Timely Word*.

15. Williamson and R. J. Allen, *Adventures of the Spirit*.

16. Sigmon, "Engaging the Gadfly"; Sigmon, "Preaching from the Perspective."

17. I have added two short pieces to this literature, "Preaching as Conversation

While process theologians share many things in common, the particular contributors to this movement have their own distinguishing and differing points of view. I do not presume to offer the definitive homiletic arising from process theology. The present volume is really "Ron Allen's take on preaching from a process perspective." Hence, the subtitle of this book is not *Preaching from **the** Perspective of Process Theology* but is *Preaching **a** Perspective on Process Theology*. I try to follow the main currents of process theology, but here and there idiosyncratic points of view slip into the mix.[18]

PROCESS THEOLOGY
AND CONVERSATIONAL PREACHING

Current scholarship in preaching broadly distinguishes between two kinds of preaching: sermons that *proclaim* interpretations of Christian life to congregations and *sermons that are genuinely conversational* in character. Most preachers today operate in the proclamatory mode. In proclamation the preacher declares something the congregation should believe about God, the world, and the congregational response. Through exegesis the preacher typically discovers what a biblical text calls people to believe, commends that belief to the congregation, and applies what it means in practical terms to the life of the congregation. Proclamation is not simply a style but is a theological mindset. It can be expressed in wide range of sermon styles from those that are "in your face" through sermons that are straightforward and direct though not "in your face" to sermons that are artful and even inductive and indirect.

I need to say clearly that process theology can be preached in the proclamatory way. A preacher can announce a process God and a process world with sermonic finality similar to Barthian preachers announcing news from the God from above. The process preacher's theological content with regard to God and God's activity in the world and the human response would be quite different from that of, say, evangelical or neo-orthodox preachers, but the clarity and confidence of the process preacher's theological claims could be similar.

While the preacher in the process tradition can approach the pulpit in a proclamatory way, I do think a conversational approach is more natural for a preacher informed by process.[19] In the conversational approach, the

among Proposals" and "Preaching as Invitation."

18. Roland Faber offers a taxonomy of different nuances among process interpreters in *God as Poet*, 17–44.

19. While we have a serious conversation about conversational preaching in Chapter

preacher engages in a conversation (1) with the text, (2) with other voices in tradition and (3) with contemporary theology, (4) with the congregation, (5) with the preacher's own life, and (6) with voices beyond the congregation. Preacher and congregation search together for a theological interpretation of life. When process theology is a voice in the conversation, the search is for an interpretation of life that points towards optimum becoming, or inclusive well-being for all.[20]

As is developed more fully in subsequent pages, this conversational approach is indebted to the theological method of mutual critical correlation as articulated by David Tracy.[21] For Tracy the community first identifies what the biblical text invites the congregation to believe and do in the context of its worldview, and then compares and contrasts those things with what people today believe and would like to do in the context of our worldviews. The community then determines what parts of the witness of the text should be formative for today and those parts that are no longer authoritative (usually for theological/ethical reasons.). Simultaneously, the community determines the parts of the text that challenge what today's community believes and prefers to do and that correct today's perspectives. The conversation involves give-and-take between then and now, and it often results in the community shifting its perspective on how the biblical material relates to today as well as how people today understand ourselves. The conversation might lead the preacher to affirm the text, to affirm parts of the text but to reject others, or to reject the authority of the text altogether.

In the proclamatory model, the outcome is predetermined. The preacher will develop the sermon to articulate the claim of the text (as the preacher discovers it through exegesis and hermeneutics). In conversational preaching, the outcome depends upon what happens in the conversation.

In this book, the biblical text is at one end of the correlation. Process theology is at the other. Multiple voices of tradition, other theologies, congregation, preacher, and world are in the middle. Frankly, such a conversation can be messy. But then, life is often messy.

3, I now call attention to O. W. Allen, *Homiletic of All Believers*, as the best introduction to conversational preaching. O. W. Allen and R. J. Allen expand this approach in *The Sermon without End*. Additional literature is given in *Sermon without End*, 108–14, and in R. J. Allen, *Interpreting the Gospel*, 229, "Chapter 6," note 2. Doug Pagitt offers an approach to preaching that is conversational in character in his *Preaching Re-Imagined* (reissued as *Preaching in the Inventive Age*).

20. The term "inclusive well-being" comes from Marjorie Suchocki as a summary of God's purposes for the communities of humankind and nature. Suchocki, *Fall to Violence*, 13, 18–19, 42–44, esp. 66–80, 86, 101–11, 158; Suchocki, *End of Evil*, 122–30, 133.

21. For discussion, see R. J. Allen, "Note on Mutual Critical Correlation."

In my work, I have long tried to hear others from the perspectives from which they seek to be understood. I have tried to reflect critically on viewpoints under discussion, including identifying strengths and weaknesses, gains and losses. I try to continue that pattern here with respect to other theological families as well as to other voices within the process household.

THE TITLE

The title of the book is adapted from the pre-Socratic philosopher Heraclitus (about 535–475 BCE) whose thoughts are preserved in fragments. In one such fragment, the pre-Socratic philosopher says, "You cannot not step twice into the same river."[22] Heraclitus apparently emphasizes here that life is always in flux.

In a similar way a preacher can never stand in the same pulpit twice because the elements of the event of preaching are always in process. From one occasion of preaching to the next, the cultural context is different. The dynamics of the congregation are different. The preacher is different. The differences may not be of the same magnitude as the differences between night and day, but even small differences can significantly change perception, expressiveness, receptivity, and possibilities. The preacher needs to be aware of such changes and to adapt within the range of the preacher's theological commitments, keeping in mind, of course, that changes in perception may prompt the preacher to reassess her or his commitments.

THE PROCESS GOD AND THE PROCESS SERMON

The nature and purpose of the sermon takes is character from the nature and purpose of God. According to Whitehead, "the nature of God is dipolar."[23] God has both a primordial nature and a consequent nature. While identified by two designations, the primordial and consequent natures of God are not essentially different but are two completely interrelated dimensions. The primordial nature of God is God's ongoing concern to seek the inclusive well-being of all things. This broad purpose never changes. Through the consequent nature, God prehends the world and adapts the specific expression of that purpose to particular situations. God offers particular situations

---

22. Cited in Wheelwright, *Heraclicus*, 29. For "You Could Not Step Twice into the Same River."

23. Whitehead, *Process and Reality*, 345.

distinctive opportunities for inclusive well-being according to the possibilities that are available in the situations.

The primordial and consequent natures never work against one another. They are always consistent. The consequent nature adapts the expression of the primordial will in light of what is possible in a particular local setting.

The sermon, similarly, has a dipolar character. From week to week and season to season and year to year, preaching should share the primordial aim of seeking inclusive well-being for the congregation, for the community beyond the congregation, and for the wider world. This broad purpose is always the same. Like God, however, preaching also has a consequent dimension. The preacher must help the congregation identify the specific implications for inclusive well-being that are appropriate for the actual circumstances of congregation, community, and world when the sermon is preached. The preacher helps the congregation identify and respond to the possibilities for inclusive well-being that can actually be realized in the congregation's situation.

Before leaving this subject, I stress the importance for the preacher of having an actual "primordial theology," that is, a consistent set of core convictions regarding God's nature and God's purpose that remain consistent over time. I make this remark because I continue to hear preachers whose theological utterances differ from week to week (often in response to the different lectionary readings with their differing theological views). Such preachers do not simply adapt a well-thought-out and coherent theology to new and different weekly settings (in the manner of the consequent nature) but set out different notions of God's purposes., and even different notions of the nature of God. Such preaching can be confusing to the degree that it creates a sense of theological unwell-being in the congregation that works against the very thing preaching is intended to foster, the move towards inclusive well-being.

I TRY TO SAY WHAT I MEAN

In this volume I seek to talk plainly about what I think about the nature and purposes of God, the nature and extent of divine power, appropriate responses to God's initiatives, and realistic possibilities for life. I intend to say what I really believe in language that is as precise and unmistakable as it can be. Having cut my homiletical teeth on story and image, I do think I understand many forms of aesthetic expression. I acknowledge, further, that we can say some things only by metaphor or other figurative ways of speaking.

But, in this book I intend to say as much of what I mean as clearly as possible. This approach may sometimes seem raw and unbecoming to readers who are accustomed to more elevated and nuanced articulations. But I take the risk of putting off nuanced readers for the sake of clarity.

At the same time, trying to speak as clearly as possible does not mean complete and full understanding. We finite beings cannot have infinite and unerring understanding. Postmodern thinkers rightly emphasize that every act of perception is interpretive. As Williamson says, "Human beings are always interpreting everything. To find a record of uninterpreted experience, you will have to ask an inanimate object for its autobiography."[24]

Does uninterpreted reality exist? Yes. But we do not have access to it: we never have pure, unadulterated awareness. Moreover, to use the evocative expression of Bernard Meland, "More" is going on than we can recognize or name.[25] Indeed, some things we know cannot be articulated in conventional ways. As Whitehead says, "Mothers can ponder many things in their hearts which their lips cannot express."[26]

However, many people use the fact that we cannot explain everything as an excuse to stop thinking prematurely. I would like to have a dollar for every time a student has said something like, "You can't put God in a box," "God's ways are not our ways," "Who can understand the mind of God?" While such declamations may sometimes be intended to signal limits with respect to what we can know and say about God, I often hear them as rationalizations for shutting off thought. Such verbalizations provide convenient escapes from theological struggle. Process theology does not claim to offer clinical, irrefutable statements about God. But process does seek the most adequate interpretation available for a given time and context. Indeed, the very name "process" suggests that its points of view are open to reformulation in response to new awareness. Even if we cannot fully say what could be said, we need to say as much as we can. As David Tracy says, we seek an *adequate* interpretation of life.[27]

---

24. Williamson, "Preaching as Conversation," 74. Williamson echoes Whitehead's famous statement, "Our habitual experience is a complex of failure and success in the enterprise of interpretation. If we desire a record of uninterpreted experience, we must ask a stone to record its autobiography." Whitehead, *Process and Reality*, 15.

25. Meland, *Fallible Forms and Symbols*, xiii, 43, 49, esp. 174–75.

26. Whitehead, *Religion in the Making*, 67.

27. Tracy, *Blessed Rage for Order*, 70–72, 79–81.

PROCESS THEOLOGY AND CONVERSATIONAL
PREACHING IN A POLARIZED CULTURE

Thoughtful friends raise the question of the pertinence of process theology and a conversational approach to preaching in the highly polarized culture of the United States in the 2020s.[28] This season is one of misperception, caricature, name-calling, demonization, misrepresentation, lying, and the brute use of power. While politics is the first arena to come to mind that is characterized in these ways, such impulses are also manifest in other areas, including in religion. Many religious groups are so confident of their interpretations of God's purposes that they do not believe they can dialogue with others. The only thing they believe they can do is dictate their convictions to others. They take a radical proclamatory approach to preaching with little apparent recognition of their finitude.

The threats to inclusive well-being in our era are so pervasive and savage that some people think that process theology is impotent with its emphasis on a God whose power is based on persuasion. Where process theology envisions the mutually supportive relationship of all created things, many groups today thrive on disrespect, exclusion, creating partisan division, exploitation, and threat. Moreover, such reflective friends note that the best conversations typically involve the willingness to listen to others, whereas many individuals and groups in the present ethos are unwilling to listen to others; they will only make declamations to others with no intent of being open to rethink their own perspectives. Indeed, I repeatedly experience people talking in the same space not even waiting for others to articulate their points of view before attempting to speak over them. Someone suggested to me, "We need to confront force with greater force. It's all they understand."

On the one hand, a process approach to the world in a conversational framework offers an alternative to the present antagonism as process invites us towards a world of well-being that comes from mutual support. Process thinkers do not want to be shallow triumphalists in this regard. But process theology does affirm that God never gives up, even in the face of the most hateful interactions. In every situation God invites participants towards the highest available good. The opportunity for some level of inclusive well-being is always present. The mission of the pulpit includes joining God in setting out such invitations.

Over the course of history, as far as I know, every self-centered, exploitative, and idolatrous empire which has based its rule on violence has

28. I deal with these issues in more detail in R. J. Allen, "Building Bridges," 47–58.

eventually collapsed under the weight of its own injustice. I believe the same thing can happen again to the various empires today. The invitation to inclusive well-being is irrepressible. But at what point in time might such changes occur? How many more people will suffer, some in almost unimaginable ways, while we live, occasion by occasion, towards cultural transformation? How long do we give persuasive invitations a chance before the human suffering becomes unbearable?

Having been an exponent of nonviolence most of my adult life, it is hard to write these words. But I wonder if the time may come when the path towards inclusive well-being that involves the least total suffering might pass through the raw assertion of power on the part of human agents.

I do not believe that God actively causes people to feel pain (as they would in such force-to-force confrontations). Nor do I believe God wants people to feel such pain. All suffering grieves God. Moreover, through internal relationship, suffering touches all persons and communities even when they are not conscious of it. Yet I wonder if the anguish of the relatively smaller number in the short term might lessen the suffering quotient in the world than if we wait for a long-term creative transformation. Elsewhere I have written that such an eventuality should

> take place not with the kind of flag-waving that launches wars, but by displaying the kinds of flags that mark cars in a funeral procession. A dramatic move with force would be accompanied not by bands playing patriotic marches, but by bands playing dirges. Preachers would not rally the congregation for battle but would lead in confession of sin. The mood in the pulpit would not be cheering but would be regret that the choice before the community is the lesser of two evil behaviors.[29]

For the time being, we have not reached such a point. But I do believe the extent of inclusive well-being is in a precarious situation. I have been ordained since 1974. I cannot remember a time in my ministry when the stakes of the responses to the possibilities for inclusive well-being have been higher.

I hope we will continue to point to possibilities for *inclusive* well-being (and not just the well-being of the few) in the confidence that God is ever present and ever seeking the best for all. It may not look that way on *Fox News*. But the mystery of God is not God's inscrutability. God's purposes are clear and bold. The mystery of God is God's inexhaustibility. God ever and always invites us towards inclusive well-being. The path to such

29. R. J. Allen, "Diversity Is Diverse," 19.

comprehensive well-being is still open. This moment calls for us to join God with our best and most persistent efforts.

THE CHAPTERS AHEAD

Some of the ideas in this book have appeared in my earlier writings. However, they are here under new management in that this book is my first *comprehensive* attempt to interpret the occasion of preaching through the lens of process theology. Moreover, I have already written extensively on conversational preaching in the mode of mutual critical correlation but not with the intense focus on process theology as the contemporary pole in the correlation. I name many of the categories and discussions in this volume in the language of process theology so readers can get an uninterrupted perception of how process theology functions in the ecclesial practice of preaching.

Chapter 1 traces the origin and appeal of process theology. Chapter 2 summarizes a process worldview. Chapter 3 unfolds a process understanding of preaching in concert with a conversational approach to preaching. Chapters 4 through 9 discuss a series of things that preachers do when preaching from process perspectives: identify the invitation of the text or topic (chapter 4), bring the invitation into conversation with other invitations (chapter 5), reflect in a critical theological way on the invitations, and establish a direction for ethe sermon (chapter 6), shape the sermon in a way that invites conversation (chapter 7), and embody the sermon in a conversational mode (chapter 9). I use the parable of the talents (Matt 25:14–30) as a case study beginning in chapter 4 and continuing through the rest of the volume and as the basis of a sample sermon (chapter 10).

Many Christian communities are at defining points in their lives and witnesses early in this third decade of the twenty-first century.) I place this book in the hands of the church in the hope that it will help the church consider the process alternative for preaching that has life-transforming potential. I know. I have been transformed by it.

1

The Worldview of
Process Theology

PEOPLE OFTEN BEGIN A new theological movement when they have fresh
perspectives on a mix of several things: developments in their communities, events and trends in the larger culture, evolution in philosophical and
theological ideas, and occurrences in their own lives. The birth of process
theology was such a mix involving shifts in the tectonic plates in science
from Newtonian to quantum physics, the search for a believable hope after
the catastrophic effects of World War I, and personal matters in the life of
the originating process thinker, Alfred North Whitehead. The latter include,
I believe, his gentle spirit and the death of one of his sons in World War I.[1]
Paying attention to this mix opens windows into the main themes of the
process worldview and helps us understand its distinctive character.[2]

1. While process ideas do not unfold in a single strand of development across the
centuries, historians of philosophy cite writers from the ancient world through the
nineteenth and early twentieth centuries whose ideas resemble process conceptuality. For example, Heraclitus (ca. 535–475 BCE) famously described the nature of the
universe in his memorable saying, "Everything flows and nothing abides. Everything
gives way and nothing stays fixed. You cannot step twice into the same river, for other
waters and yet others go ever flowing on" (Heraclitus, *Fragments* 20, 21, cited in Wheelwright, *Heraclitus*, 29). A classic study of the presence of process themes in the history
of philosophy is Hartshorne and Reese, *Philosophers Speak of God*. Some representative
thinkers who put forward ideas that resemble those of process thought include Ploti-
nus (205–70 CE), G.W. Leibniz (1646–1716), Charles. S. Pierce (1839–1914), William
James (1842–1910), Henri Bergson (1849–1941), and John Dewey (1859–1952).

2. In addition to Whitehead (1861–1947) the second most formative voice in process thought is that of Whitehead's student and colleague, Charles Hartshorne (1897–
2000). Whitehead's work is broadly philosophical with implications for theology. Much
of Hartshorne's work is more overtly theological than Whitehead's, but Hartshorne

This chapter briefly sketches main lines in process worldview with an eye towards their implications for preaching.[3] We begin with a focus on Whitehead's shift from the philosophical interpretation of existence reigning at the beginning of his work—that is, existence as made up of substances—to another mode of interpretation, namely, to the notion of existence comprised of life process, often characterized as "becoming."[4] We move to process theologians rethinking significant components in many traditional concepts of God.[5] The chapter concludes with a statement of why I find

is more a philosophical theologian than a theologian per se. His work concentrates on issues usually discussed under the doctrine of God and seldom engage the broad range of theological issues in the manner of contemporary systematic or constructive theologians.

3. For the sake of brevity, this book concentrates on process conceptuality with respect to Christianity in the Western world. Over the last two generations, process thinkers have discovered that they have much in common with some Eastern traditions, such as Buddhism. E.g., Cobb, *Beyond Dialogue*, and Cobb and Ives, *Emptying God*. Process thinkers are also engaging a wider range of traditions, e.g., Faber, *Becoming of God*; Griffin, "Religious Pluralism"; Williamson, "Dialogue Between Christians and Jews"; Long, "Whiteheadian Vedanta"; Lubarsky, "Covenant and Responsible Creativity."

4. Many writers provide an overview of process conceptuality. I find the following to be particularly direct and accessible (in alphabetical order): Cobb, *Christian Natural Theology*; Cobb, *Process Perspective II*, 3–29; Cobb and Griffin, *Process Theology*, 13–29; Coleman, "Introduction to Process Theology"; Epperly, *Process Theology: A Guide*; Epperly *Process Theology: Embracing Adventure*; Faber, *God as Poet*; Hosinski, *Stubborn Fact and Creative Advance*, which is unusually informative; Keller, *On the Mystery*; McDaniel, *What Is Process Thought?*; Mesle, *Process Theology*; Mesle, *Process-Relational Philosophy*; of the many books by Norman Pittenger, *Picturing God* is a nice summary; Williamson and R. J. Allen, *Adventures of the Spirit*, 7–36. I continue to keep Sherburne, *Key to Whitehead's Process*, at the desk as a guide to difficult concepts.

5. While neither Whitehead nor Hartshorne focus on traditional theological topics, in the manner of a systematic or constructive theologian, process theologians take the next steps in drawing out the explicit theological implications from many of the leading ideas in process conceptuality. Space permits naming only a few theologians in the process tradition whose works are accessible (in alphabetical order): Charles W. Allen, William A. Beardslee, Donna Bowman, Kathlyn Breazeale, Robert Brizee, Philip Clayton, John Cobb, Monica Coleman, John Culp, Daniel Dombrowski, Bruce G. Epperly, Ronald L. Farmer, Patricia Adams Farmer, Roland Faber, Lewis Ford, Terrence E. Fretheim, Robert Gnuse, David Ray Griffin, Nancy R. Howell, Lucinda Huffaker, Tyron Inbody, J. Gerald Janzen, Carol Johnston, Catherine Keller, Harold Kushner, Bernard Loomer, Sandra Lubarsky, David J. Lull, Jay McDaniel, Bernard Meland, C. Robert Mesle, Mary Elizabeth Mullino Moore, Leslie Muray, Robert Neville, Schubert M. Ogden, Thomas J. Oord, Norman Pittenger, David P. Polk, Russell Pregeant, David Roy, Casey T. Sigmon, David Grant Smith, Helene Tallon Russell, Jeanyne Sletom, Paul Sponheim, Marjorie Suchocki, Daniel Day Williams, Clark M. Williamson, Barry Woodbridge, and Henry J. Young. To honor process's emphasis upon the distinctiveness of each person/event, it is important to note that these (and all) process theologians interpret process in their own ways.

process theology to be persuasive. The chapter introduces how process thinking helps people make theological sense of the ever-changing qualities of life, and how process interprets some vexing theological issues.

We find some theological themes once particularly associated with process now commonplace in voices across the theological spectrum. For instance, the permeating emphasis on relationship among all things, a trademark of process, is now characteristic of many theological families.[6] The process movement itself sometimes prompted theologians outside the process corral towards this awareness. But perspectives similar to those of process are also emerging spontaneously in wider cultures. The fact that ideas similar to those found in process bubble up without contact with process thinking testifies to resonance between process perspectives and early twenty-first-century perceptions. As is typical of brief reviews of this kind, I sometimes oversimplify issues for heuristic purposes.

A SHIFT IN A MAJOR ISSUE IN PHILOSOPHY: FROM SUBSTANCE TO PROCESS

Beginning with the ancient Mediterranean world where Western philosophy was born, the landscape of philosophy has been dominated by questions about the nature of existence. What compromises existence? Philosophers seek to explain what is—what exists—in ways that are logically coherent.[7]

Traditional Western Philosophy: Existence as Substance

For the ancients, questions about existence were not idle abstractions. The questions were sparked by the perception that life is tenuous, often unpredictable and threatened. Human existence was temporary and ended in death. Traditional philosophy sought to explain existence in such a way that people had a sense of what they could count on. Philosophy offered people an understanding of the world that gave them a feeling of security in the face of unpredictability, threat, and the final insignificance of death.

---

6. Several years ago, one of my colleagues in the field of preaching who subscribes to another theological family burst out, "You process theologians think you have a trademark on the concept of relationship. But you don't. We're concerned about relationship, too."

7. Faber, *God as Poet*, 45–80, surveys philosophical issues in the background of the emergence of process.

The Western philosophical tradition resolved these questions by thinking of existence in terms of substance or being. Existence is made up of substances. Each substance is unchangeable and eternal, with its own essence and its own properties. Although the essence of a substance does not change, the properties can change. This perspective provides for continuity (the unchangeable essence of the substance) and an acceptable level of change through the change of the properties. An important point: while human beings can be aware of the attributes of a substance, human beings cannot have real and direct knowledge of the substance itself.

An analogy catches the spirit of the substance way of thinking. Existence is like a wall built of cement blocks. Each block is a chunk of substance. The blocks can be painted different colors—some gray, others green, still others blue and red. The colors may change, but the essence of the blocks does not change, thus guaranteeing that the garage will stand. From the traditional point of view, all of existence is made up of substances like blocks. Change is as superficial as painting a gray block green. After painting, the block may be a little more colorful, but it is still a block that sits alongside other blocks. The blocks make a wall, but the blocks do not really affect one another.

While we take up the relationship of God to existence more fully in the next section, we should note that for much classical philosophy and theology, god or God is a substance. Like other substances, God is above time, and, like a cement block, God does not change. To be sure, God is not just one substance alongside other substances but is a kind of super-substance. Indeed, the changeless God is the guarantee of the changelessness (and, hence, reliability) of the world.

Process Philosophy:
Existence not as Substance but as Becoming

Whitehead's move towards process thought is rooted in empirical observation.[8] Whitehead, like Heraclitus, observed that existence is not static but is constantly active process.[9] Existence is not made up of fixed entities but is

8. Process seeks, as much as possible, to describe existence as it really is. I say "as much as possible" because process recognizes that all perception involves interpretation. We never have pure, uninterpreted awareness. Furthermore, process thinkers recognize that our interpretation of existence can change in response to fresh insights. In a sense, every interpretive statement is provisional.

9. Indeed, change is the very nature of existence. The universe is made up of tiny atoms which are themselves made up of tinier particles that are constantly whirring. An atom is not a tiny substance but is itself constituted by its moving parts. Constant

a constant flux. Process thinkers often use the language of "becoming" to speak of this constant movement. Existence is not made up of static entities bumping into one another but is a perpetual process of becoming. Indeed, becoming is the very nature of existence.[10]

The process of becoming involves occasions which are made up of three moments. The first is the past opening into the present. What happened in the past does not unilaterally determine the present, but the effects of the past contribute to the present, even when people in the present do not directly remember or recognize those effects. The second is the immediate moment that comes to life in response to the past, in response to circumstances at work in the present, and in response to possibilities that are available to the present and are yet unrealized. The third moment is the present ending as it becomes the past and opens into the future, which immediately becomes its own present as it unfolds. Process thinkers sometimes use the notion of "perishing" to speak of what happens to the present moment when it gives way to the next emerging moment.

In the strict sense, of course, the present moment does not even last a heartbeat before it starts to perish and to become the initiating phase of a new moment. Life is *constantly* in process. However, with respect to practical perception, some moments last relatively long times.

As the living moment perishes, it does not simply disappear. Its effects become the past out of which the next moment begins. Indeed, in process conceptuality the possibilities and actualities that came to life in the past continue into the present and future, albeit often in decreasing awareness. While the immediacy of the past, and the sense of potential associated with it, usually diminishes with time, those things never completely vanish. To a process thinker, the past is not simply a deposit but is a living resource.

It is easy to see the process of becoming forming the lives of individual human beings and human communities. It is also easy to see this process in the world of animals, and in the broader purview of ecology. The process of becoming is not as obvious in things that appear to be more dense, solid, and long-lived such as the wooden table on which my computer sits, and the computer itself. But, strictly speaking, since the table and the computer are made up of atoms whose parts are themselves in constant motion, there is a distant sense in which the table, the computer—and other dense things—are not lifeless but have their own lives in reduced states. An important point:

---

motion, then, is the essence (so to speak!) of existence

10. A fuller account of the origins of process thought and its distinctive character can be found in Williamson and R. J. Allen, *Adventures of the Spirit*, 37–60.

from the process point of view, each thing has its own integrity and its own worth.

Living entities have different levels of complexity, consciousness, and sensitivity. As far as we can tell, a human being is typically more aware, critically reflective, and more sensitive than the rabbit sitting in the euonymus in the backyard outside my study window.[11] The rabbit seems to manifest these qualities more than the maple tree and certainly more than the chain-link fence that separates the yard from the alley. In process parlance, with respect to consciousness and responsiveness, a human being is a higher-grade organism than a rabbit who in turn is a higher-grade organism than a chain-link fence. Though I do not like to use the expression, some process thinkers would refer to the maple tree and the chain-link fence as lower-grade organisms.

At the same time, all things have the ability to be responsive—and to become—according to their level of complexity. The tree is ever changing, often in ways that are imperceptible to me. The becoming of the chain-link fence is even more imperceptible, but over the course of the forty years we have lived in this house, the fence itself has changed, and continues to change.

While the change involved in becoming is ever present in everything in every moment, some things do continue for long periods of time so that we count on them. However, this stability should not blind us to the possibility that the sub-electrons and atoms and systems that make up the enduring object are actually always in motion.

The qualities of a moment come about through the ways in which participants respond to the various elements that are present. A person, for instance, can respond to things unfolding from the past on a spectrum from a strong "Yes" to a strong "No." The same spectrum of response is at work regarding possibilities in the present and in the future. We can say "Yes" and "No," and we can also say, "Maybe. I am taking the time to consider this possibility."

Process philosophy sees the responses of the various participants in the living moment as key to what the moment becomes. We make choices. To be sure, our choices do not imperially determine what happens in the moment because other participants are also making choices. These choices interact with the effects of the past and the possibilities of the present to create the present and to open the door towards the future.

---

11. I say "typically" because human beings sometimes operate as if they have no capacity for critical reflection and are insensitive to many other entities. Indeed, humans beings can even be insensitive to themselves.

Making choices, however, is not always neat, clean, and self-aware. Human beings make some choices in conscious, critically reflective ways. When we are aware of issues, complications, and possibilities, we have the opportunity to choose options that we hope will enhance the quality of life for as many people and other elements of the world as possible both in the moment and in the future. The opportunities for choice and the outcomes of such choices are always affected by the choices of others in the networks of entities involved in the choices.

However, we cannot be consciously aware of all the factors present in a situation. Some factors in the depth of the past and present do not rise to the level of consciousness. We make many choices intuitively, often not even recognizing that we are making choices. Without reflection, we simply do, think, or feel. We do some things out of habit and others in the spontaneity of a moment. While such responses can move toward the good for the self and its many communities, they can also cooperate with forces that diminish the experience of the self and the communities of which the self is part.

Chapter 3 contends that one purpose of preaching in the process tradition is to encourage the congregation towards recognizing the important choices at hand, the issues involved, and the possible outcomes—all in a context of critical reflection so the congregation can make decisions that are as informed as possible.

It is important to note that the process of becoming does not mean that the quality of life always improves with change. The process view is not a version of the old proverb, "Things are getting better and better every day in every way." Some changes diminish the quality of life for those involved.

ALL THINGS ARE RELATED

One of the most important themes in process philosophy and theology is that everything in existence is related. All things are inherently in relationship.[12] Indeed, Monica Coleman says, "We do not have relationships, we *are* relationships. We are constituted by our relationships to other people, to our environment, to our past lives, our potentials, and God."[13] Because we are

12. Whitehead initially referred to his emerging thought as "philosophy of organism" thereby calling attention to the fact that the elements of life work with one another in the same way that the parts of a living organism work with one another. Some process theologians recently tried to refer to the process movement as "relational theology," but theologians from some other theological families cried, "But we think theologically about relationships, too." Suchocki constructs a process systematic theology around the language of relationality in *God, Christ, Church*.

13. Coleman, "Introduction to Process Theology," 16. Emphasis is Coleman's.

inherently related, each member of a relationship (human and non-human) affects and is affected by the relationship. The one always affects the many, and the many always affect the one.[14]

In the process world, relationships are manifest at two levels. The more obvious level is the external, fully articulate relationship in which the dynamics of the relationship are at work so that participants are immediately cognizant of what is happening. People know they are affecting others and/ or being affected by them. For example, the preacher steps into the pulpit and speaks the content of the sermon. Preacher and people are aware that they are in the event of preaching and listening. They are aware of being affected by the event and of affecting it. As we note below, however, even when conscious of relationships (and of being affected and affecting) our consciousness is seldom complete.

The other level, internal relationship, is much less visible. Indeed, a person may not be aware of being in relationship with another person (or other entities) and yet is affected by other entities affects them.[15] We experience most internal relationships as intuition and feeling much more than as conscious awareness. For example, I may feel some of the pain of a person in another country who is dying because of hunger, and, because all things are connected, I am affected by that death.

Relationship and Awareness

Discussion of levels of relationships—external and internal—intersects with the consideration of levels of consciousness introduced above. Conscious awareness also takes place in different degrees in different organisms. Some organisms—such as people—often have a relatively high degree of consciousness of things happening around, to, and in them. They may also be conscious of being in relationship with others, and of participating in choosing how others respond to the events in which they are involved.

However, the human capacity for perception is limited, which means that we seldom consciously perceive all others with whom we have external relations, nor can we perceive any relationship in its complete array of dimensions. But even organisms with a high degree of awareness are conscious of only a small part of life process. We are affected by others at transconscious levels in which awareness is intuitive and is seldom formulated in direct speech.

14. On the one and the many, see Whitehead, *Process and Reality*, 21–22, 154–55, 341, 347–49.

15. Whitehead, *Process and Reality*, 58–59, 308–9.

Other organisms have lower degrees of consciousness. Animals, fish, and birds have degrees of awareness appropriate to their needs of functioning in the world. When equipped with pertinent mechanisms—such as the capacities to yap or meow or cuddle or writhe—they can communicate some things, but they can never communicate the depth of their experience.

Still other organisms, such as trees or rocks, do not appear to have consciousness and do not appear to attempt to communicate in meaningful ways to others, though I have to say, candidly, that it is not clear to me whether the tree I cut down in the front yard had any consciousness of being related to me or any awareness of distress as I used a chainsaw to remove the limbs, fell the tree, and cut up the trunk. At the same time, my limited capacity for perception cautions me from blithely assuming the tree has utterly no awareness. Regardless of what the tree may or may not feel, I experience the loss of the tree as loss of relationship. The presence of the tree has affected me in its living and its dying.

In the fullest sense, since all things are connected, we are related to all events that take place in the universe. We are affected by everything that happens, and we affect everything that happens. Some relationships are external. Many more are internal. To be sure, the human capacity for awareness is so limited that we cannot process all the things that affects us and that we affect. Because so many things are happening in and around us all the time, we cannot consciously choose how to respond to all of them. But we hope to be a part of patterns of response—conscious and instinctual—that promise a rich quality of experience for all concerned.

Amid the flux, we benefit from communities that can help us identify, prioritize, and reflect critically on the relationships at work in our immediate worlds and beyond. Others can often perceive the dynamics of the moment in ways that we cannot. Others can often raise questions that may not come to us. Others may name possibilities that do not occur to us.

A SHIFT IN UNDERSTANDING DIVINE POWER: FROM OMNIPOTENCE TO LEADING PARTNER

There is a reciprocal relationship between the ways in which communities experience and interpret the world and the ways in which they picture God. On the one hand, a significant part of the way a community portrays God affects how the community understands the world. The community takes its cues for values and behavior from its image of God. The one often affects the other. The substance view of existence points towards a substance view of God, which is the dominant portrayal of God in Christian history. The substance picture of God reinforces the substance view of existence. A similar structure of thought is true for process communities. The ever-changing relational view of a world whose elements feel one another points towards a God who is at home in change. The view of God as empathetic, relational, present in change, and ever offering possibilities for good, informs how a community views what should happen in the community's life.

While a fair number of people outside the process family resonate with the general notions of becoming and relationship, I find that a smaller number are drawn to the more specific process understanding of God. My experience as a teacher in theological seminary, and as a preacher and Bible study leader in local congregations, leads me to think that most people operate with shades of traditional understandings of God. Many people, however, are troubled by aspects of those understandings and are open to fresh configurations, such as the one offered through process theology.

Traditional Pictures of God

Contemporary theology rightly emphasizes the diversity of voices within theological tradition. Indeed, some scholars speak not of "tradition" but of "traditions." Nevertheless, we may describe a picture of God that has played a far-reaching role in Christianity, and which is alive in various degrees today. Its roots include the substance worldview of Greek philosophy (per above). The substance way of thinking about God emerged formally in Christian circles by the time of Clement of Alexandria (roughly 150–215 CE). Langdon Gilkey, who taught theology at the Divinity School of the University of Chicago, summarizes the classical view. God is

> eternal in the sense of utterly non-temporal, necessary in the sense of absolute independence, changeless in the sense of participating in and relating to no change, purely spiritual instead of in any fashion material, unaffected and thus seemingly unrelated and even unrelatable to the world.[16]

In less technical language, this view holds that God is beyond time, that is, God does not need time. God exists independently, apart from time, and is not truly related to other things. God cannot be moved by the situation of the world. God does not change. This God is entirely self-contained and does not truly empathize. Indeed, God does not suffer. Moreover, God has the kind of power that enables God to intervene directly in history and to do whatever God wants. God may practice self-limitation in the exercise

16. Gilkey, "God," 93.

of that power, that is, God may choose not to act, in a certain circumstance, but the potential for complete and total intervention is always there. Process thinkers often refer to this mode of power as coercive power: God can simply force God's will. God is omniscient, that is God knows all things.[17]

Whitehead identified three common ways that people in the ancient world described their deities that manifest aspects of this traditional picture: "the ruling Caesar, the ruthless moralist, and the unmoved mover."[18] Elements of these characterizations have persisted through history to this very day in many traditional understandings of God.

To be sure this picture is not the universal view of the church through history. Different theologians, churches, and theological movements interpret it with their own nuances. For example, most theological families today say that God has more empathy and relationship with the world than do the pure voices of the unmoved mover perspective. Some theologians who differ with the traditional model describe it in caricature in order to make their own viewpoints stand out more distinctly.

Nevertheless, aspects of the classical approach permeate much popular Christian thinking about God, especially regarding divine power. In a popular adaptation of this model, all things are under divine control: God either initiates or permits all things. Since God has absolute power, God either directly *causes* things to happen or God *allows* them. This point of view offers believers a certain security: life is under ultimate control even when things occur that seem arbitrary and hurtful. For example, not long ago someone in the congregation to which I belong who contracted a serious illness voiced a widespread perspective by saying, "God has reasons for everything that happens, even this disease. We human beings may not know those reasons in this life. We just have to trust that God knows best." I often hear people say, "God never gives people more than they can bear." This way of thinking is often accompanied by the idea that at death (or at the second coming), God will remove the faithful from the present world and give them a home in heaven that magnifies the blessings of the present life and that is free of the pain, sorrow, and death that diminishes the quality of life in the present.

These people live with a view of a God who causes or allows hurtful things, even for unknown reasons, because that view promises that things are under divine control. They can get through whatever happens because they believe God will ultimately make things right. Some people consciously

17. For a process view that affirms a certain coercive power in God, see Janzen, "Modes of Power."

18. Whitehead, *Process and Reality*, 343.

choose to adopt this perspective. Others drift into it because they do are not aware of other points of view. They just assume that "Christians believe these things." Still other people who are troubled by aspects of the traditional view find process to be a saving alternative.

A Process Picture of God

As we noted above, a community tends to have a reciprocal relationship between its view of the world and its picture of God. For process theologians, the changing and relational nature of existence points to a God who is present in change and becoming, who is always in living, compassionate relationship with all things, and who seeks the good for all things. God is ever involved in life process, both affecting it and being affected by it. To be sure, God is more than one entity alongside others, but, as Whitehead famously says, "God is not to be invoked as an exception to all metaphysical principles, invoked to save their collapse. [God] is their chief exemplification."[19]

Two Dimensions in the Divine Nature: Primordial and Consequent

To say that God is present in change does not mean that everything with God is up in the air all the time. Process theology speaks of two dimensions of the divine nature: "primordial nature" and "consequent nature." The primordial nature is an aspect of God that does not change. Through the primordial nature God always seeks optimum experience for the cosmos and all in it. Marjorie Suchocki describes this desire as "inclusive well-being."[20]This desire does not change. In all the flux of life, God consistently seeks community for all. We might think of the primordial nature as an infinite storehouse of possibilities that can come to expression in real life.[21] All of the possibilities in the primordial nature aim for human beings, animals, and other dimensions of nature to live together in relationships of mutual solidarity, security, and abundance so that all involved can become in optimum ways.

19. Whitehead, *Process and Reality*, 343.

20. Suchocki, *Fall to Violence*, 13, 18–19, 42–44, esp. 66–80, 86, 101–11, 158; *End of Evil*, 122–23, 125–30, 133.

21. Whitehead describes the primordial aim as "the active entertainment of all ideals, with the urge to their finite realization, each in its own due season." *Adventures of Ideas*, 357.

The consequent nature of God refers to that the conviction that God is affected by the world. The consequent nature of God means that God completely understands who we are and what we think, feel, and otherwise experience. Moreover, the consequent nature is the responsive aspect of God. God is affected by all of things which thereby become a part of the way God feels the world. The consequent nature is the responsive aspect of God. God feels what happens in the world and adapts the possibilities to the situation. God changes the possibilities that are available to the world in light of the circumstances.

In every situation God seeks the optimum level of becoming for all involved in that situation. God always seeks the good. God never intends suffering or evil.[22] This broad purposes of God do not change from one situation to another (primordial nature), but God changes the possibilities so that they are truly possible in the immediate context (consequent nature).

In popular religion, people often speak about the plan of God meaning that God plans the events of life in a direct way. "I am looking for God's plan for my life" In this context, it is worth underscoring that the primordial nature of God does not mean a fixed plan of events that God can unilaterally put into motion. The possibilities are just that: possibilities. They are actualized only as entities in the world act on them. When entities in the world do act on a possibility, that possibility is not simply produced in the world according to a blueprint from God but, instead, takes shape according to the specific factors at work in the situation. A possibility "becomes" in the way that we described events taking place above—evolving from the past in response to present circumstances with an eye towards the future.

For process theology, God becomes in ways similar to human beings and other inhabitants of the world. New things are happening in every moment. God takes in what happens in the world and changes in the consequent nature in response to what God experiences. However, God never adapts in ways that contradict God's primordial nature. Rather, God changes in ways similar to the way in which I changed in my understanding of children when my wife and I became parents. The essential me did not change, but I began to see the world, in part, through the eyes of the children and to imagine what I could do to try to make their experiences better and to enhance my relationship with them. A key difference between God and me is that whereas my attempts to perceive the world through the eyes of the child is limited, God's capacity to feel the world is infinite and clear.

---

22. This statement raises the question of how to understand God in relation to the notions of divine punishment and evil. We take up these issues below.

From a process viewpoint, God is omnipresent: God is fully present in every time and place. Clark M. Williamson, who taught theology at Christian Theological Seminary for forty years, once entitled a book *God Is Never Absent*.[23] Strictly speaking, from a process viewpoint the worship leader makes a theological mistake when requesting in the opening prayer in the service, "O God, we ask that you be here with us." God is already present. The congregation needs to become more cognizant of that presence. A more appropriate prayer would be, "O God, thank you for your presence always with us. We pray that we will be open to that presence and to the ways in which this hour of worship might heighten our responsiveness to your desire that we live in love, peace, justice, solidarity, and security."

What Does God Do?

Not only is God omnipresent, but God is always doing all that God can do to offer possibilities for optimum experience in every given situation. God never withholds the fullness of divine help. God never hides from a person or a situation. But the possibilities for what can happen are often limited by the circumstances of the context.

If God is always doing all that God can do, the question comes up, "What *does* God do?" The background to the answer to this question is a distinctive understanding of divine power in process thought. As we have already pointed out, God cannot intervene from outside history with unilateral and coercive force. Rather, God operates by way of invitation: God invites human beings and other entities to participate with God in becoming in optimum ways.[24]

Clark Williamson used an illustration that became famous in our seminary community. God aims for people who are hungry to have the food they need to live. However, God cannot directly make a peanut butter sandwich. God offers the aim of making peanut butter sandwiches to a congregation

---

23. Williamson, *God Is Never Absent*. Williamson wanted to entitle this book *Faith is a Verb* in order to emphasize the becoming character of the life of faith.

24. Process theologians sometimes speak of the lure" of God or of the "persuasive power" of God. However, in everyday language usage, these expressions may be confusing. In the heightened awareness of sexual misconduct in the early twenty-first century, the word "lure" may unintentionally be associated with such behavior. The word "persuasion" may be associated with manipulation. The term "invitation" captures the spirit of how God's power works in the world: God invites other beings to consider possibilities, and to make their own decisions regarding which possibilities—if any—to embrace.

who can then create the sandwiches. The food would not appear if the hands did not make it. But the aim comes from God.

As we noted above, the situation is more complicated in the case of organisms who do not have consciousness similar to the human family.[25] Human beings have the capacity to make direct choices in favor of cooperating with—or turning away from—God's invitations. Intuition and spontaneous reaction may also play significant parts in responsiveness. Beyond that, according to process conceptualities, other entities can respond to the divine purposes to the degree that they are able. On a beautiful, lush day—the sun lolling in the sky, the water quietly splashing in the brook, the tadpoles leisurely swimming upstream, the squirrel using a tree limb as a bridge—the elements of nature respond positively to the aim of living together in mutual support. God offers the possibility of such a day, but the elements must cooperate in bringing it to expression.

But what about negative, community-denying aspects of nature, such as big fish eating little fish, and tornados cutting across cities like lawn mowers cutting grass? God does not intend such events. God invites community. God invites elements of creation into community in modes of expression befitting their perception. The invitation towards mutually supportive becoming comes from God in forms like intuition, feeling, or magnetic attraction. Community-denying aspects of life among animals and among the rocks and trees occur when participants do not accept God's invitation. Because the elements do not have a high degree of consciousness or articulation, it is difficult to offer an opinion as to why they do not respond to the highest possibilities.[26]

25. Process theologians give quite a bit of attention to the natural world and to the relationship between humankind and the natural world, e.g., Mesle, *Process-Relational Philosophy*, 37–38; McDaniel, *Of God and Pelicans*; McDaniel, *Earth, Sky, Gods and Mortals*; McDaniel and Adams, *Replanting Ourselves in Beauty*, especially Epperly, "Dogs and Divinity," 77–80; Epperly, *Process Theology: A Guide*, 23–24; Farmer, "Numinosity of Rocks," 80–87; Brown, "Respect for Rocks."

26. The human relationship with the natural world—and relationships within the natural world itself—are now complicated by ways in which the human community aggressively rejects God's invitation for mutual solidarity with nature, and, instead, exploits nature for human comfort without regard for the integrity of nature itself or for the future of nature or humankind, thereby eroding the highest possibilities for life for all. While it is philosophically puzzling to explain why some participants in nature form a tsunami, in the current moment, human influence in the world of nature often creates conditions in which nature itself is positioned to behave in ways that are against its own good.

The Power of God: The Power of Invitation

One major difference between God's power and the power of other entities is that God's power never runs out. No matter what happens in a situation, God has the power to continue to offer possibilities for richness in becoming. Even if pertinent parties actively reject God's initial aim, then God reformulates and offers another invitation. As a student who commuted a long way to school wistfully said, "God has a bottomless gas tank."

Since God's power works by invitation, and cannot effect unidirectional change, it requires response on the part of human beings or the natural world for fullest effect. According to process theology, human beings and other parts of the world are partners with God in moving towards God's desire for richness of experience and for inclusive well-being. Indeed, process sometimes thinks of people as co-creators with God. When I first discovered process thought, I was, frankly, put off by the term "co-creator" as it seemed to move in the direction of *hubris*, claiming more for the creature than is theologically justified. However, for process, God has the primary role. Without response on the part of human beings or others, God's initiative does not reach its fullest potential. Indeed, God may have to rethink the invitation. God's partnership with us (when we are responsive) does bring about genuinely new becomings. But God is always the prior actor. Something of the difference is suggested by the difference between the pilot and the co-pilot or the producer and the co-producer or executive producer.

An important thing to note in this discussion is that human attitudes and actions make a real difference not only in the world but also to God. For, as we have noted, God is affected by everything that happens. Human choices can affect God along a spectrum from enriching to disappointing. God becomes in response to the choices of human beings and other elements of the world.

There is an important contextual dimension here. God invites people towards possibilities that are realistically attainable within the situation. Some situations can change in response to the divine invitation, especially where human agency or other forms of agency are present. For example, as a part of seeking inclusive well-being, God seeks a human community in which people of different races and ethnicities live together in love and covenantal relationship with the natural world. God cannot bring about such a community by divine fiat. Such a community can come about only when people join God and one another as partners in living together in respect and solidarity.

But some situations are unlikely to change. For example, a terminal illness is usually just that. God cannot singularly bring about restoration.

The patient is unlikely to get well. Within such a situation, God's invitation may be for all concerned not only to be aware of the divine presence but also to realize that God feels fully with everyone involved. The situation may not change, but the perspectives of patients and others can change when they realize that they are not alone. To draw an analogy: one of the most important things that happens in many Al-Anon groups is for relatives and friends who live with people who struggle with alcohol to realize that they (relatives and friends) are not alone. "Other people understand." That awareness may not change what happens with the person who abuses alcohol, but it often helps relatives and friends make their way day to day.

Whitehead thus speaks of a God as "the great companion—the fellow sufferer who understands."[27] A companion sometimes says or does something that changes circumstances. But sometimes a companion is simply present, and the awareness of that presence is itself a redemptive change in perspective. "I am not alone."

WHY THE PROCESS PERSPECTIVE IS PERSUASIVE

Many people who encounter Christian faith through traditional theological worldviews simply continue to assume those points of view without being aware of other possibilities in the Christian house. Becoming aware of the process perspective often has the effect of prompting people to consider the degree to which they *really* believe in God in traditional ways. To draw on a crude similarity, settling upon a theological perspective is somewhat like choosing a car. Buyers decide the qualities that are more and less important. Buyers settle on those things they really want, those things with which they are willing to live, and those things they will not accept.

Different theological viewpoints offer distinctive perceptions on God, the world, and life possibilities. Scholars, preachers, and others must decide what they most deeply believe about God, the world, and life. We must decide those theological affirmations and denials that are more and

27. Whitehead, *Process and Reality*, 351. Scholars of Whitehead's generation seldom spoke of their personal lives. One of Whitehead's sons, Eric, was killed World War I. To my knowledge, Whitehead did not refer in a formal way to the effect of this event on his thinking. Whitehead's biographer does note that Whitehead was an agnostic for many years prior to World War I but took a turn towards "philosophical theism" in the wake of the social and personal tragedy of that war. Lowe, *Alfred North Whitehead*, 1:5. Lowe believes that Whitehead "was looking for something that [would] give meaning to what happened: in Whitehead's case, to the carnage of the First World War and Eric's death in it." Lowe, *Alfred North Whitehead*, 2:188. This autobiographical element could account, at least in part, for Whitehead turning away from the traditional model of God outlined above to the vision of a God of invitational power who is a companion in suffering.

less important, including those things with which we are willing to live and those things with which we are not willing to live. A student from a traditional background once put it this way, "When I read process the first time, it put me on the spot. It forced me to answer the question, 'Do I believe this way or not?'"

Without intending to stereotype or to be reductionistic, my colleague Helene Tallon Russell notices that some people are initially attracted to process thought because its theological ideas speak to festering intellectual issues.[28] I fell into this category. Others are often initially drawn to the process pattern of thinking because its relational dimension is truer to their experience than notions of relationality in other theological families. Of course, once inside the room with process thought, these two emphases become mutually interpreting.

I turn now to why I have committed my theological life to a process perspective. The key issue for me is implied in the student's question above: What can I *really* believe? In view of the scientific way in which I interpret the world, what can I credibly and deeply believe about God, God's purposes for the world, and our response?[29]

Process accounts more adequately for my experience of the world than traditional substance-based thinking or any other mode of thought with which I am familiar.[30] I do not perceive existence as a bunch of substances bumping into one another but as a dynamic arena in which change is always taking place. I experience myself as ever becoming, along with my immediate network of social relationships, the broader culture, and the creation itself. Process makes theological sense of the totality of my life experience in the wider context of the world. It offers assurance and affirmation while simultaneously challenging me to enlarge my sense of connection with others, and with the world.

28. Personal conversation.

29. While science was once regarded as something like a Pharaoh of understanding, it is now evident that many perspectives in science change from one era to another, indeed, sometimes more quickly. Moreover, some of the assertions of science are themselves open to interpretation. Nevertheless, I find the basic scientific construal of the world expressed in the Modern perspective to continue to be persuasive. Of course, process conceptuality is always open to reconsideration, but especially so when basic perspectives change.

30. My experience confirms what Whitehead sought. His process perspective "is the endeavour to frame a coherent, logical, necessary system of general ideas in terms of which every element of our experience can be interpreted. By this notion of 'interpretation' I mean that everything of which we are conscious, as enjoyed, perceived, willed, or thought, shall have the character of a particular instance of the general scheme. Thus, the philosophical system should be coherent, logical, and in respect to its interpretation, applicable and adequate." *Process and Reality*, 3.

Process theology offers a way of dealing plausibly with the most difficult theological issues. Without having put it this way, I had previously believed in a "God of the gaps," that is, I explained as much of the relationship between Christian faith and my everyday world as I could on the basis of the typical scientific view of reality, but when it came to a difference between that worldview and the claims of religion, I assumed that God somehow intervened to fill the gap. By contrast, process offers theological perspective that takes account of the whole cloth of life.

Process thought resolves the aching theological issue of the relationship of God to the suffering of the innocent. The clear-thinking Clark Williamson points to a logical inconsistency in the classical model of God on this point. If God has the absolute power to intervene in history and can thereby end the suffering of the innocent, but does not do so, then God is not fully moral.[31] As noted, the process God does not have the kind of power necessary for such an intervention. God is fully present to all involved in situations of such suffering and is doing all that God can do.

Process thought also provides an adequate reframing of how to make theological sense of the notion—present in the Bible and in Christian doctrine—that God actively punishes those who are disobedient. This punishment typically invokes some kind of suffering. As noted, in my view God who is unrelenting love does not actively wish suffering on anyone or anything. However, in my process perspectives, human beings invite consequences on ourselves when we disrupt God's purposes for community. God does not aggressively mete out punishment. We bring punishment on ourselves. Consequences may be immediate as when a community serves the interests of powerful corporations by building a dam in a poor location and bypassing safety regulations only to have the dam burst and wipe out the very industry it was intended to make profitable. But consequences may also take longer to develop. The Roman Empire was centered in idolatry and self-serving power, ruled by violence, enforced servitude and poverty on generations, and often practiced injustice. Rome ruled a long time, but by 476 CE, the violence by which Rome ruled had become the very means by which the Empire in the west was destroyed. While the God of unrelenting love does not directly punish, people are held accountable for their attitudes and behavior and consequences do befall them.

I struggled for a long time with *how* God works in the world. Process offers a perspective on this phenomenon that is at home in the scientific worldview. Many theologies, especially since the Enlightenment, hold that

---

31. See further Williamson and R. J. Allen, *Credible and Timely Word*, 20–21.

the world operates on an everyday basis according to the laws of nature.[32] In order to do something, God must intervene in history by suspending the laws of nature, that is, God must act supernaturally. Thus, to account for God's action in the world, those who assume this viewpoint must suspend the ways in which they ordinarily presume the world to operate. Moreover, the question just discussed comes into play: if God has the power to intervene in the world but does not use it—especially to relieve suffering—then God is not fully moral. In Whitehead's formulation from above, process does not regard God as an exception to the basic patterns by which existence takes place but operates through them in the mode of invitation.

Williamson notes, further, that in its extreme form in classical theology, human actions are meaningless since they take place under the aegis of a God who is all-powerful, unchangeable, and who already knows what will happen in the future. The notion of such a God "simply cannot be reconciled with the reality of human freedom and responsibility."[33] If our actions cannot affect the impassable God, and if God already knows what will happen, "Then the ultimate and final truth is that what happens on and to the earth, what we do and fail to do, are simply and finally unimportant."[34] Our actions do not really matter because they are not really our own, and they do not really affect the course of history.

In its fully blown form, the traditional approach to God loses sight of essential insights regarding the nature, purposes, and behavior of God pictured in the heart of the Bible and the earliest Christian faith. Indeed, the God of pure classical theism is almost a different God from the one portrayed in the Bible.[35] While the Bible and tradition are diverse in the ways in which they picture God in these matters, the Bible repeatedly portrays God as loving, and compassionate and seeking to bless Israel, the church, and the wider human family and world. God is not simply an unmoved mover but is responsive to the communities of humankind and nature. Indeed, at several points in the Bible God "repents" of decisions or actions that God has made

---

32. The premodern worldview, which the church largely assumed from antiquity to the Enlightenment, did not distinguish in the sharp way between the natural and the supernatural that became common in the Enlightenment-modern worldview. On differences in premodern, modern, and postmodern worldviews, see R. J. Allen, *Preaching and the Other*, 7–28.

33. Williamson, *Way of Blessing*, 20.

34. Williamson, *Way of Blessing*, 21.

35. Whitehead identifies his core understanding of God specifically with "the Galilean origin of Christianity." *Process and Reality*, 343. A closer look at the Bible itself reveals that the themes that are important to Whitehead are found not only in "the Galilean origin" but also in other strands of the diverse and complicated biblical traditions.

or taken (e.g., Exod 32:14; 2 Sam 24:16; Jonah 3:10). Subsequent chapters say more about the Bible and process perspective

In the end, I have to say that the process approach to life *feels* right. I use the word "feeling" here not simply in reference to emotion but in the process sense of the thick fabric life that includes awareness that is seldom articulate in conventional language but is often in touch with the deep streams of life.[36] After reading a passage in Susanne Langer's philosophy of art which expands on this epistemology, I thought, "This just *feels* right." To be sure, feeling alone, can seldom be the determining factor in what we believe. But critical reflection on feeling often leads to the conclusion that the feeling has something to commend it.

Many people do not find the process perspective persuasive. Accustomed to believing in an all-powerful God, they sometimes think, "Process theology offers no security. With all that emphasis on change, what can you really count on? The process God cannot really do anything. It all depends on human effort." A student once dismissed process with two words, "Wimp God."

However, here is a point at which a preacher must simply choose those things with which to live and those things to set aside. I would rather live with the process view because I find it to be more intellectually credible than the alternatives. I can *really* believe in the God whom it describes. This God offers both continuity and adaptability with respect to working with the constantly changing aspects of life. This God is not a wimp, for this God is fully present in *all* contexts, including the ones that are most painful, and feels everything about them. The awareness of this presence in every single moment and the confidence that God is ever inviting the world to the highest possibilities that are available in a particular context offers its own kind of security. God empowers partnership among the divine, the human family, and nature. This God cannot do everything for the world. But the certainty is that God unrelentingly does everything that God can do. Consequently, every situation has a hope particular to that situation. I not only believe in such a God, I trust that God.

The next chapters narrow the focus from this broad worldview of process theology to more specific background matters for preaching—a process understanding of epistemology, a process perspective on language, a theological method for using process theology in preaching and in broader theological reflection with special attention to the nature and role of the Bible and to the relationship between the Bible and experience.

---

36. The best exposition of this understanding of feeling is Langer, *Philosophy in a New Key*, 76–115.

2

Perception and Language

What Happens When We Speak and Listen?

LANGUAGE IN THE EVERYDAY WORLD,
THE BIBLE, AND THE SERMON

ON SUNDAY MORNING (OR Saturday night), the last strains of the song led by the praise band slowly fade into the worship space. The preacher rises to the pulpit or the speaking stand, or simply steps in front of the congregation, then reads from the Bible, looks up and straightens up, pauses for a moment, looks the congregation in the eye, and begins to speak. What happens when the preacher speaks? What happens when the congregation listens? What does language do in the rarefied atmosphere of preaching, and in the more everyday world?

In the process worldview, language is powerful because it can connect individuals and communities with the deepest reaches of existence. Speaking and listening is a full-bodied *event*, per chapter 1. Language *is* an event. Language *interprets* events, language *contributes* to events. Language can be an *impetus* for subsequent events. Language can help us understand aspects of existence, and it can shape and generate aspects of reality. Because language is powerful, preachers need to be aware of how they use language and of what happens when congregations receive language so preachers can speak in ways that are theologically appropriate and that make intellectually credible statements.

To understand what happens when preachers speak and congregations listen, we must consider the relationship between perception and language. This chapter first explores relationships between these two things. We distinguish between two modes of perceiving and speaking that are fundamental for the preacher—presentational immediacy and causal efficacy. We take account of how these two modes of perception and language relate through symbolic reference, and we pause over the fallacy of misplaced concreteness, one of the most persistent stumbling blocks in perception, speaking, and hearing, and a typical error in theological thinking and preaching. Along the way, we note how language functions in the Bible, in the interpretation of the Bible, in Christian doctrine, and in preaching.

A PRELIMINARY NOTE:
THE LANGUAGE OF THE BIBLE
AND CHRISTIAN DOCTRINE

We pay special attention to the Bible not because the biblical worlds of language are different in nature and function from language in other spheres of life, but because the Bible has such a central place in Christian communities.[1] The congregation reads from it in public worship. The preacher typically engages it in the sermon. Bible study is constituent to many efforts at Christian formation. Churches draw from it when trying to formulate what they most deeply believe. Congregations often use biblical texts to justify particular positions on social issues. Excerpts from the Bible appear on bumper stickers and tweets. Furthermore, the interpretation of the Bible is often a point of conflict within congregations and among Christian communities. My observation—supported over many years in many different ecclesial settings—is that virtually all groups in the church want the Bible to support their views on theology, personal morality, politics, social issues, and other matters.

Christian doctrine, likewise, plays a central role in Christian communities. A doctrinal statement summarizes the core beliefs that a church—at a moment—considered essential. In many churches, those who wish to participate in full-bodied ways in the church must affirm these statements. Churches often follow formal statements of doctrine, such as the Apostolic Affirmation of Faith. But churches sometimes also take informal doctrinal positions for granted. Moreover, while churches often say the Bible informs doctrine, the typical case is more complicated in that the church's *interpretation* of the Bible informs doctrine; the church, in turn, then interprets the

---

1. By "languages" of the Bible, this discussion has in mind not Hebrew, Aramaic, and Greek—the languages in which the extant biblical manuscripts are written—but the more general reference to the nature and function of oral-aural and written expression.

Bible through the lens of doctrine. The church's use of the Bible in relationship to doctrine thus has a circular nature.

One of the major emphases in biblical studies in the last fifty years is on the diversity within the Bible with respect to historical settings in which its parts came to expression, literary genres within its sixty-six books, and multiple theological viewpoints with distinctive nuances that vary from theological family to theological family. Indeed, scholars today sometimes say that the Bible is not *a* book but a library. Such *différance* in parts of the Bible make it difficult to speak about "*the* Bible" in a comprehensive singular expression as in "*the* language of the Bible." In truth there are *languages* in the Bible with respect to worlds of thought.

The same is even more true in the broad expanse of Christian doctrine. Different churches often take different slants on specific elements of Christian doctrine. For example, understandings of the Holy Spirit can be quite different from Reformed to Pentecostal to Wesleyan to Roman Catholic. Different theological families can also cross the lines of denominations and movements, as, for instance understandings of salvation in evangelical and liberation streams. An evangelical Baptist may share more theological common ground with an evangelical Lutheran than with a progressive Baptist.

However, these languages have enough theological similarities that, in this chapter, we can make some general statements about the Bible and doctrine and their languages under an umbrella that both notes and respects the specific qualities of different voices within the sacred pages and ecclesial affirmations.

PERCEPTION AND LANGUAGE

Thinking about the relationship of perception and language in process perspective begins with the conviction that there is *something* to perceive.[2] The thing we perceive, of course, is not bricks of substance but is the process of life itself as events come into existence, flourish, and perish, becoming sources for subsequent events, as described in chapter 1. By way of anticipating motifs that will play important roles further in this chapter, we note two things about language in the process view. First, language evokes something of the experience that lies behind it. Language refers to prior realities

2. The conviction that human beings have pre-linguistic experience—that is, experience that is direct and is not mediated by language—differentiates the process perspective from some other philosophies of language. Moreover, some approaches to language claim that the meaning of linguistic expressions emerges only in the sphere of perception that language itself creates.

of existence. Language is grounded in something beyond itself and is not simply part of a self-enclosed world defined by its own usage. Language arouses awareness of the larger world and evokes a sense of relationship with it. Language seeks to describe the world as it actually is, a world that includes the great reservoir of past experience. But second, language, even at its most precise, is typically "incomplete and fragmentary."[3] While language can be powerful, even at its best it is never co-terminus with the fullness of experience.

Going a step further, the process notion of perception holds that human beings perceive in two related levels—the more basic and deep perception in the mode of causal efficacy and the more immediate and specific perception in the mode of presentational immediacy. People use language in ways that correspond to these two manners of awareness. In everyday perception we relate these two modes of perception by means of a process Whitehead calls symbolic reference.

To put the matter plainly from the perspective of my own practice as someone who interprets the Bible, Christian doctrine, and wider life through a process lens, I try to use language to describe what really happens in the world as accurately as possible, taking into account the fact that just as our perception is often imprecise—especially in causal efficacy when perception is usually dim and unformed—so our language is often "fragmentary and incomplete."

Moreover, our perception of the world sometimes changes. "A problem, . . . is that the world in which we live is hardly stable."[4] Williamson illustrates:

> Our scientific understandings of [the world] keep developing and recently have served to give new credence to pondering the classic mysteries. Why is there something and not nothing? Why is the world understandable? How is that we can, seemingly, comprehend it? Big bang and quantum scientists raise new questions. Not only that, new social-ethical issues arise and demand attention. Some of us put in entire careers teaching in seminaries while having to figure out how to deal with issues that we had never imagined because they were actually novel or had long been ignored. Our patriarchal and misogynist understanding of women was rightfully challenged. The Holocaust made us aware of the long Christian tradition of teaching and practicing contempt for Jews and Judaism, an issue that is still far from being widely faced. Also, the civil rights movement,

3. Whitehead, *Adventures of Ideas*, 291–93.
4. Williamson, "Preaching as Conversation," 73.

in which some of us participated, is still motivating churches
to face their own racism. And the new issues abound: the ordi-
nation of gays, lesbians, bi-sexual, and transgender people, for
instance.[5]

On the one hand, I try to use language as accurately as possible in light of
what I perceive. On the other hand, perception is always somewhat provisional. Everything is not always up in the air. We count on some things, a
least for now. But the door is always open for fresh ways of perceiving.

While we cannot use language to describe all aspects of our experience
in the world with permanent, technical scientific precision, we can use language, in concert with our experience, to offer adequate ways of conceiving
and relating to God, one another, and the wider world in the light of our
best present perception. Even if language is inadequate to account for the
fullness of experience, it can help disclose relationships in the vast networks
that make up existence and it can help us articulate what we can and cannot
typically expect from God, from one another, animals, and the ecosphere.

PERCEPTION AND LANGUAGE
IN THE MODE OF PRESENTATIONAL IMMEDIACY

Whitehead calls the simpler mode of perception "presentational immediacy."[6] As its name implies, it refers to perceiving a piece of the world in the
immediate moment as that piece is presented to us. As a student said, "What
we see is what we see. What we hear is what we hear."

Whereas causal efficacy is a massive network of feeling the effect of
the past on the present (see below), presentational immediacy takes place
in the moment and largely involves what we take in through the senses.[7]
In presentational immediacy we focus on a limited arena of life. with consciousness, clarity, and precision. In a manner of speaking, we cut away
extraneous elements and concentrate on one nucleus as the center of our
perceptual fields and we pay little attention to surrounding elements. While
this image oversimplifies, presentational immediacy is like taking the card-
board tube around which the toilet paper was wound, and holding it up to
one eye, closing the other eye, and looking with one eye through the tube
at the world. We can see a circular piece of the world very clearly, but we
cannot see other things, including things that are taking place just outside

5. Williamson, "Preaching as Conversation," 73.

6. On presentational immediacy, see Franklin, *Speaking from the Depths*, 185–209.

7. Whitehead, *Symbolism*, 13–16; Whitehead, *Process and Reality*, 171–72.

the circle of view. We can typically describe the things that come to us in the mode of presentational immediacy with quite a bit of precision.

Steno-Language Serves Presentational Immediacy

My longtime colleague at Christian Theological Seminary, J. Gerald Janzen, calls attention to some of the most precise and beneficial expressions in presentational immediacy. "The languages of the special sciences, logic, mathematics, and rational philosophy have as their ideal the development of terms that are univalent, conceptually focused, precisely defined."[8] Janzen compares language in the mode of presentational immediacy to "steno-language" in Philip Wheelwright's well-known study, *The Burning Fountain*.[9] In steno-mode, language has a one-to-one correspondence with the things to which it refers. Janzen points out that such language is "enormously useful for the formulation of rational explanations and for exercising control over the world for specific purposes."[10]

A circular situation can develop between perception in the mode of presentational immediacy and the language we use to report the perception in that mode. We perceive an aspect of experience in presentational immediacy which prompts stenographic language to refer to the perception. When we use steno-language, it encourages those who read it or hear it to perceive the world in the dimension of presentational immediacy.[11] Steno-language is clear and to the point.

Here are some examples of things that come to us through presentational immediacy and that we typically discuss in steno-language, the language of plain sense.

- The address label on the package the postal carrier left on the porch
- The binary language that makes it possible for computers to operate
- The prescription for the anti-cholesterol medication that allows me to enjoy a wide variety of foods that would otherwise be inadvisable because they contribute to the risk of heart disease

---

8. Janzen, "Old Testament in 'Process' Perspective," 492.

9. Wheelwright, *Burning Fountain*, 15–17, 186–89.

10. Janzen, "Old Testament in 'Process' Perspective," 492.

11. Of course, as we note below, through symbolic reference, perception that begins in presentational immediacy and one-dimensional language can meld into perception in the mode of causal efficacy and depth language.

- The utterance "I am hungry" when I come upstairs from our morning workout and declare, "My stomach is empty and growling. I am
  hungry."

- The elder at the sacred table saying, at a certain point in the service of
  worship, "Let the deacons come forward."

Steno-language is the language of plain sense in which a word means what
it appears to mean in a one-to-one correspondence between the word and
that thing to which it refers.

Biblical scholars and preachers today often think broadly of the language of the Bible as depth language. To be sure, we cannot interview the
many individuals and communities who created and shaped the Bible regarding what kind of language they had in mind. But, it stands to reason
that at certain points in the long and complicated evolution of the biblical
traditions, some of the shapers of the Bible conceived of some of the biblical
material in steno-dimensions.

Similarly, one positive way of understanding why the church generated some of its affirmations of faith and other theological statements is to
see the councils and theologians seeking to bring into clear focus what they
understood as core elements in Christian faith. In the midst of the doctrinal controversies that beset the early churches, specific leadership groups
within the church developed affirmations of faith and other theological
statements to define the boundaries of Christian belief and practice. Many
decision-making bodies ruled that members of the churches had to believe
certain things about Jesus and could not believe other things. Without
claiming that the language of the affirmations of faith originated as entirely
steno-language, we can nevertheless say that many efforts moved in a one-
dimensional, defining way. For purposes that sometimes helped maintain
identity and empower mission, the church has often used steno-approaches
to affirmations of faith, Christian doctrine, and theology for the purpose of
building fences around community.

Regardless of the degree to which the earlier communities may have
perceived parts of the emerging and final biblical tradition as steno-expression, some Christians today think of the Bible in whole (or in their favorite
parts) in steno-ways. Indeed, one of the points of conflict in the contemporary church is the degree to which Christian communities interpret the
Bible (and Christian doctrine) in steno-terms or depth terms.

Whitehead laments the reduction of depth understandings of religious
language to one-dimensional meanings.

Religions commit suicide when they find their inspirations in
their dogmas. The inspiration of religion lies in the history of
religion. By this I mean that it is to be found in the primary
expressions of the intuitions of the finest types of religious lives.
The sources of religious belief are always growing, though some
supreme expressions may lie in the past. Records of these sources are not formulae. They elicit in us intuitive response which
pierces beyond dogma.[12]

Yet, plain talk can have a positive role in Christian preaching from a
process point of view. While presentational immediacy and one-dimensional language are easiest to see in connection with technical matters, physical
sensations, and physical objects, people can also perceive ideas and beliefs
in a kind of presentational immediacy and can speak about ideas in steno-
language. That is, people can write and speak intending to call forth one-
to-one correspondence between the expression and the reality to which it
refers. With respect to preaching and the life of the church, this capacity can
enable preacher and congregation to be pretty clear about what they believe
and what they do not believe.

As an example, a preacher in the process tradition sometimes employs
low-intensity steno-approach to language when indicating what the preacher does and does not expect regarding the second coming of Jesus, an event
that most writers of the gospels and letters anticipated in their relatively
near futures. Hope for the second coming in a steno-way climaxes many of
the major historic affirmations of faith across the centuries. A preacher in a
process community might, by contrast, summarize in direct plain talk the
fact that the preacher does not believe such an event will occur. In place of a
singular interruption of history by Jesus returning from outside the universe
(so to speak) the preacher believes that God is ever present, offering the
divine lure towards qualities of life that are similar to those expected in the
apocalyptic tradition in the new heaven and the new earth. Such language
has a steno-character as it deals in a direct one-to-one way with what the
preacher believes—and with what the congregation might believe—while
also having a depth character.

12. Whitehead, *Religion in the Making*, 138–39.

PERCEPTION AND LANGUAGE
IN THE MODE OF CAUSAL EFFICACY

In the mode of causal efficacy, we perceive life much more deeply than in the presentational immediacy.[13] Since life process is constantly taking place across the face of the universe, causal efficacy is utterly massive. As life process moves forward, it does not leave a trail of inanimate pieces of trash that the Department of Cosmic Public Works can shovel into a truck and haul to the dump. Rather, streams of experience come together in a moment of becoming which perishes and then feeds streams of experience from that moment into the continuing flow of life. Life process is constantly alive, and the effects of the past are ever alive in continuing life process—and ever accessible to some level of perception—albeit typically dimly, diffusely, and with subdued force.

The designation "causal efficacy" refers to the fact that elements of the vast and often undifferentiated past have effects in life that continue after an event has perished. Experiences from the past—especially feelings—influence subsequent experiences, sometimes in ways that are invisible but occasionally in ways that are more pronounced. Causal efficacy pertains to all elements in existence, and not just to human beings. Susanne K. Langer, a student and friend of Whitehead, notes that the mass of experience at work in causal efficacy has its own quality and patterns.

> Human feeling is a fabric, not a vague mass. It has an intricate dynamic pattern, possible combinations, and new emergent phenomena. It is a pattern of organically interdependent tensions and resolutions, a pattern of almost infinitely complex activation and cadence. To it belongs the whole gamut of our sensibility—the sense of straining thought, all mental attitude and motor set. Those are the deeper reaches that underlie the surface waves of our emotion and make human life a life of feeling instead of an unconscious metabolic existence interrupted by feelings.[14]

We can perceive aspects of this fabric of feeling. However, we seldom perceive aspects of causal efficacy in ways that a crisp and clear.

David Roy puts it this way. Causal efficacy is "a means of direct, non-mediated perception that arises from the background. It is the world in us, that feeling in our guts, that intuition that arises from the background. It

---

13. On language in the mode of causal efficacy, see Franklin, *Speaking from the Depths*, 124–39; 232–41.

14. Langer, *Philosophical Sketches*, 89.

accounts for knowledge that comes to us from others about their condition that is not the result of visual or auditory perceptions."[15]

Prehension: What Happens When We Perceive in the Mode of Causal Efficacy

Whitehead uses the term "prehension," adapted from the word "apprehension," to call attention to the particular character of what happens in perception in the mode of causal efficacy.[16] In prehension, the self receives data from the past and incorporates it into particular events of becoming. Although prehension can involve receiving cogently stated thoughts and other kinds of clear and definite data, prehension goes far beyond to include the full range of experience, most of which exists at pre-linguistic levels of feeling and intuition.

When we prehend the past, we do get more than simple data about the past. Much more: we feel the effects of the past in the way Janzen and Langer describe above. We may decide consciously what to do with these effects in the present moment of becoming. However, as we have noted previously, the awareness of these things may never rise to the level of consciousness. Often, these things become a part of our awareness and decision-making process at the level of feeling and intuition. As a part of prehension we can sometimes name the effects of perception, especially of the past, and can then deal with them consciously and critically. But often prehension remains at the level of inarticulate feeling.

Depth Language Serves Perception in Causal Efficacy

Just as perception in the mode of presentational immediacy has a correlate in steno-language, so causal efficacy has a correlate in language that is sometimes called "depth language," "expressive language," or tensive language."[17] Indeed, Stephen Franklin entitles his magisterial study of experience, perception, and language in Whitehead, *Speaking from the Depths*.[18] A person or community can use language so as to express perception that arises from the depths of causal efficacy. The notion of speaking from the depths, of course, implies listening to the depths. That is, the language of the speaker

15. Roy, "Creative Adventure of Pastoral Counseling," 109.

16. Whitehead, *Symbolism*, 39–48; Whitehead, *Process and Reality*, 168–83.

17. Wheelwright, *Burning Fountain*, 12–17, 73–171.

18. Franklin, *Speaking from the Depths*.

can stir the awareness of the depths in the heart of the listeners. However, the speaking can seldom express the deepest of the depths. Even the most charged language can only go so far in evoking the gravity of the depths.

What kinds of language can covey depth expressions? In the first instance, Whitehead notes that "the deeper truths must be adumbrated by myths."[19] Whitehead has in mind here not the casual use of the word "myth" to refer to something that is not true but to stories and other imagistic expressions that seek to explain aspects of reality. Susanne K. Langer notes that the "ultimate end" of mythic expression "is not wishful distortion of the world, but serious envisagement of its fundamental truths; moral orientation, not escape." Indeed, myth exists "essentially for understanding actual experience."[20]

Myth is peculiarly well suited to function in this way. In its fullest literary form, a myth uses setting, characters, and plot to describe how the mythmaking/myth-telling community feels about the world and what it is like to experience the world and life. When a myth has a large place in a community's understanding of itself, a speaker or writer can evoke the whole myth, or significant aspects of it, with a phrase or a word.

Wheelwright calls attention to poetry as another mode of expression that conveys depth-meaning. Yet, as Wheelwright implies, expressive language can occur in many literary forms.[21] Susanne Langer points out that the arts can help express awareness that comes through causal efficacy. Using media appropriate to their talents, artists express what they know about aspects of the life of feeling through things such as music, dance, painting, sculpture, and the fabric arts. As already noted, language can function in this way via poetry and various forms of narrative ranging from myth through short story and novel.[22]

In their own cultural contexts, the arts often communicate at the deepest levels when they are presented directly to the receivers without intermediate commentary. To make two observations that are important to biblical, theological, and homiletical interpretation: at one level, the arts often communicate what the creator knows about the life of feeling even when transported from one culture to another. However, at another level, the receiving community's engagement with an artistic expression can often be significantly enriched with some interpretation of background matters that the originating culture assumed.

19. Whitehead, *Modes of Thought*, 10.
20. Langer, *Philosophy in a New Key*, 176–77.
21. Wheelwright, *Burning Fountain*, 73–101.
22. Langer, *Philosophy in a New Key*.

Depth expression is less a matter of form and more of function. Janzen describes how this mode of language works.

> Employing multivalent words, laden with innumerable asso-
> ciational and evaluational and emotional ligatures, this mode
> of languages conveys the essential connectedness and concrete
> particularity of things. With its disconcertingly capacious tol-
> erance, and even demand for referential congruity, contextual
> variation, plurisignification, soft focus, paralogical dimension-
> ality, assertorial lightness, and paradox, this mode of language
> is ill-designed to serve the limited functional purposes of, say,
> the special sciences. But these same features enable it to report
> the empirical world most richly and concretely for human,
> understanding.[23]

Janzen calls Whitehead to mind on this point. Such "language is expression from one's past into one's present. It is the reproduction in the present of sensa which have intimate association with realities of the past . . . An
articulated memory is the gift of language."[24]

Depth Language in the Bible and in Affirmations of Faith and in Other Theological Statements

The Bible itself contains much depth language. The history of the interpretation of the Bible has depth dimensions, and the Bible itself, as a collective
book, is a depth symbol. At the simplest level, of course, the Bible contains
myth, poetry, narrative, and other forms of depth expression. Interacting
with a biblical text—especially when illuminated by exegesis—can invoke a
powerful sense of connection with the past. Indeed, the psalmist has direct
reference to the immediate existential experience of chaos when saying,
"Out of the depths, I cry to you" (Ps 130:1). Beyond the immediate moment, the cry evokes the penumbra of causal efficacy in a way that often
happens: when we read the Bible, we become aware of depths in existence.
In this spirit, many preachers "feel a text," that is, they have the sense of
knowing something about a text that they cannot initially articulate. Often
this impression is a result of causal efficacy.

The Bible plays a key role in helping the Christian community come to
clarity with respect to our deepest conviction about God and the world and

---

23. Janzen, "Old Testament in 'Process' Perspective," 493.

24. Whitehead, *Modes of Thought*, 33, cited in Janzen, "Old Testament in 'Process' Perspective," 493.

in making theological sense of life.[25] The community often uses the Bible as part of this task. At the same time, because it comes from cultures and worldviews that are so different from many today, the community needs to make theological sense out of the Bible itself. The relationship between making theological sense of the Bible and using the Bible to make theological sense of life is reciprocal and ongoing. David Tracy, a theologian who taught for many years at the University of Chicago, refers to a form of this interaction as "mutual critical correlation."[26]

Whitehead seldom comments in a broad way on the nature of the biblical witness and on how it might be part of the reciprocal conversation aimed to making theological sense of life. But Whitehead does speak broadly of "rational religion" in a way that helps explain why the Bible has had and continues to play a formative role in Christian community. Rational religion is one

> whose beliefs and rituals have been reorganized with the aim of making it the central element in a coherent ordering of life—an ordering which shall be coherent both in respect to the elucidation of thought, and in respect to the direction of conduct towards a unified purpose commanding ethical approval.[27]

A rational religion, Whitehead continues, "appeals to the direct intuition of special occasions, and to the elucidatory power of its concepts for all occasions. It arises from that which is special, but it extends to what is general."[28]

Such a religion involves much more than the Bible or even conversation with the Bible. A rational religion is a comprehensive statement of deep theological convictions expressed through worship, creed, congregation, and broader life through which a community embodies a theological view of God, the world, and life in a way that is intellectually and morally credible. A rational religion helps a community see how all the pieces of the world fit together in a meaningful and believable pattern of relationship. As indicated above, the church draws on perspectives from the Bible for contribution to the vision of the coherent ordering of life and interprets the Bible from the perspective of that vision, and sometimes takes positions over and against the Bible.

25. For a magisterial view of the importance of the Bible in Christian community from a neo-process perspective, see Williamson, *Way of Blessing*, 73–96; cf. Williamson and R. J. Allen, *Credible and Timely Word*, 71–90; Williamson and R. J. Allen, *Adventures of the Spirit*, 113–36.

26. R. J. Allen, "Preaching as Mutual Critical Correlation."

27. Whitehead, *Religion in the Making*, 31; cf. Williamson, *Way of Blessing*, 64–66.

28. Whitehead, *Religion in the Making*, 32.

In a similar way, though writing under the heading of the traditional theological category of revelation, H. Richard Niebuhr, who taught theology at Yale for many years, resonates with Whitehead when Niebuhr describes revelation.

> Revelation means for us that part of our inner story which illuminates the rest of it, and which is itself intelligible . . . The special occasion to which we appeal in the Christian church is called Jesus Christ, in whom we see the righteousness of God, [God's] power and wisdom. But from the special occasion we also derive the concepts which make possible the elucidation of all the events of our history. Revelation means this intelligible event which makes all other events intelligible.[29]

The different churches and theological families have different views of the nature of the Bible and on how they draw on the Bible in formulating their versions of rational religion and revelation. Nevertheless. Indeed, the Bible does not itself constitute the whole of "rational religion" nor is the Bible by itself a comprehensive instrument of revelation. But churches and theologians nearly always find the *über*-narrative(s) of the Bible, or particular biblical passages or themes, to function analogously to the "special occasions" that give rise to the "elucidatory power of its concepts for [many other] occasions." Elements from all the sixty-six books of the Protestant Bible—and not (per Niebuhr's formulation) just the twenty-seven books focused on Jesus Christ—are part of the inner history and consciousness of the church that "illuminates the rest of it," and, indeed, make "all other events intelligible."[30]

Elements of the Bible may themselves have arisen from "special occasions" with "elucidatory power." Over the centuries, the church has found that engaging the Bible provides opportunity not only to explain those special occasions but to experience the engagement with the Bible in the church's contemporary context as themselves events that "make other events intelligible."

While churches may have articulated many affirmations of faith and many other theological statements in a mindset of theological presentational immediacy, affirmations of faith often have a depth character. To be sure, the precise meanings of the words and grammatical constructions are important, and preachers and theologians do need to help congregations wrestle with the theological constructions as clearly as possible. Indeed, Bernard Meland notes that while the "realities of faith" are

29. Niebuhr, *Meaning of Revelation*, 93.
30. Niebuhr, *Meaning of Revelation*, 93.

energies within experiences that are now immediately upon us, it is nevertheless true that awareness of [these things] within the structure of experience among any people rests back upon, or in some subtle way issues from, a cultic or cultural legacy of long-standing which may best be expressed in terms of themes or motifs of the faith. I have come to regard these primal themes or motifs as the enduring basis of our Christian legacy, rather than any formulated doctrines or creeds; for the latter, while they have their claim to importance for specific purposes, cultic or otherwise, must be regarded as various renderings of this primal legacy. Doctrines have proven expendable; yet the legacy of faith persists.[31]

Hearing and reciting an affirmation of faith can prompt self and community to go beyond considering the specific concepts set out in the affirmations to the deeper and wide sense of movement of God and human response across history.

SYMBOLIC REFERENCE

The self and community often operate in the modes of presentational immediacy and causal efficacy at the same time. That is, in ordinary, everyday perception, we take in the world simultaneously through presentational immediacy and through causal efficacy. Whitehead uses the designation "symbolic reference" to refer to the process whereby the self relates these two patterns of perceiving.[32] Ronald L. Farmer, a biblical scholar and theologian who works in the process framework, explains,

> Whereas presentational immediacy merely presupposes causal efficacy, symbolic reference integrates the two modes so that there is both clear location in a contemporary region (presentational immediacy) and the power of continuity with the past and an efficacy for the future (causal efficacy).[33]

In presentational immediacy we perceive a piece of the world with clarity and directness but in isolation from the fullness of life. In causal efficacy we sense the piece in wider relationship to the whole fabric of life, although this sense sometimes remains inarticulate.

---

31. Meland, *Fallible Forms and Symbols*, 31.
32. Whitehead, *Symbolism*, 18–20; Whitehead, *Process and Reality*, 168–83.
33. Farmer, *Beyond the Impasse*, 87.

Symbolic reference is a mixed mode of perception in which, as the designation "symbolic reference" implies, the self works out how presentational immediacy and causal efficacy and their corresponding modes of language relate (refer) to one another.[34] Whitehead describes how symbolic reference works.

> There is "symbolic reference" between the two species when the perception of a member of one species evokes its correlate in the other species, and precipitates upon this correlate the fusion of feelings, emotions, and derivate actions, belong to either of the pair of correlates, and which are also enhanced by this correlation.[35]

In the mode of symbolic reference, language typically associated with one mode of perception can evoke awareness in the other mode. A symbol in one mode of expression can refer to experience in the other mode of expression.

Stephen Franklin notes that symbolic reference moves towards limiting the "shallowness" of presentational immediacy by placing the presentational symbol in the wider and deeper context of causal efficacy. Symbolic reference simultaneously seeks to sharpen the specificity of causal efficacy by eliminating some of its "vagueness."[36]

Consider some examples introduced earlier but amplified to take account of how symbolic reference can bring the experience and language associated with presentational immediacy into interaction with the experience and language of causal efficacy.

- The label on the package that sits on the front porch may have been affixed as steno-language, but, when I see the return address on that label, I am stirred by the awareness of my long and deep relationship with the sender.

- The physician wrote the prescription for anti-cholesterol medication as a steno-symbol, but when reference to that prescription in conversation around the dinner table evokes the forceful awareness of people in my wider family damaged and killed by heart disease, that prescription is a powerful symbol of the desire to live.

- When I come upstairs from our morning workout and declare, "I am hungry," I report the sense of hunger in my abdomen. But when I hear the reading from Matt 5:11 in worship on Sunday regarding those who

34. See further, Franklin, *Speaking from the Depths*, 210–23.
35. Whitehead, *Process and Reality*, 181.
36. Franklin, *Speaking from the Depths*, 212–14.

hunger and thirst for righteousness, the reference to hunger evokes the visceral memory of being hungry for food and casts the yearning for righteousness—that is, for all things in the cosmos to live towards inclusive well-being—in visceral terms similar to the hungry body's yearning for food. I *feel* the hunger and thirst for righteousness.

- At a certain point in the service of worship, the elder at the sacred table says, "Let the deacons come forward." While the elder may have intended to use the words as a steno-signal, the act of the deacons coming forward represents the congregation seeking grace and offering itself for service to and in that grace.

In symbolic reference, a steno-expression can arouse an experience of causal efficacy either apart from or in conjunction with the intention of the speaker or author. Similarly, people can hear a depth expression on a steno-channel.

THE FALLACY OF MISPLACED CONCRETENESS

One of the most egregious uses of language—one of its most fallible uses—is the fallacy of misplaced concreteness. Whitehead uses the phrase "fallacy of misplaced concreteness" to refer to a common mistake that people make in perception. Whitehead introduces this idea by pointing out that it is impossible to give an adequate account of "a bit of matter" by simply plotting the object's present location in space and time. Instead, to have a more adequate understanding of the "bit of matter," one must describe it in much fuller contexts of its becoming. In misplaced concreteness, people sometimes look at something specific and assume that what they see is the whole of the situation when more is actually involved, often beyond the range of immediate perception.[37] Often the fallacy is that they mistake the part for the whole.

The fallacy of misplaced concreteness can take place in all modes of perception, including language both written and oral-aural media. In regard to language, it is the fallacy of misplaced understanding of language. A writer or speaker can use a word or phrase (or develop a sentence, paragraph, or book) as if the expression has but one, limited meaning, when, in fact, the expression is connected to a wide range of associations. A person can speak or hear in the mode of presentational immediacy or steno-language without taking account of the fact that the expression is but one piece of a much larger network of associations.

37. Whitehead, *Science and the Modern World*, 52–55; Whitehead, *Process and Reality*, 7, 19, 93–94.

A complicating factor for the preacher is confusion that can result when the preacher uses an expression in resonance with causal efficacy, but the congregation (or some members) commit the fallacy of misplaced language by hearing the expression in the guise of presentational immediacy. The people hear only a part of what the preacher intends. Of course, the opposite can be true. A preacher can speak in the mode of presentational immediacy when the congregation (or part of it) hears an expression resonant with causal efficacy.

Through symbolic reference, language that begins in the mind on a steno-channel can connect to causal efficacy in such a way as to evoke more than the speaker intended. It is important for the preacher to recognize that the reverse flow can also happen in something we might think of as symbolic reduction. A person or congregation can receive a message arising from the depths and charged with causal efficacy and reduce it to a steno-like message. This, of course, is the fallacy of misplaced concreteness.

However, even when a person or community engages in this kind of symbolic reductionism, the language itself is still charged with causal efficacy. Indeed, one dimension of many renewal movements in the church is precisely this phenomenon. A generation takes the faith of the church experienced in causal efficacy and expressed in depth-language and reduces it to limited experience expressed in steno-language. But as time passes, a person or community connects afresh with the dimension of causal efficacy so that experience regenerates self and community. The same words that had recently been spoken and heard in presentational immediacy resonate with causal efficacy and function in depth ways.

CRITICAL REFLECTION IS KEY

Perception and language can be quite powerful. However, preachers should not lapse into rhapsody about them. Whitehead notes that people must make judgments.[38] Coming to clarity on these matters of what a community *really* believes is often a complicated affair in the light of the theological diversity of the theological traditions about which we can be conscious as well as the fact that causal efficacy contains inarticulate vectors from the past—including its most destructive moments—that play into prehension. We should also add the human impulse towards oversimplification as a complicating factor.

On the one hand, a preacher should honor the otherness of all experience, perception, and language. On the other hand, if—as chapter 1

38. Whitehead, *Process and Reality*, 256–57.

proposes—God's ultimate purpose is for all entities in creation to live together in mutual support towards inclusive well-being, then some experiences, perceptions, and uses of language are more consistent with God's purposes than others. Indeed, inappropriate judgments can be expressed in either steno- or depth language, as appropriate judgements can be. Just because a feeling comes from the depth does not mean that the feeling is commendable. The past is filled with brutal, self-undermining and community-destroying experiences whose effects linger through causal efficacy. A preacher needs to help the community distinguish points at which experience, perception, and language are more and less consistent with our best understanding of the divine aims at a given moment in time.

As noted above, Christian communities often turn to the Bible and other voices in Christian tradition to help with this sifting process. The scriptures and voices in history often alert the community to possibilities for becoming that the community has forgotten, or not considered, or even not imagined. However, Meland joins other process theologians in pointing out that a community's beliefs must withstand the test of lived experience.[39] Something that an ancient community, such as Israel or the church, regarded as elucidatory or making intelligent in the Bible or in a historic affirmation of faith, today's community might view as antique, obfuscatory, or even wrong-headed. Russel Pregeant puts the matter succinctly. Whether from the Bible, official pronouncements of the church, theologians, or preachers, "Religious language (like all other modes of discourse) may be misleading."[40] In particular, religious statements can sound so direct and precise that we face "an overwhelming temptation to treat religious statements as literal," thus short-circuiting the many limitations in our perception and language and drifting into the fallacy of misplaced concreteness.[41]

As indicated above, I have found that steno-language can be helpful, even if it is not always adequate. For the hallmarks of the language of presentational immediacy are clarity and precision. Speaking in this mode can help the preacher state *as clearly as we can* what we believe—and do not believe—about God's nature, God's power, and God's purposes. While such language can be reductionistic, it also puts us on the spot to articulate plainly what we really believe God can do—and what we think God cannot do. It helps us name our deepest convictions about God. It helps us identify what we can count on in the way of divine presence and operation, and what we cannot. And, of course, language in presentational immediacy helps us

39. Meland, *Fallible Forms and Symbols*, 27.
40. Pregeant, *Christology beyond Dogma*, 38.
41. Pregeant, *Christology beyond Dogma*, 39.

come to clarity with respect to how we can respond to the divine invitation, what we can do and what we cannot do. As we noted above, and expand more fully below, churches often use language in this mode in affirmations of faith (creeds) and formal theological statements.[42]

Remember the Finitude of Human Perception and Language

Yet, as already noted, steno-language does not account for the fullness of experience. This is especially true of language in the service of religion. Even when we speak as precisely as we can, steno-language seldom accounts for the fullness of religions experience and perception. The language that *accounts most adequately* for religious experience and perception is language that arises from the depths of the speaker and touches the depths of the listener.

Two key phrases in the immediately preceding exposition are italicized: *as clearly as we can* and *accounts most adequately*. Whitehead famously points out, "Mothers can ponder many things in their hearts which their lips cannot express."[43] Bernard Meland puts it this way: "We live more deeply than we can think."[44] Even the language of the depths does not capture the fullness of the experience of living. Consequently, "No formulation of truth out of the language we use can be adequate for expressing what is really real, fully available, fully experienced within this mystery of existing, in the mystery of dying, or in whatever surpasses these creatural occurrences of such urgent moment to each of us."[45] Indeed, Meland notes,

> Our language is rarely of a depth to apprehend, least of all to comprehend, the realities of which our lives are made, and within whose context they exist. Yet when we speak, we speak out of a depth of existing; and, to a degree, in terms of it. And that may be the best we can hope for.[46]

This is why Meland thinks of language as "fallible forms and symbols." At its best, language points toward realities of lived experience, but language seldom captures the fullness of experience. What we seek is not absolute

---

42. In the next chapter, I present three criteria adapted from the work of Clark M. Williamson that help the preacher evaluate texts, doctrines, broader ideas, and experiences in a process theological frame of reference.

43. Whitehead, *Religion in the Making*, 67.

44. Meland, *Fallible Forms and Symbols*, 24.

45. Meland, *Fallible Forms and Symbols*, 24.

46. Meland, *Fallible Forms and Symbols*, 30.

certainty. Indeed, because of the relativities of perception and language, that is not attainable. But we can move towards "reassurance, confidence, in a response of trust."[47]

---

47. Meland, *Fallible Forms and Symbols*, 32.

3

Preaching from
a Process Worldview

Conversation among Invitations

As WITH SO MANY other things in the ever-generative sphere of process theology, we cannot speak of *the* process way to prepare and preach or of *the* singular process understanding of the sermon. From the perspective of the process family, every sermon is a distinct occasion of homiletical becoming. Indeed, there can be as many approaches to preaching in the process theological household as there are preachers and sermons. Perhaps more than any other theological movement, process conceptuality resists formulaic thinking about preparing and preaching the sermon, about the nature and purpose of the sermon, as well as about considering the effects of the sermon.

This chapter puts forward *a* process approach to preaching, not with the idea of setting out an imperial homiletic but with the hope of articulating a way of thinking about the nature of preaching is in continuity with core perspectives of process conceptuality while keeping the window open for creatively adapting these things in light of the ever-changing circumstances in which preaching takes place.[1]

---

1. As noted earlier, only a few preachers and scholars have set out comprehensive approaches to preaching in process perspective. These include Pittenger, *Proclaiming Christ Today*; Pittenger, *Preaching the Gospel*; Beardslee et al., *Biblical Preaching*; Suchocki, *Whispered Word*; Sigmon, *Engaging the Gadfly*; Sigmon, "Preaching from the Perspective"; Williamson and R. J. Allen, *Credible and Timely Word*; Williamson and R. J. Allen, *Adventures of the Spirit*, 137–58; R. J. Allen, "Preaching as Conversation among Proposals."

To help the conversational approach to preaching stand out, the chapter begins by summarizing common features of the different exegesis-application method of preaching. We then turn to something that is fundamental to this process approach to preaching: the notion of invitation (proposal, proposition) in process conceptuality. The preacher develops the idea of the sermon as conversation among invitations with an eye towards helping the congregation identify and respond to invitations that hold promise for the inclusive well-being of all in the congregation and in the other communities. The chapter identifies several important functions of the sermon and concludes with a discussion of a conversational approach to the sermon in relationship to prophetic preaching. We take these concerns into more practical matters of methods of preparing and preaching in subsequent chapters.[2]

A BIRD'S-EYE VIEW OF THE EXEGESIS-APPLICATION APPROACH TO PREACHING

At the outset, I note a commonplace assumption about preaching in many theological families that is quite different from the perspective of *You Never Stand in the Same Pulpit Twice*. Most preachers share the assumption that the work of the preacher is to identify a message from a biblical text and apply it to situations today.[3] We refer to this phenomenon as "the exegesis-

2. These considerations are developed in chapters 4–9. While that part of the book presents developing a sermon from a process point of view in a series of linear chapters—very much like steps that follow one another—in actual preparation, the elements of preparation may take place in different sequences, including the possibility that several could occur at the same time. It is not important that the preacher follow a particular series of steps but that the preacher brings such matters into self-conscious and critical view.

3. Theologians are divided on the question of whether Christian preaching *must* deal in a serious way with a biblical text in order for the sermon to be a real sermon. Most books published in the field of preaching today assume that the sermon will center in a biblical text or biblical theme. However, topical preaching can have an honored place in the pulpit. In the topical sermon, the preacher interprets a topic—e.g., a doctrine or a personal or social issue—from the perspective of the preacher's deep theological convictions rather than from the specific perspective of a text. See R. J. Allen, *Preaching the Topical Sermon*, and Rzepka and Sawyer, *Thematic Preaching*. In the current volume I focus on preaching in conversation with a biblical text, but the principles can easily be adapted to preaching from topics. In addition to *Preaching the Topical Sermon*, see R. J. Allen, *Interpreting the Gospel*, 97–140.

I should note that while most preachers today claim to preach the text, some preachers never interact in a significant exegetical way with the text but use the text as a springboard to a discussion of a topic, often one that the preacher already had in mind before preparing the sermon. It might be more honest for this preacher to take a

application approach to preaching." This approach assumes that every biblical text contains an authoritative message the preacher can identify and
commend. The preacher builds a bridge from the ancient world to today.
The traffic of meaning moves one way on the bridge from the past to the
present. The sermon is a truck carrying a payload of meaning from the past
to the present where today's preacher will unload the truck and delver the
meaning. As Edward Farley characterizes this viewpoint: every biblical passage contains a "preachable x."[4] Or, as a popular epigram puts it, the task of
the minister is to "preach the text."[5]

Through exegesis, the preacher must find a theological message that
is pertinent for today and then draw out the implications of that message.
Three of the most important criteria for evaluating a sermon in this paradigm are the degrees to which the preacher (1) offers a plausible exegesis of
the text, (2) focuses the sermon on the actual exegetical-theological content
of the text, and (3) makes the intent of the text come alive for today's world.

The preacher translates the meaning of the text into comparable
meaning for today. The preacher *proclaims* the message to the congregation.
Indeed, some preacher and congregations view the sermon as God's own
word.

Under this umbrella, preachers can bring all manner of data into the
sermon ranging from personal experience to public issues, including information from the social and physical sciences to the arts and philosophy. But
the preacher uses this data in the service of clarifying the meaning of the
text in the past and drawing out the significance of the text for the contemporary community.

As already noted, the theological content of the text is the norm by
which to measure all other perspectives. If the preacher comes upon a text
that appears to present a theological, moral, or scientific difficulty, then the
preacher might make some of the following moves. For one the preacher
can work harder at exegesis to find things in text itself (or in its historical or literary contexts) that resolves the difficulty. This approach is often
at work behind sermons with titles such as "What Paul Really Says about

---

topical approach.

4. Farley, "Preaching the Bible," 76. Farley offers extensive critical reflection on
the bridge paradigm for preaching. His approach recurs in nearly every historic and
contemporary theological family, as we can see in the discussions in R. J. Allen, *Thinking Theologically.* Different families do perceive the content of the "preachable x" differently, but the assumptions of such an "x" and the movement from then to now is
commonplace.

5. Strictly speaking, of course, the preacher does not simply preach "the text" but
"preaches "the text as the preacher interprets it."

Homosexuality" wherein the preacher tries to show that the apostle was really a first-century advocate of LGBTQAI+ rights.

For another approach, the preacher can take a hermeneutical tack that allows the preacher to leave behind some of the baggage associated with the text while bringing the central message of the text into the present world in an authoritative way. Demythologizing is a familiar example. The preacher recognizes that a text makes use of ancient mythological descriptions of the world that differ from contemporary scientific understandings. The preacher then argues that the mythology is just the husk in which the real meaning is wrapped, so the preacher strips away the scientifically inaccurate mythology and presents the theologically meaningful core meaning that the preacher can apply to today. For example, when Ps 75:3 refers to God steadying the pillars of the earth, the reference is to a three-story universe in which the earth sits on pillars over a primeval chaos. When the psalm says that God steadies the pillars of the earth, the psalm means that God prevents the earth from descending into chaos. The preacher today can leave behind the three-story universe while claiming that God continues to steady the world.

For a third approach, a preacher may make an analogy between the function of the text in ancient world and the function of the text and the function of the text in the world today. Caesar and the Roman Empire, for instance, ruled the Mediterranean world at the time of the Gospels and Letters. The Empire is noted for idolatry, for most of the resources being concentrated in the hands of the few elites, for rigid social hierarchy, and for rule by threat of violence. The Roman Empire is no more. But nations and other systems and communities in the contemporary setting function analogously to the Roman Empire in antiquity. If the text challenges some aspect of Roman culture or rule, the preacher can often angle from the ancient challenge to contemporary challenges to empire.

As I have noted already, a preacher in the process movement can preach in this exegesis-application model with many biblical texts. When faced with difficulties of worldview, culture, or theology, the preacher can often make the kinds of hermeneutical moves just reviewed. I know. I sometimes take such steps. However, in my view, some biblical passages are so theologically intractable the preacher is compelled to preach against them (or against part of them). The two steps of the exegesis-application model sometimes lull the preacher into forgetting conversation with other voices that that can enrich the sermon. Moreover, in the exegesis-application model, the preacher can become so accustomed to finding a "preachable x" in the text that the preacher can overlook theological (and other) problems with texts and can also overlook some possibilities invited by the text.

PREACHING AS CONVERSATION
AMONG INVITATIONS

I join some other preachers and scholars in the process family in thinking of preaching as conversation among invitations (or proposals) with an
ear towards discerning which invitations offer optimum opportunities for
becoming to the congregation and to the world. A preacher in the process
household is not obligated to find "a preachable x" *in every text*. Instead, a
preacher engages in a conversation with a text and other sources and aims
to help the congregation to better identify and respond to possibilities for
more inclusive well-being. The preacher's *conversation with the text* rather
than the text itself generates the possibilities that the preacher brings to expression in the sermon.

This approach requires understanding what process means by "invitation" as well as what we mean by "a conversational approach to preaching."
"Conversation" has been a buzzword in theology for the last generation.
Multiple times every day I hear people refer the importance of having
conversation about significant subjects. Getting something into "the conversation" is a buzzword. However, conversation has a particular frame of
reference in a conversational approach to preaching.[6]

---

6. Conventional approaches to preaching often envision the purpose of sermon to
be "proclaiming the word of God," as if the preacher has a clear window into that word
and can announce it to the congregation. To be sure, as this book makes clear, I think
God offers specific aims to individuals and to communities. However, human finitude,
especially with respect to the relativity of perception, means that we do not have immediate and confident access to the fullness of God's word, or to God's purposes for
each person and occasion. The top-down model of authority invoked by the language
of "proclaiming God's word" invests preachers with a level of authority that exceeds
our own actual. Moreover, history is replete with preachers "proclaiming God's word"
when that word turned out to be a projection of their own prejudices and a platform
to establish their own exploitative power or that of groups or systems which they sa-
cralized by speaking God's word over it. One thinks of the Eurocentric preaching that
blessed slavery in the ante-bellum south or the "German Christians" who consecrated
Nazism. While those examples are extreme, even preachers who are more theologically
alert and critical are subject to our own relativities and to those of the various groups
and cultures in which we participate. Hence, rather than "proclaiming God's word," I
think it is more honest to speak of the preacher offering interpretations for God's aims.

The conversational model is especially helpful to preachers in a process modality
since others can often help us notice things we might otherwise overlook. Preachers
bouncing their ideas off others, and vice versa, are, perhaps, less like to move toward
absolutizing or even idolizing their own interpretations. But there is no guarantee conversation will help preachers or congregations avoid misrepresenting the divine aims.
Nor will conversation always lead to correctly naming God's purposes and means of
inclusive well-being. As we know so well in democracies, the will of the people is not
always in the best interests of the community. Indeed, the will of the people can erode

What Are Invitations?

I begin this discussion by nuancing the vocabulary at its center. Process thinkers sometimes use different expressions for a similar thing—"proposals," "propositions," "theories" or "concrete possibilities." While I sometimes use all these words for the sake of variety, as I commented above, I prefer the word "invitation" as I think that people outside the process orb can more easily recognize its function. An invitation urges people to make a personal investment. The word "invitation" seems to me to have more immediate existential connection with people today than "proposal" or "proposition."

Whitehead describes an invitation (a proposal) as a "lure for feeling."[7] As we mentioned earlier, "Feeling" in this context is much more than emotion in the sense of an immediate, natural, instinctive wave of sensation; it is a network of understanding that involves trans-verbal awareness as well as articulate thought.[8] David Lull describes invitations as possibilities for "how things could be."[9] In their most dramatic form, invitations envision "the transformation of 'the way things are'"[10] William Beardslee describes an invitation as "the indispensable vehicle of imagination which reaches out from that which has already been experienced towards possibilities as yet unrealized."[11] Casey Sigmon notes that the sermon that offers such an invitation expands the hearer's world.[12] An invitation assumes the influences carried by causal efficacy from the past into the present and if offers the actual opportunities towards becoming that are available in the present circumstances. An invitation offers self or community—human, animal,

---

the public good. Similar things can happen in conversational preaching.

The journal *Encounter* offers a spirited discussion of the value of the notion of proclamation in the entire issue: "Is the Goal of Preaching Still to Proclaim?" 78.2 (2018), edited by O. Allen).

7. Whitehead, *Process and Reality*, 25, 185–207. Cf. Franklin, *Speaking from the Depths*, 17–27.

8. Recall Susanne K. Langer's explanation. "Human feeling is a fabric, not a vague mass. It has an intricate dynamic pattern, possible combinations, and new emergent phenomena. It is a pattern of organically interdependent and interdetermined tensions and resolutions, a pattern of almost infinitely complex activation and cadence. To it belongs the whole gamut of our sensibility—the sense of straining thought, all mental attitude and motor set. Those are the deeper reaches that underlie the surface waves of our emotion and make human life a life of feeling instead of an unconscious metabolic existence interrupted by feelings" (Langer, *Philosophical Sketches*, 89).

9. Lull, "What Is 'Process Hermeneutics'?" 190.

10. Lull, "What Is 'Process Hermeneutics'?" 190.

11. Beardslee, "Whitehead and Hermeneutic," 34.

12. Sigmon, "Preaching from the Perspective," 000[x-ref].

nature—the opportunity to shape the next moments of becoming according to the possibilities invited by the invitation.

In the process approach to sermon preparation, as in every moment of life, God offers preacher and congregation an "initial aim." God's initial aim is an invitation to the congregation. Marjorie Suchocki elegantly describes this aim.

> In Whitehead's model, consciousness is a late phase of each mo-
> mentary being, but the initial aim is the beginning phase. The
> content of the aim provides direction for how we might become
> ourselves in each moment; it offers a possible integration of the
> past in light of a best future.[13]

While this aim is always present, human beings and other elements of world do not always recognize it or respond to it appropriately. Preachers hope to discover a form of this aim and bring it into the flow of sermon preparation.

Process preachers—including me—sometimes rhapsodize about invitations as if they all come from God and as if they only offer opportunities that enhance inclusive well-being. While God's initial aim is always present, so are other invitations from a variety of sources. Some invitations pose next steps that undermine inclusive well-being. One of the callings of the preacher is to help the congregation identify invitations and sort through them to determine which are more and less likely to enhance inclusive well-being.

Invitations can concern the whole sphere of life. In the theological arena, preachers focus particularly on three dimensions of invitations. (1) What does an invitation invite its recipients to believe about God and God's purposes (2) What does an invitation invite its recipients to believe about the world, and what is possible in the world? (3) What does an invitation invite its recipients to do? We will return to these issues repeatedly, but it is good to have these theological foci running in the background.

Invitations come in as many forms as there are forms of life. Some of the most obvious invitations are in verbal form. Invitations can take the form of steno-language (in the mode of presentational immediacy) or depth language (in the mode of causal efficacy). Proposals in steno-speech are typically the easiest with which to work because they are so explicit. The invitation is stated directly so that preacher and congregation can immediately grasp it, identify its implications, and reflect theologically on it. A preacher may immediately be a little suspicious of an invitation in steno-language because it may appear to be shallow. Yet, the preacher should remember that an invitation that appears to be steno in character may have depth

---

13. Suchocki, *Whispered Word*, 7.

dimensions that do not immediately come to the attention of the preacher or congregation.

Large parts of Christian tradition are handed on in the form of words. Christian doctrines—especially those stated officially by denominations—often explicitly state invitations. The historic creeds, for instance, invite those who recite the creeds to organize their worldviews around the elements of the creeds. Voices from the history of the church—including signal figures like Augustine, Aquinas, Luther, Calvin, and Wesley—are often quite pointed in what they invite listeners or readers to believe and do. Churches and theologians debate the degree to which to understand such statements as steno-language or depth language. My informal sense is that churches towards the conservative end of the theological spectrum tend to take doctrinal language in more steno-modalities while churches towards the progressive end of the spectrum tend to take these invitations as more depth language. I am thinking here only of tendencies and not bunker-like positions. In real ecclesial life, I know conservatives who appreciate depth language and progressives who think and speak in steno-ways.

Going beyond verbal formulations, Ronald Farmer, speaking for many process thinkers, reminds us that many invitations "do not function at the conscious level."[14] Many invitations are trans-linguistic in the sense that they come to us at the levels of feeling and intuition without coming to direct verbal expression in consciousness. From Whitehead's perspective, "We think with our bodies."[15] Bernard Meland puts it this way: "We live more deeply than we can think."[16] Meland eloquently expands: "perceptual experience is a richer event than conception can possibly be, providing every occurrence of awareness with a 'fringe,' implying a 'More,' much of which persistently evades conceptualization."[17]

Such awareness is more than passing emotion. Awareness is a fabric of feeling. Though neither preacher nor congregation may be able to explain this phenomenon fully, they are often aware of it. In each moment and circumstance, there is More than meets the eye. Because the self is a perceptual *Gestalt*, a proposal affects thoughts, emotions, and behaviors.

Invitations come from the breadth and depth of life itself. Beyond straightforward statements, many proposals come to articulation less directly, but with great power, e.g., in poetry, fiction, visual media, cinema dance, digital imagery. Invitations, whether in steno-language, depth language, or

14. Farmer, *Beyond the Impasse*, 92.

15. Cited in Meland, *Fallible Forms and Symbols*, 50.

16. Meland, *Fallible Forms and Symbols*, 28.

17. Meland, *Fallible Forms and Symbols*, 43.

in other media, invite us to imagine the world as it is or might be from the perspective articulated in the expression.

Recipients often respond intuitively to invitations without giving the invitation conscious, evaluative attention. When an invitation truly embodies God's aim, individuals and congregations can thus accept qualities of the invitation into their everyday lives of feeling and behavior, so their experience is enriched accordingly. But when an invitation discourages optimum becoming, individuals and congregations can unthinkingly integrate the invitation into patterns of feeling and action that sabotage God's purposes of love and justice for each and all.

Going beyond the Preacher's Conundrum

The preacher often faces a conundrum here. On the one hand some invitations come in language that is clear and easy to understand. The preacher and congregation can easily identify this invitation and work with it theologically. Yet, many invitations come to the preacher in forms that are difficult to describe in language. The "More" is present in the invitation—often quite forcefully—and the preacher feels something but cannot articulate it fully in written or spoken speech. On the other hand, the sermon is a public act in which the preacher must use language that offers the congregation a real opportunity to take part in the conversation. The preacher cannot simply stand in the pulpit and point or groan (except, perhaps, in a special circumstance). The preacher must talk about the invitation with the congregation in language that makes communication possible, even if the invitation itself is expressed in a way that is trans-linguistic.

One of the preacher's fundamental tasks, then, is to *name* the invitations that are present in the conversation. This task is relatively easy in the case of proposals that are stated in direct verbal ways, whether in steno- or depth modes, as in biblical texts, voices from Christian history, theological tomes, cultural expressions, or matters specific to the immediate context. Many of these sources state directly what they invite the congregation to believe about God's purposes, the world, and how to respond. But in the cases of more indirect expression, the preacher must try to articulate—as straightforwardly as possible—what the proposal invites the congregation to believe about God and the world and what to do in response.

However, the task is more complicated when the proposal is expressed in an aesthetic medium, such as a novel, a painting, or dance. Indeed, since the meaning of such a piece is inextricably tied to its form of expression, neither preacher nor congregation can translate the full meaning of the proposal into straightforward statements.[18]

The task is most complicated when a proposal does not pass into expressive form but remains at the level of intuition and feeling. However, for purposes of discussion in the sermon, the preacher typically needs to try to set out the heart of the proposal in conventional speech. The preacher can never fully capture the significance of intuitive awareness in conventional speech, but the preacher can formulate a statement on which the congregation can reflect as fully as circumstances permit.

"It Is More Important That a Proposal Be Interesting Than It Be True."

Whitehead famously remarks, "In the real world, it is more important that a proposition be interesting than it be true."[19] Whitehead's point is that the act of considering invitations can help a community come to clarity regarding which invitations are more and less promising. An invitation asks us to think about what the world would be like if we say to the invitation, "Yes" or "No" or "Maybe" or something else. As William A. Beardslee and his colleagues point out, taking into account a wide range of invitations—even those that finally prove to be less promising—help "pave the way along which the world advances into novelty."[20] Moreover, Beardslee and colleagues note that becoming aware of the options available for interpreting life enhances the freedom in an individual or community.

As we note below, some biblical texts and voices in Christian theology put forward invitations that preachers and congregations who operate out of the process worldview find problematic. But the act of considering such proposals can help the church come to clarity regarding what it most deeply believes; it helps the church articulate why it finds such statements difficult; and it helps the church identify appropriate ways to respond.

18. An eloquent statement of the irreducible unity of form and feeling is Langer, *Feeling and Form.*

19. Whitehead, *Process and Reality,* 259. Whitehead adds, "The importance of truth is that it adds interest" (259).

20. Beardslee et al., *Biblical Preaching,* 24.

PREACHING AS CONVERSATION IN THE MODE
OF MUTUAL CRITICAL CORRELATION

The conversation that leads to the sermon and that then becomes the sermon itself typically takes place through an adaptation of the method of mutual critical correlation. This approach to theological method grew out of Paul Tillich's famous method of correlation. People in the present raises theological questions to which they turn to the tradition for answers. However, when doing so, they encounter a gap between the ancient and contemporary worlds.

With respect to the gap, Tillich called attention to two things: (1) differences in *language and cultural expression* between the worlds of antiquity and today, yet (2) similarities of *experience* between then and now, even when names and cultural forms differ. The preacher seeks to overcome the hermeneutical gap by correlating ancient language and experience with a contemporary language and experience.[21] In a sense, the preacher translates the meaning from antiquity into comparable meaning for today.[22] For example, in one of his most famous sermons, "You Are Accepted," Tillich correlates the experience "grace" from the world of the Bible to the experience of acceptance today.[23]

David Tracy, one of Tillich's students and an influential theologian at the University of Chicago who is sympathetic to the process worldview, notices that Tillich's method of correlation did not take full account of another dynamic present in the relationship of the present to the past.[24] While the past can provide resources for the present, the present can also raise questions about the adequacy of the past with respect to both aspects of worldview as well as theological and ethical perceptions.[25] Mutual critical

21. While Tillich called particular attention to differences between the worlds of the Bible and today, the same kinds of "gaps" often occur between other sources of invitations (and their historical and cultural contexts) and the worldviews and cultural contexts of congregations today.

22. Tillich, *Systematic Theology*, 1:30–31, 60–66; 2:13–16.

23. Tillich, "You Are Accepted."

24. Although Tracy has a certain affinity for process thought, especially in his early writings, the method of critical correlation can function with other theological families whose theological content allows for truly critical evaluation of materials from the Bible and other historic and contemporary sources as well as evaluation of the present from the standpoint of traditional points of view. In mutual critical correlation in this book, the process perspective is the theological viewpoint with which the Bible and other sources are correlated in a mutually critical way.

25. Tracy, *Blessed Rage for Order*, 45–47; 97–81; Tracy, *Analogical Imagination*, 371–72; 405–11; 421–23; Tracy, "Theological Method," 52–59; Tracy, "Hermeneutical Reflections," 334–62. Cf. R. J. Allen, "Preaching as Mutual Critical Correlation"; and

correlation explores the possibility of a Tillichian correlation in which the past informs the present, albeit sometimes in different language and cultural dress.

Going beyond Tillich, the preacher practicing mutual critical correlation also explores the possibility that voices in the past may have misperceived some dimensions not only of how the world operates but may have missed some important elements in interpreting God and God's purposes for the church and world. Consequently, to be faithful to what today's community believes to be optimal opportunities for becoming, the sermon may need to criticize some ancient thinking and actions and reformulate ideas from the past with more adequate forms of thought and behavior.[26] In the model proposed in this book, process theology is the center of the contemporary pole for the critical correlation.

When using process theology to practice mutual critical correlation, it is important to remember that both the method of critical correlation and process thought are truly *mutual*. That is, they seek ways in which the past can offer advice of great value to the present while also recognizing that things in the past can be problematic from the standpoint of philosophical assumptions, theological claims, and ethical guidelines. The word "critical" in the expression "mutual critical correlation" has to do with making a clear analysis of those things from which communities can still benefit as well as those things that need to be corrected or rejected.

From Bridge to Conversation

Because advocates of traditional approaches to preaching often speak of traffic moving one way on the bridge from then to now, I have often described a conversational approach to preaching as traffic moving two ways on the bridge from then to now back to reconsider our perception of then. While that image is helpful, conversations have many more possibilities for movement then simply going from then to now and back again.

A better bridge-related image for conversational preaching is a multi-level highway interchange where several roadways come together. The interchange contains exit ramps and entrance ramps from which proposals enter and leave the flow of traffic. Invitations sometimes intersect with one another, as with merging traffic, but they sometimes pass through the

---

R. J. Allen, "Note on Mutual Critical Correlation." For a similar proposal, see Farley, *Practicing Gospel*, 71–82.

26. When engaging in mutual critical correlation, the preacher often brings the hermeneutic of suspicion into play.

interchange at the same time on different levels without touching. Accidents and breakdowns slow and even stop the flow of traffic.

However, the movement on a multi-level highway interchange is still too limited an image to represent the movement that can happen in conversation among preacher, text, congregation, and voices from church history, theology, the church, and the wider culture. On a roadway—especially on a bridge—the lanes are fixed. The cement and steel are almost immovable. Even with cars moving constantly on multiple levels, the roadways predetermine—and limit—where travelers can go except when unusual things occur, as when a car flies off the interchange and crashes or when an earthquake brings down the interchange.

By comparison with a traffic interchange, conversation is much more living. It is a form of life that is more dynamic than traffic on a bridge or on an interchange. As David Tracy explains. "Conversation in its primary form is an *exploration of possibilities*."[27] Conversation involves the "movement of question and response, give and take, as the partners in the dialogue clarify issues and seek resolution."[28] Tracy notes that in such dialogue, "We find ourselves by allowing claims upon our attention, by exploring possibilities suggested by others, including those we call texts."[29] In this mode of interaction, "we notice that to attend to the other as other, the different as different, is also to understand the different *as* possible."[30] In conversation, "We must speak clearly, respect others, and be open to changing our own opinions when other viewpoints prove convincing."[31]

When I visit Goodwill in search of clothing, I slip into the changing room to try on prospective jeans or sweatshirts. In a similar way, a sermon can be an occasion when the congregation tries on how they might experience becoming from the perspectives of the invitations in the sermon. Some proposals fit better than others. Looking in the mirror in the try-on closet, I sometimes think, "Just right." I sometimes surmise, "Not quite me." I sometimes grimace, "This garment was a mistake. It should never have been made."

In a real conversation, participants seek to perceive the perspectives of others from the standpoints from which the others want to be perceived.

27. Tracy, *Plurality and Ambiguity*, 20. For a broadly-based overview of Tracy's program, and by extension of a conversational paradigm, see Okey, *Theology of Conversation*. On the church as a community of conversation, see O. W. Allen, *Homiletic of All Believers*, 16–37.

28. O. W. Allen, *Homiletic of All Believers*, 16.

29. O. W. Allen, *Homiletic of All Believers*, 19.

30. O. W. Allen, *Homiletic of All Believers*, 20.

31. O. W. Allen, *Homiletic of All Believers*, 19.

This does not mean that participants will agree with one another on all aspects of the topic, but it does mean that participants will try to understand the points of view of others and will try respect those perspectives. Authentic participation in conversation includes being willing to reflect critically on one's own viewpoints and to be willing to consider changes.

Conversations sometimes come to resolution. The sermon sometimes identifies a particular invitation that is the outcome of the conversation. Preacher and congregation can be confident with what the conversation has concluded are responsible things to believe about God and the world, and how to respond. They can then conceive how best to respond accordingly in view of their actual possibilities—their resources and context.

But life is such a continuous process that resolutions are often provisional. In this spirit, a student once opined of a certain proposal, "This statement is the best we can do right now, but we need to keep the door open for fresh perspective." A conversation can begin at one place and move to another entirely unexpected place. Of course, conversations are not always electric and exciting. They can unfold along predictable lines. And, frankly, occasional conversations can unfold in obvious ways or can even be dull.

PURPOSES OF PREACHING

Preaching viewed from the process house has several purposes. Of course, since everything in the universe is related, these purposes connect with one another. But certain purposes sometimes rise more fully to the surface than others in connection with particular occasions and particular sermons.

Conversations involving preacher, congregation, and invitations take place at all levels of the preaching event—sermon preparation, the sermon itself, and what the congregation does with the sermon after the preacher stops speaking.[32] During sermon preparation, the preacher identifies the various invitations at work in the listening congregation—in the biblical text or the sermon topic, in the history of the church, in theology, in local congregational dynamics and in the congregation's cultural setting. In the sermon itself, the preacher has a conversation with the congregation to identify and evaluate invitations that are most relevant in the congregation and in its world. The preacher seeks to help listeners name both promising

32. The best discussion on the nature of conversation in preaching is still O. W. Allen, *Homiletic of All Believers*, 16–57. Cf. Rose, *Sharing the Word*; O. W. Allen and R. J. Allen, *Sermon without End*, especially the bibliography of advocates of conversational preaching, 108–14; Lose, "Preaching as Conversation"; Pagitt, *Preaching in the Inventive Age*; R. J. Allen, *Interpreting the Gospel*, 63–96, especially the bibliography on 299: "chapter 4," note 1.

and unpromising elements in the invitations before them, and to move towards adequate assessment of the invitations, and, hence, towards appropriate responses.

To Invite the Congregation (and World)
toward Inclusive Well-Being

Casey T. Sigmon summarizes the larger purpose of preaching in this tradition. "Preaching as a process theologian is a practice of amplifying God's [aims] in worship so that more of us can be in tune with God's range of liberating possibilities within the grasp of every living thing at any given moment."[33] Sigmon joins Bruce Epperly in stressing, "The interdependence of life challenges us to consider the impact of our actions on the non-human and human futures, as well as on our lives and the lives of our immediate companions."[34]

My eye pauses over the notion of the sermon "amplifying" our awareness of possibilities. Through the sermon, the preacher seeks to amplify the congregation's awareness of the invitations that are consistent with God's purpose and that, when embraced, can lead congregation and world in the direction of love, peace, justice, abundance, and mutually supportive relationships among all created entities. Many of those possibilities are already present in the world of the congregation. But the congregation may not be aware sufficiently aware of them. Through the sermon, the preacher seeks to amplify the invitations so that the congregation can better identify and respond to them. At the same time, the sermon should help the congregation recognize invitations that do not embody the highest hopes for inclusive well-being that are pertinent to the circumstances as well as invitations that lead to unwell-being.

Just as recipients are free to accept an invitation to a wedding or a class reunion, so communities are free to accept an invitation or not. Indeed, Communities can respond to invitations along a spectrum that ranges from directly embracing the invitation to directly rejecting the invitation. In between are all manner of response, including the possibility that the consideration of the proposal will transform the ways in which preacher and

33. Sigmon, "Preaching from the Perspective,"282. Sigmon actually writes of "proclaiming God's living Word in worship." I have explained my hesitation about expressions like "God's living word." In my mind, preachers amplify their interpretations of God's aims or God's invitations to liberating possibilities or possibilities for inclusive well-being."

34. Sigmon, "Preaching from the Perspective," 281-282, citing Epperly, *Process Theology: A Guide*, 104.

congregation understand the questions, issues, and other dynamics related to the proposal. Moreover, participants may place proposals on hold while further consideration takes place.

In the process house, the mutual critical correlation takes place among voices from across the past (especially the Bible and Christian tradition) and the voice of process theology. Process provides the categories for exploring how other voices portray the nature and power of God, the purposes of God, and how human beings and nature respond to God and one another.

At its best, the sermon itself can participate in God's manner of relating to the world. That is, just as God offers each moment the highest relevant possibilities for becoming, the sermon can help the congregation name optimum opportunities for becoming. Participants then have the freedom to respond.[35] If the community responds optimally, their becoming can take place in full and rich ways. If the congregation responds less optimally, the immediate becoming is diminished, but God subsequently offers other invitations appropriate to their revised patterns

A good question to ask of each sermon is: in specific terms, how does this homiletical conversation invite the congregation towards more inclusive well-being?

To Help the Congregation Make Sense of Life

One of the oldest purposes of religion is to help a congregation make sense of life, that is, to offer a perspective that shows how people can understand the various pieces of life working in relationship to one another that we can understand. Whitehead himself points to this function of "rational religion" as religion

> whose beliefs and rituals have been organized with the aim of making it the central element in a coherent ordering of life—an ordering which shall be coherent both in respect to the elucidation of thought, and in respect to the direction of conduct towards a unified purpose commanding ethical approval.[36]

35. Of course, sermons do not automatically offer congregations optimum opportunities for becoming. Preachers, congregations, and sermons can set out proposals that offer limited chances to become. For example, preaching can easily fall into the fallacy of misplaced concreteness.

36. Whitehead, *Religion in the Making*, 31. Whitehead's hope for philosophy is also a statement of the hope for preaching, namely, "to frame a coherent, logical, necessary system of general ideas in terms of which every element of experience can be interpreted" (*Process and Reality*, 3). 15.

Process theology offers "a coherent ordering of life," that is, a way of explaining how things relate with one another, how things happen, and what is possible in life. In suggesting that religion points "to conduct towards a unified purpose commanding ethical approval," Whitehead has in mind behavior that is consistent with assumptions and values of the religion so that we experience continuity between what we say we believe and how we act and so that these behaviors serve the optimum good. Religion invests life with meaning, sets out the most important values, shows how the various pieces fit together, and guides the community in living.

As I mentioned in the previous chapter, H. Richard Niebuhr used the language of "revelation" to call attention to an important aspect this phenomenon.

> Revelation means for us that part of our inner history which illuminates the rest of it and which is itself intelligible . . . From that special occasion we also derive the concepts that make possible the elucidation of all the events in our history. Revelation means this intelligible event which makes all other events intelligible.[37]

While I no longer use the term "revelation," the point is still useful. At one level, the preacher in the process tradition helps the congregation explore ways in which events and texts from the past help us make sense of the present, especially from the life of Israel and the emergent stories of Jesus and the church. At another level, in the conversational model, the preacher explores the possibility the possibility that concerns from the contemporary world might prompt reconsideration of the illuminative power of ancient voices.

The authors of *Biblical Preaching on the Death of Jesus* point out, further, that "the task of preaching" in these regards "involves helping congregations themselves look at public affairs" in the light of inclusive well-being.[38] This task, of course, is part of helping the congregation make sense of life (as mentioned above). The preacher wants to help the congregation identify tendencies towards and against well-being. This conversation can be especially difficult as it can involve trying to listen to voices on an issue that are quite different, even diametrically opposed, to our own. Yet, such listening is often necessary in order to give a fair and accurate evaluation of values and practices that we ultimately find unacceptable.

Preaching is an important way—though by no means the only one—whereby the church articulates its most compelling understanding of

---

37. Niebuhr, *Meaning of Revelation*, 93. Cf. Williamson, *Way of Blessing*, 65–66.

38. Beardslee et al., *Biblical Preaching*, 59.

inclusive well-being and invites the congregation to live in response to the possibilities of that animating center. Preaching should offer the community the opportunity to "get" how the pieces of life work together from process points of view—including past, present, and future.

In the first third of the twenty-first century in North America, this function becomes ever more important as some religious groups set out religious visions that are particularly sectarian and self-serving. Indeed, some religious visions in the contemporary world actively seek to invoke the divine against the well-being of many in the community of the universe. Consequently, the preacher needs to be able to help the congregation compare and contrast the different religious visions.

To Articulate Invitations Appropriate to the Context

The sermon should set out an initial aim that is both appropriate to God's fundamental purposes while also being appropriate to the context of the congregation. The limitations within a context may limit the possibilities for well-being in that context. Indeed, in some settings—such an impending death at the end of a long illness—possibilities may appear to be quite limited. In such cases, the aim may be quite modest, e.g., that all circled around the hospital bed may be aware of the divine presence in suffering and support as the patient slips away from this life and towards whatever come next. In other cases, the context may offer much more dramatic possibilities as in the late spring of 2020 when the Black Lives Matter movement invited the larger population towards a process of social transformation that could increase justice, equality, dignity, freedom, mutual respect, security, and mutual solidarity for all.

The context includes both individuals and communities.[39] Of course, from process perspective individual and community are not separate entities because all things are always related. An individual becomes, in part, in response to community even while contributing to the becoming of community. Because of this soluble relationship between self and community, it is sometimes helpful for a preacher to think of a sermon as having slightly different foci even as both individual and community are always in the homiletical view. That is, a preacher may prepare a particular sermon with the idea of helping individuals struggle with personal issues. For example, a preacher might devote a sermon to how the knowledge of God's presence helps us with experiences like dying (as in the illustration above). A preacher

39. See Suchocki, *Whispered Word*, 28–36, for an eloquent description of preaching as relating individual and community.

might focus a sermon on helping the congregation interpret the communal dimensions of its life, perhaps in relationship to an issue. For example, the congregation as community, as part of larger life systems, needs to make a congregation-as-community response to the Black Lives Matter movement.

Because of the community-destroying effect of radical individualism in North American today, I emphasize that thinking of the sermon as addressing matters of particular concern to individuals is not a retreat from community. The end goal is to help the individual so the individual can become a more supportive member of the community which, in turn, can help the community itself become a more vital agent of creative transformation. Along the way, the preacher can often help individuals wrestling with particular issues discover that others are also doing so, so that listeners become more aware of being a part of a community struggling with similar matters.

To Build Up the Church as a Community Embodying and Inviting Inclusive Well-Being

To some readers, the phrase "to build up the church" may have an institutional ring.[40] "Oh, the sermon is to help the church maintain its life as an institution through such things as attracting members, raising money, persuading people to serve on committees, promoting church programs, fostering institutional loyalty, and helping the church take its place alongside other institutions in the community."[41] To be sure, like all human communities, churches need to attend to their own health. But many people functionally view the church as an end itself. Indeed, some clergy view the ministry as a path to social standing in the community and as a path to serve their own career goals. Moreover, many congregations are notoriously reluctant to accept invitations to become in ways that differ from their present mode of being.

However, churches should not be a conventional social institutions. The mission of the church is twofold. First, in the spirit of Isaiah and the tradition that viewed Israel and the followers of Jesus as "light of the world," churches should embody inclusive well-being for everyone in the church (Isa 42:6–7; Matt 5:14–16). Regardless of the details of its organizational life, the church should be a model of inclusive well-being for other groups. Preaching seeks to build up the church as a community of well-being within itself.

---

40. Beardslee et al., *Biblical Preaching*, deal brilliantly with this issue, 50–56.

41. Preaching in a process vein can certainly serve such tasks, albeit interpreting them through a process lens.

The fact, of course, is that churches continue to say and do things that subvert well-being. Here the process model offers exceptional help as it asserts that no matter how grievous the church's failure, God continues to offer the church possibilities for creative transformation. Preaching can try to help congregations recognize such invitations. Preaching continually invites the community towards this aim of renewal.

A second aspect of the mission of the church is related to the first. The church invites others towards paths of inclusive well-being in settings beyond the church. Churches have sometimes mistaken this task as one in which the church has perspectives on well-being that it can impose on others without regard for the possibility that others may have viewpoints on well-being that may have escaped the church's line of vision. Conversation with these viewpoints can help the church not only relate more constructively with others but may even help the church reflect on ways in which it might increase the well-being in its own life. Preaching helps build up the church by helping the church engage in conversation about the invitations it can and should offer to communities beyond itself. Preaching can also help churches enter into conversation about invitations to think afresh about its own understandings of well-being that come from the world beyond the edge of the parking lot.

I have heard several scholars of preaching use the image of preaching as a figure to speak about the vocation of the congregation in the larger world. Metaphorically speaking, on Sunday the preacher speaks with the congregation. From Monday through Saturday, the congregation preaches in the world, that is, the congregation stirs conversation about possibilities for amplifying well-being across the many settings of life. A key role of the preacher in the congregation in this regard is to invite the congregation towards greater consciousness of its role through the week.

To Evoke Feeling Consistent with Invitations to Well-Being

An invitation is a lure for feeling. The reader will remember that in this context, "feeling" includes the whole range of perception, recognizing that a relatively small amount of perception is conscious thought and that most perception is inarticulate awareness in the depths of the self.[42] Invitations speak to the whole of the self, conscious and unconscious. While this is true, I have been clear that I think the preacher must try to be as clear as possible,

---

42. The discussion in this section is important background on the notion of feeling for the discussion in chapter 4 on working back to discover the feelings that are part of giving rise to biblical texts.

in direct speech, in describing invitations that come to us. I stress that "feeling" involves more than passing emotion. But because feeling is such an important part of perception, it deserves more consideration.

William Beardslee and his colleagues seem to use the notion of "emotion" in line with the broader interpretation of "feeling" when they note:

> Humans are emotional beings more fundamentally than they are thinking beings. The great forces that help shape history have depended as much on tribal and national feelings as on the ides and images that express and arouse them. Indeed, action never follows from ideas and images alone. It is always motivated in part by emotions that attach to these.[43]

To see this phenomenon in action one needs only recollect the loyalty to certain political persona that has less to do with specific policies advocated by the person (or group) than with identification with the senses of grievance aroused by the person and with the yearning for power even when the power is to be used for ends that destroy the well-being of many.

Beardless and his associates are on target when they say, "Preaching that does not move its hearers is a failure."[44] They add the important caveat that this awareness does not mean that the preacher should try to manipulate the congregation.[45] Attempting to evoke feeling in the congregation should be connected to the purpose of the sermon. "The primary consideration remains that of the end to which they are moved and whether the pattern of the emotions aroused is appropriate to the gospel."[46] The appropriateness of the message to inclusive well-being is the most important consideration.

At the same time, the theological adequacy of the sermon is "meaningless if it is simply a matter of accuracy to the preacher."[47] The following statement is true for many listeners. "The reality of preaching is its impact, that which is actually felt by the hearers, and that is as much a matter of the emotions elicited as of the objective pattern of ideas and images, they are led to entertain."[48] Yet it would be reductionistic to assume that all hearers are the same in this regard. I am aware of some listeners who have been profoundly affected by ideas *qua* ideas. The writers do contend, "The finest preaching is that in which the message is spoken with utmost objective

---

43. Beardslee et al., *Biblical Preaching*, 62.
44. Beardslee et al., *Biblical Preaching*, 62.
45. Beardslee et al., *Biblical Preaching*, 62.
46. Beardslee et al., *Biblical Preaching*, 62.
47. Beardslee et al., *Biblical Preaching*, 62.
48. Beardslee et al., *Biblical Preaching*, 62.

faithfulness in the rhetoric that is most likely to elicit the appropriate emotional response."[49]

One important question for the preacher is how to evoke feeling. Because of the diversity of preachers and listeners, there is no single formula here. One of the most effective ways to bring feeling to expression is to tell stories with which congregations can identify and which can stir depth experience in listeners. Most of the time, I think the most powerful stories with this capacity come from real life. They can also come from novels, short stories, movies, television episodes, and wherever stories occur. The key is for the characters, plot, and setting of the story to have the complexity of real-life experience. But preachers do not always have to tell an entire story to invoke feeling. A preacher can sometimes use a single word or an image to call into expression a whole network of feeling. A preacher can describe an event from the past or present. As long as the preacher is honest about the source of the story or other evoking material, preachers can use their imaginations to create materials for the sermon that evoke feeling consistent.

I grew up in a congregation of the Christian Church (Disciples of Christ) in which our Bible school teachers repeatedly told us, "Our faith does not depend on what we feel. It depends upon the facts."[50] By "facts" they had in mind not scientific facts but the "gospel facts," that is, the confidence God has acted objectively on behalf of the human family through Israel and through Jesus Christ. The deeds of God work in our behalf regardless of whether we respond to them with feeling. While Beardslee and his co-authors emphasize the importance of the sermon evoking a fabric of feeling, they share the caveat of my Bible school teachers as they write,

> Preaching must communicate . . . the good news that we are
> accepted, forgiven, and loved quite apart from our religious
> feelings, and that its call to us is not primarily to cultivate the
> conscious awareness of the Spirit but rather to receive the Spirit's
> gifts and to respond in appropriate service to the Spirit.[51]

---

49. Beardslee et al., *Biblical Preaching*, 62.

50. Some other churches in our community claimed that God gave a high-voltage emotional experience to people to assure them of God's good pleasure toward them. Such churches claimed that unless people had such a feeling, they could not be sure that God loved them. By contrast, the Disciples of Christ emphasize that God's assurance comes not in the form of a feeling within the self but from the objective articulation of the promises of God in the Bible and in Christian theology. These promises do not depend upon our feeling. They are trustworthy because God is true to them.

51. Beardslee et al., *Biblical Preaching*, 64.

Given the conversational nature of the entire preaching event, it is pertinent here to mention that the process of preparation should include the preacher giving attention to the feelings associated with invitations that inclusive well-being. As we have already said, the preacher wants to understand counterproductive invitations from their own standpoints, and these standpoints include feelings as well as ideas, and as Beardslee and colleagues point out, feelings often take precedence over ideas. If the occasion and sermon present the right circumstances, the preacher might be able to reflect candidly with the congregation about the dangers associated with such feelings and might even be able to present a comparison and contrast of the experience of embracing such trans-verbal awareness with that of embracing feelings that empower inclusive well-being.

SERMON AS HIGHWAY MARKER

In process ecclesiology, a sermon is not a final destination. A sermon is a moment like all other moments: it comes into expression, happens, and then leaves its trace in the flow of life. At the conscious level, a sermon is much like a highway sign indicating where the preacher and congregation are located on the great theological roadway of life.

At a deeper level, a sermon is a moment that perishes into the causal efficacy of the church and the world. This latter point should be a great encouragement to preachers who sometimes think that a particular sermon, or even seasons of sermons, has not had any effect. The invitations posed by the sermon enter into the deep subterranean life of the congregation and can influence the congregation long after the preacher takes her or his seat.

The distinctive character of the sermon is to seek to affect other moments by inviting the congregation to continue becoming in ways that bring people and nature into mutually supportive community. A preacher may see the community take up life-affirming, community-building proposals as a result of interacting with the sermon. But even if the preacher does not see immediate effects, the preacher can take heart in the process perspective that the possibilities the sermon offers to the church and world still live through the medium of causal efficacy and may resurface in another sermon or another place in the world.

PROPHETIC PREACHING AND
CONVERSATIONAL PREACHING

Concern for prophetic preaching animates many clergy in the first decades of the twenty-first century. I have been in several groups in which ministers attempt to contrast conversational preaching with prophetic preaching, as if the two have quite different concerns.[52]

The concern for prophetic preaching comes from our awareness of the many forms of injustice in our era of history. To name just a few: injustice related to race, ethnicity, and culture, injustice related to gender and sexuality, injustice related to economic exploitation, injustice related to ecology, injustice related to religion, and the use of threat and violence to support injustice. Vast, powerful international systems work together to limit life possibilities for many people and nature, so that a few can live in luxury. The latter have the power to serve their own ends.

Contemporary preachers sometimes describe the prophets as outsiders who denounce perpetrators of injustice and who call for systemic change. In a confrontational style, prophets speak with certainty represented by the phrase, "Thus saith the Lord." The prophetic preacher is sometimes pictured as angry, speaking in thunderous tones. The prophet threatens that God will bring about judgement unless the community repents. From this point of view, prophetic preaching is bold, in-your-face, and risky. The prophet speaks the word in uncompromising terms and lets the chips fall where they will.

By contrast some contemporary preachers caricature conversational preaching as soft, exploratory, insufficiently authoritative, and insufficiently confrontive. A student who was distraught and angry at injustice and who was electrified by the previous notion of prophetic preaching once dismissed conversational preaching as "puny," even "coddling."

I reply that neither of these pictures does justice to its subject.[53] In the broad picture, the prophet is like a theological ombudsperson who measures the quality of life in the community according to the values and practices of covenant, identifies points of imbalance, and calls the community to return to the covenantal perspective and action. Prophets sometimes call attention to social imbalance and urge the community to repent. Hosea is one of many such prophets who come to mind. But prophets also identify moments when the community does not sufficiently trust in the promises

---

52. For a consideration of prophecy from a process perspective, see Gnuse, *Old Testament and Process Theology*, 125–40.

53. This argument is further developed in R. J. Allen, "Building Bridges," 47–58.

of God and urges the community to believe. The second Isaiah, whose voice sounds in Isa 40–55, is such a figure.

In conversational preaching, conversation is not its own end but is intended to help the community come to an adequate theological understanding of its current context and to respond appropriately. While conversation is sometimes gentle and muted, it can have hard, animated, edges.

Charles Hartshorne, a shaping voice in process thought, wisely observes that when a contrast contains two elements that appear to be opposed, one element in the contrast is often actually the larger one and embraces the other.[54] Preachers often contrast pastoral and prophetic preaching, as pastoral (caring) "versus" prophetic (challenging). But from the point of view of Hartshorne's schema, the pastoral is the larger element: God's ultimate purposes are pastoral, that is, caring for (building up) the community. The prophet appears when the community behaves in ways that undermine the well-being of the community. The prophet seeks to alert the community to an imbalance in the community's life so that the community can take restorative action.

While Dale Andrews, who taught preaching at Vanderbilt University, was not a process thinker per se, he voiced a notion sympathetic to process concerns by speaking of prophetic preaching as "prophetic care."[55] The prophet expresses care for the world by naming forms of injustice and imbalance, calling for repentance, and inviting the community towards ways of living in mutual support through "living in covenant" or "living towards the realm of God."

From this latter point of view, conversational preaching from a process base can have a prophetic focus. The preacher recognizes thinking, feeling, and acting that undercuts patterns of living that lead to optimum becoming. The preacher calls for changes of direction (repentance) hoping that members of the community will cooperate with God and others in moving towards optimum circumstances of becoming. Preaching in both the traditional prophetic mode and in the prophetic mode in process thought seek these values. Where the traditional prophet may sometimes be more confrontive and dismissive, the process preacher seeks to invite bridges of understanding, invitation, and relationship with those who work against the divine purposes. Yet, the two ways of approaching prophecy share the

---

54. Hartshorne, "Logic of Ultimate Contrasts," 99–110. Long ago, J. Gerald Janzen called my attention to this article.

55. Andrews' insight is explained and explored by twenty-seven scholars in a book edited by Sheppard et al., *Preaching Prophetic Care*. Tisdale, *Prophetic Preaching*, takes a similar approach and offers wisdom for preaching prophetically in ways that have good chances of connecting with the congregation.

common end of strengthening love, justice, peace, abundance, and relationship for all.

In the end, if some people reject optimum opportunities for becoming, the preacher in the process universe should not dismiss them. Rather, the preacher should take a cue from the manner of God working with difficult circumstances by continuing to offer redemptive invitations that have some chance of engaging the minds and hearts of the recalcitrant. As one of my colleagues said, "The great thing about God is that God never gives up." The same should be true of the prophet operating out of process conceptuality. Even if destruction should befall a people as a result of their community-destroying behavior, the preacher can point to some possibility for assurance within the circumstance.

4

Identifying Invitations
in the Text or Topic

THE PREACHER DOES NOT need to learn an entirely new way of preparing the
sermon to preach from a process worldview. Certain things are common to
sermon preparation regardless of the preacher's theological family of origin.
Nevertheless, preaching from a process perspective does reshape aspects of
the preparatory work that takes place on the way from life through the study
to the pulpit.

We now consider some process elements in the practical approach of
moving from a text or topic to a sermon.[1] We begin the chapter by setting
out a significant goal of the exegesis of a biblical text as a key element in
sermon preparation. We follow with stern words for preachers regarding
the importance of being honest about one's social location and agenda for
the sermon and for making decisions about the text or topic as the starting
point for sermon preparation. After a brief review of methods and resources

---

1. In this chapter and succeeding chapters, I set out these matters as if they always
occur in a sequence: step 1, step 2, step 3, etc. As a linear thinker, this is almost always
my custom. However, preachers—linear and non-linear thinkers alike—sometimes
take account of the concerns of the steps in different sequences. Indeed, preachers may
think they have completed one aspect of sermon preparation (one step, so to speak)
only to find that a later discovery prompts revisiting the earlier perspective. While
such rethinking occurs in sermon preparation in preachers in all theological families,
a preacher in a tradition whose name is "process" should be especially sensitive to the
possibility of fresh insights prompting a second or third look at earlier considerations.
However, regardless of the sequence of tasks in which preachers work on sermons, it is
important for the preacher to take an occasional timeout to make sure the preacher is
covering the necessary areas of research, reflection, and creativity. When the adrenaline
is rushing, it is easy to short shrift important considerations and reconsiderations.

for exegesis that are common to virtually all patterns of sermon preparation, the chapter concentrates on identifying invitation(s) in the biblical text or topic that is the focus of sermon preparation through a process lens. The chapter concludes with a case study identifying possibilities towards which the parable of the talents invites the listening community (Matt 25:14–30.).

LEAVE THE SERMON IN
THE THEOLOGICAL MULCH PILE FOR AWHILE

Given the instant gratification and impatient mindset of many people in the early twenty-first century, I note that one of the root meanings of the word "school" (from the Greek *scholē*) is leisure or free time from which comes the idea of school and scholarship as activities requiring the time to do what is necessary to engage the subject in a satisfactory way. This is especially true of subjects that are complex and/or combustible. To be sure preachers develop their own patterns of preparation, but I notice that most sermons benefit from preparation that is not rushed.

Sermon development is usually like the compost pile in the backyard. We put the leaves on the pile in the fall and over the winter they turn into rich dirt. Most sermons are well served if the preacher begins early in the week and finds the quality time needed to identify and consider the various invitations from past, present, and future that are related to the focus of the sermon. Parts of the sermon often mulch in the mind of the preacher. Over time, associations come to consciousness from the causal efficacy that contribute to the process of developing the sermon. Even when the preacher does not directly use everything that come out of the homiletical mulch, considering those possibilities helps the preacher think critically about what might and might not contribute to the emerging sermon.

CLARIFYING THE PREACHER'S
PERCEPTUAL LENS

I began my exegetical life as a university student in the late 1960s when many preachers believed they could interpret the Bible using scientific approaches to exegesis that would lead them to *the* meaning of a biblical text.[2] We believed we could look at the Bible through a clear lens and get

---

2. Bultmann had already argued that exegesis is always accompanied by presuppositions on the part of the interpreter, but this perspective penetrated slowly into my circles. See Bultmann, "Is Exegesis without Presuppositions Possible?"

an objective, uninterpreted view of the text. We thought we could discover *the* meaning of the text by suspending our presuppositions and by engaging the text according to scientific principles of analysis. However, Ronald L. Farmer, a process biblical scholar and theologian, points out, "Every interpreter reads the biblical text looking through 'tinted lenses.' Moreover, no two interpreters wear glasses with exactly the same tint because tint is the result of the experiences each interpreter has had."[3] These lenses are colored by the range of things that make up a person's social location, including (but not limited to) gender, race, ethnicity, sexual orientation, age, social class, education, political commitments, and theological worldview. The tint also includes the preacher's personality and the causal efficacy in which that preacher stands.

Moreover, my long-time colleague Helene Russell points out that these things often combine to give the preacher an "embedded theology," that is an interpretation of life that the preacher takes for granted and about which the preacher has not given much careful, critical theological reflection. The preacher needs to move from such naïve embedded theology to more deliberative theology, that is, theology that recognizes the tint of the preacher's lenses and which the preacher consciously, critically, and deliberately chooses—recognizing the strengths and weaknesses of the lenses.[4]

Preacher and congregation come to the text or topic—and to the sermon—in the flow of causal efficacy. The preacher *cannot* approach the text as a blank slate, nor can the preacher perceive the text in a completely objective, unbiased state. As we have noted previously, all awareness is interpretive. But preachers who have their eyes open to their lenses can make their interpretive moves with a critical perspective on what they are doing, and why, and what they gain and lose.

Preachers and others tend to favor interpretations of biblical texts that support their social locations. As a Eurocentric, heterosexual, retired, upper-middle-class male, for instance, I tend to be drawn to interpretations of the Bible that allow me to continue to enjoy my very comfortable life. An African American woman might be more innately attracted to a mode of biblical interpretation that gives a heavier emphasis to a social world of justice, dignity, freedom, and equity.

Farmer points out two important implications of the awareness of the "tintedness" of all interpretation. First, preachers and other interpreters

---

3. Farmer, *Process Theology and Biblical Interpretation*, 6.

4. Stone and Duke help the preacher recognize and reflect on the differences between embedded associations and deliberative perspectives with which preachers approach texts in *How to Think Theologically*, 3–28.

should be as aware as possible of the tint of our interpretive perspectives.[5] We can never be "interpretation-free" when working with a text, but we can try to be as cognizant as we can of the colors in our lenses. Preacher and congregation come to the text or topic—and to the sermon—in the flow of causal efficacy. The preacher *cannot* approach the text as a blank slate. However, process theology points out that we do not have to be prisoners of our embedded worldviews. Process theology invites me as a privileged Eurocentric, heterosexual, upper-middle-class male to recognize that I am related to all other people and all other elements of creation and to seek justice for all which, ultimately, means better qualities of relationship for me as well as for others.

Second, we should try to be aware of the colors of the tints in the glasses of others.[6] Some qualities of the contemporary mindset can interfere with hearing aspects of the ancient mindset off text, while others can serve as positive points of contact with the text. For example, identity in Eurocentric culture in North America is largely individualistic whereas identity in ancient communities was largely communal. The individualistic mindset can obscure relational implications that ancient peoples would have assumed. To take another example, the whole of the Gospels and Letters assume life under the conditions of empire. While awareness of contemporary empire today are not always on the surface of the consciousness of contemporary people, a preacher can often help a contemporary congregation awaken to similarities in the empire then and now as a way of deepening the contemporary community's understanding of what biblical texts invite as response to empire.

Furthermore, the tints of the lenses of others of whom preachers should be aware include theologians, biblical scholars, the congregation, and others beyond the ecclesial world.[7] When we are aware of the coloration in the

5. Farmer, *Process Theology and Biblical Interpretation*, 6.

6. Farmer, *Process Theology and Biblical Interpretation*, 6.

7. As a preacher in the process tradition, I share dimensions of a recent trend in theology in preaching while maintaining a respectful, critical distance. Many preachers and scholars privilege certain positions of social and theological locations so that preachers come to the biblical text looking for ways that the text will serve people in their particular theological viewpoint and social location. The preacher interprets the text through the lens of a theological system or through a particular theological/social location. For example, many preachers who subscribe to the various forms of liberation theology come to the biblical text looking for ways in which the text can support their struggle for liberation. As we have noted, preachers who come to a text or topic from a process/conversational point of view look for resonance with that worldview in biblical materials themselves as well as in the ways in which the church has interpreted texts and topics through the centuries. Preacher and congregation can then engage in conversation about the theological appropriateness of these materials.

interpretive perspectives of others, we can try to shape sermons in ways that promote the possibility of real communication and that minimize the possibility of stepping on land mines in the minds of the listeners.

The tint of the lenses through which we look at the Bible, theology, and life sometimes has a wide effect in sermon preparation—and one that is often unrecognized. The common wisdom in preaching circles is that the preacher should begin with the biblical text. That is, the preacher should take the cues for the direction of the homiletical conversation from the biblical text or the topic. In fact, I think preachers sometimes have a sense of what they want to say before opening the Bible (or looking at the lectionary) to choose a text. This sense may not be conscious and articulate. A preacher may not directly think, "I want to speak about issues in support of Black Lives Matter or the LGBTAQI+ liberation movement." But the causal efficacy related to such matters may be so powerful in the preacher's life that the preacher will read them into the purview of the text even if the text does not offer natural points of connection.

A preacher can legitimately think, "I need to preach on a particular issue, event, situation or idea this week." One of the preacher's important tasks, after all, is to help the congregation come to a comprehensive theological interpretation of life. But the preacher needs further to consider the most propitious means for doing so. A topical sermon may be the preacher's best friend at such a homiletical juncture. If the preacher moves towards a text, the preacher needs to be as mindful as possible in considering whether there is a natural hermeneutical point of contact from the issue to the text or whether the preacher might force the connection in a way that violates the text, the issue, the preacher, and/or the congregation.

To be sure, preachers can plausibly interpret the Bible so as to advantage particular social locations. However, the issue of authority often lies behind the impulse to privilege particular social and theological locations. As we have pointed out, preacher and community frequently want the authority of the Bible on their side. Interpreters so *want* a text or a topic to support their values, aspirations, and behaviors that they can read their own desires—including worthy ones—into texts even when texts do not manifest such desires in either surface current or undercurrent. Theological progressives can easily spot this phenomenon in the case of religious groups on the theological and political right who take texts as endorsements for self-serving things like nationalism, sexism, racism, social exclusivism, and restrictive political views. Yet, theological progressives often following a similar structure of exegetical analysis to serve more progressive theological and social agendas.

STARTING POINTS FOR SERMON PREPARATION

One of the first decisions in sermon preparation is the focus of the sermon. "On what shall I preach this week?" The preacher needs to make this choice carefully and critically. The preacher seeks a conversation that will help the congregation understand aspects of the past, come to a responsible theological interpretation of the present, and envision a future that is appropriate to God's purposes of mutual solidarity among all pieces of creation.

Many preachers and theologians in the process movement (including me) share the opinion of most scholars of preaching that conversation with the Bible should be the typical practice for preaching.[8] Such preaching has the proven experience of helping the church maintain important elements of its life and witness through history. To be sure, the church has misused the Bible, and, not only that, but the Bible also contains parts that are themselves theologically problematic. But conversation with the Bible continues to help the church ponder what we most truly and deeply believe and practice. At the same time, conversations with sources beyond the Bible can also help the church recognize and respond to invitations towards inclusive well-being.

Because God is omnipresent and issuing invitations in every situation, the starting points for the preaching conversation can be as broad and deep as life itself. But for purposes of discussion, we may think of three basic starting points for sermon preparation.

Preaching in Conversation with a Biblical Text

For one, a consensus has emerged across the theological spectrum from conservative to progressive that the exposition of the Bible should typically be central to the sermon.[9] While process theologians typically share the

8. See note 8 above.

9. Process interpreters respect the Bible and believe that preaching in conversation with the Bible is important to the life of the church. Indeed, As John Cobb says, "an historical emergent is best grasped in its primal form . . . Even in its primal form the distinction between what is essential to the emergent and what is difficult is not easy to make. But it is there, if anywhere, that it can be made" ("Authority of the Bible," 200). While Beardslee and his colleagues do not directly say that every sermon should include serious conversation with the Bible, they do say, "Our argument is that scripture is foundational and constitutive for preaching, but that it is not an absolute authority" (Beardslee et al., *Biblical Preaching*, 48). Indeed, there are "two basic constraints" for preaching. "One of these is that the sermon be a serious engagement with the biblical text. The other is that it be sensitive to the leading of the Spirit" (Beardslee et al., *Biblical Preaching*, 49). I nevertheless contend that occasional moments in the life of the

conviction that preaching in dialogue with the Bible can be an important source of theological nourishment in the congregation, some process theologians note that it is not necessary for *every* sermon to involve a serious consideration of a biblical text. Nevertheless, in the process world, sermon preparation often begins with the exegesis of a particular biblical text and considers how interacting with that text can enrich the life of the congregation and the world. The sermon may take up other biblical passages but does so in the interest of clarifying the text or taking account of how other biblical writers consider material related in some way to that of the text.

Preaching in Conversation with a Biblical Theme

In other cases of preaching in serious dialogue with the Bible, the preacher may take a more thematic approach by looking at a variety of texts that pertain to the main theme of the sermon. For example, a preacher might develop a sermon on the theme of "faith" by turning to a number of passages in the Bible that develop that notion. The preacher might launch the sermon from a particular passage, but not limit the sermon to bringing forward the significance of that initial passage. The sermon is more a review of passages that deal with the theme of helping listeners to understand the cumulative effect of the theme as well as to distinguish discriminate differences of perspectives found in different biblical materials.[10]

Preaching Occasionally in Conversation with a Topic

For still another approach, I continue to think that topical preaching can serve the congregation's growth in theological awareness and in becoming in ways that enhance the quality of life in the world.[11] In topical preaching,

---

congregation or world are better interpreted theologically by turning directly to one's core theological convictions. Applying his statement in a way he may not intend, Farmer indicates, "Process theology can stand on its own without biblical warrant" (*Beyond the Impasse*, 116). Of course, I agree with Farmer and others that over time, sermons should regularly engage the Bible in conversation in the pulpit, for "if one's theology is to *remain* Christian, i.e., is to maintain continuity with Christian tradition, one must attend to the Bible. Conscious knowledge and beliefs do increase the effectiveness of the past in shaping one's present existence" (Farmer, *Beyond the Impasse*, 117).

10. R. J. Allen, *Wholly Scripture*. Of course, this thematic approach calls for respecting the exegetical backgrounds of the various texts involved. This approach often leads to comparison and contrast among the various views of the various texts, especially if they are from different theological families.

11. R. J. Allen, *Preaching the Topical Sermon*. Cf. Rzepka and Sawyer, *Thematic*

the preacher does not center the sermon in the exegesis of a biblical text or biblical theme. The sermon does not have *a* biblical text or cohere around one biblical theme. Instead, the preacher focuses on a particular topic— e.g., a doctrine, a Christian practice, a personal issue, or a social issue. The sparks for topical preaching can come from such things as Christian tradition, contemporary theology, the life of the congregation, the preacher's deep theological convictions and experience, and voices beyond the Christian community. A preacher might turn to a topical sermon when the Bible does not provide a real entry into a topic that deserves detailed theological reflection or when the time is very short, and the preacher cannot give a text the exegetical attention that is necessary to respect its otherness.

In topical preaching, in a sense, the preacher's theology is the "text" of the sermon. Such a message may include reference to the Bible, but the Bible does not play the issue-setting role that it does in most preaching. The preacher interprets the topic from the standpoint of the preacher's deep theological convictions rather than from the viewpoint of a particular biblical text or theme. For instance, a preacher might develop a sermon on abortion. The Bible does not focus on this topic in the way we think of it today. The issue itself may be so complicated—and so fraught—that it is worthy of full and undivided attention in the pulpit.

While the methods and steps below focus on preparing a sermon in conversation with a biblical text, many of the steps can be adapted to interpreting a topic—a doctrine, Christian practice, a personal or social issue. While preachers and theologians typically aim to interpret biblical passages in light of their historical, literary, and theological settings, the same interpreters often draw directly from texts beyond the Bible without taking into account larger cultural settings. In a sense preachers and theologians "proof text" from sources such as Augustine, Julian of Norwich, Luther, Calvin.

EXEGESIS: IDENTIFYING WHAT THE TEXT INVITED PEOPLE TO BELIEVE AND DO[12]

One of the preacher's basic tasks is to identify what the biblical text at the heart of the sermon invited people in the past to believe about how the world

---

Preaching.

12. As already noted, the focus of this volume is on preaching in conversation with biblical material while acknowledging the validity of topical preaching and encouraging it in appropriate situations. Although focusing on interpreting and conversing with the Bible in sermon preparation, the preacher can adapt these interpretive moves to preaching in conversation with topics.

functions and about God's purposes and power, and how to respond.[13] As we have said already, after identifying the invitations put forward in the text the sermon brings them *into conversation with pertinent voices from the past and present in search of a believable interpretation of the divine purposes and an appropriate response.*[14] I underscore the fact that this perspective is quite different from identifying what a text asked people in a previous world to believe and do and then *translating* that notion into present-day terms and applying it to today.

This task comes with an opportunity particular to preachers with a process orientation as well as a caution that applies to these preachers and others. The opportunity is to explore possible resonance between the biblical material and a process interpretation of the world. While there were no Whiteheadians as such in the ancient world, process interpreters sometimes find points of similarity between process perspectives and biblical passages (or larger segments of biblical material). Process thinkers particularly find such resonance in the biblical emphases on matters of relationality among members of the human family and between humankind and nature.

13. The world of process approaches to the Bible contains a classical body of articles and books. I can list here just some of these voices: Janzen, "Old Testament in 'Process' Perspective"; Janzen, "Modes of Power and the Divine Relativity"; Williamson, "Process Hermeneutics," esp. 79–85; Lull, "What Is 'Process Hermeneutics'?"; Cobb et al., "Introduction: Process Thought and Exegesis"; Beardslee, "Whitehead and Hermeneutic"; Beardslee, "Narrative Form in the New Testament"; Beardslee, "Recent Hermeneutics and Process Thought"; Beardslee, "Process"; Beardslee et al., *Biblical Preaching*, esp. 15–22.17; Woodbridge, "Assessment and a Prospectus"; Farmer provides an overview and expansion in *Beyond the Impasse*. There are too many specific studies to list them all, but I point to some as representative: Ford, *Lure of God*; Beardslee, *House for Hope*; Lull, *Spirit in Galatia*; Gnuse, *Old Testament and Process Theology*; Fretheim, *God So Enters into Relationships*; Fretheim, *God and the World*; Fretheim, *Suffering of God*; Pregeant's *Engaging the New Testament* is one of the most theological introductions to the Gospels and Letters and has process perspective in the background. Cf. Pregeant, *Reading the Bible*; *Semeia* 24 (1982) and *Journal of the American Academy of Religion* 47 (1979) are dedicated, respectively, to process interpretation of passages from the Torah, Prophets and Writings, and the Gospels and Letters. The Chalice Commentaries for Today are sympathetic to process: Steussy, *Psalms*; Pixley, *Jeremiah*; Pregeant, *Matthew*; Beardslee and Lull, *Romans*; Lull and Beardslee, *First Corinthians*; Farmer, *Revelation*. Biblical interpreters influenced by process do not always write under the rubric of process but resonance with process appears in their work, e.g., Janzen, *Job*; Janzen, *Abraham and All the Families*; Janzen, *Exodus*.

14. David Kelsey notes two strands of interacting with the Bible among process interpreters. The larger strand approaches biblical texts much as I construe them here, namely as invitations (propositions) "expressed by the text" with the interpreter's job being "to describe the systematic universe presupposed by those propositions." The other strand regards texts as approaching "the force of straightforward descriptions, even ontological descriptions, of actualities (in contrast to ideal possibilities." "Theological Use of Scripture," 181–88.

Whitehead himself interpreted Jesus as articulating "the Galilean vision" as one that turned away from the prevailing notions of power and relationship exhibited by the Caesars, the ruthless moralism of the prophets, and the unmoved mover.[15] Indeed, many process thinkers believe that we can find the origins of the process worldview in the Bible, especially its emphasis on relationality.

The caution, of course, is to be circumspect with respect to finding elements of process theology in the Bible. I have heard a good many preachers with a process inclination rush too quickly to the conclusion that an isolated biblical text or some element of a text exhibits process inclination. This interpretive overreach often happens when the preacher focuses entirely on a particular biblical text and does not take adequate account of the larger theological worldview within which the text is expressed or does not consider cultural assumptions prevalent at the time the text was articulated.[16] The desire to shape our perception of the world according to process sensibility moves some preachers to read too much process into the Bible.

Indeed, preachers in the process school sometimes follow the model of identifying the invitations of the text in the past and simply translating those invitations into the present in process terms. Of course, this problem is not peculiar to process preachers. Preachers who operate from other theological families do this also—e.g., Barthians, Tillichians, Niebuhrians, existentialists, the various kinds of liberation theologians, the postliberals, and those who posit Radical Orthodoxy. Here we see again the importance of keeping in mind the tint of the preacher's exegetical glasses.

The Preacher on the Route of Historic Living Occasions

When the preacher prepares the sermon, the preacher steps into the "historic route of living occasions" connected with the text or topic at the heart of the sermon.[17] When beginning to prepare the sermon, the preacher may

15. Whitehead, *Process and Reality*, 342–43.

16. In its present form, the Bible contains five basic theological worldviews: Deuteronomic, priestly, wisdom, apocalyptic and Hellenistic Judaism. Handy summaries of these theological worldview can be found in R. J. Allen, *Preaching Is Believing*, 38–43. Fuller descriptions of the theological families in the Torah, Prophets, and Writings can be found in Holbert and R. J. Allen, *Holy Root, Holy Branches*, 38–56.

17. On these routes see Whitehead, *Process and Reality*, 46, 119, 161, 188 as well as Williamson, "Process Hermeneutics," 79–82; Woodbridge, "Process Hermeneutics," 84–85; Farmer, *Beyond Impasse*, 110–14; Cobb, "Trajectories and Historic Routes." Canonical criticism traces similar development, e.g., Sanders, *Torah and Canon*, and *Canon and Community*.

feel alone in the study. Physically, this may be the case. Yet, according to the process conceptuality, the preacher prehends aspects of the interpretation of the text from the past and the preacher's work with the text will contribute to the interpretation of texts in subsequent occasions. The preacher may not be cognitively aware of being affected by the forces traveling on this route, but, as we have noticed so often, a preacher can be influenced by things that may be dim though present and even powerful.[18]

Scholars in the process community often call attention to similarities (and differences) between the notion of the historic routes of living occasions and Hans Georg Gadamer's idea of "effective history."[19] Preachers and other hermeneuts often speak of a "hermeneutical gap" between the world of the text and the world of today. Gadamer points out that the "gap" is really not an empty space, a "yawning abyss." It is "filled with the continuity of custom and tradition, in the light of which, all that is handed down presents itself to us."[20] The effective history of the text is the influence of the passage upon succeeding generations as new communities interpret the text in the light of new contexts—and in the light of how the passage interprets the new contexts. Williamson and Farmer note that in process terms, the preacher is part of this historic route through internal relationship, a route that includes both the passage and the history of interpretation associated with the text.[21] Thus, for instance, "Augustine's interpretation influenced Luther's, and Augustine's and Luther's influenced Schleiermacher's, and so on down to the present."[22] Farmer continues, "This does not mean that the present interpreter 'has no immediate access to the lures elicited by reading the text itself,' but it does mean that the kind of lures the interpreter feels 'have been socially conditioned by prior feelings of the text's lures.'"[23]

Clark Williamson points to Christian anti-Judaism as a bracing example of a long-lasting effect in interpretive history.[24] Originating in intra-family tensions in particular moments in the first century CE, this ideology

18. The concept of the historic route of living occasions plays a larger role in Chapter 5 and the preacher attending to a wide range of voices in the congregation. But we introduce the historic route here because

19. Note Williamson, "Process Hermeneutics," 79–82, and Farmer, *Beyond the Impasse*, 110–11.

20. Gadamer, *Truth and Method*, 264.

21. Williamson, "Process Hermeneutics," 79–82; Farmer, *Beyond the Impasse*, 111.

22. Farmer, *Beyond the Impasse*, 111.

23. Farmer, *Beyond the Impasse*, 111, citing Woodbridge, "Process Hermeneutics," 84–85.

24. Williamson, "Process Hermeneutics," 85–88; cf. Williamson, *Way of Blessing*, 8–10.

broadened into an interpretive lens with powerful and often unconscious effect that became constitutive of the mainstream church's way of reading the Bible through the Holocaust. Only when exposed has the church in the last half century taken significant steps to recognize and exorcise this interpretive demon.

The historic route is not centered in passing along the "essence" of the text. It is a causal continuity that accounts for change."[25] Farmer continues,

> What happens in later occasions of the route is deeply affected by what happened in earlier occasions, but it is not simply repetitive. No feature of earlier occasions need be repeated unchanged in later occasions. What is distinctive about life is novelty. Identity through time for living occasions is not achieved by the endless repetition of a particular form; in fact, identity achieved through endless repetition is a form of decay because intensity of feeling and zest continually diminish from the levels present in earlier occasions of the route.[26]

Farmer cites Cobb. "Identity through time is maintained when successors include, transform, and build on what they have received." The positive dimensions of a historic route of living occasions are "more in the form of its change than in its unchanged preservation of particular forms."[27]

Every transformation in interpretation along the way is not good. Some transformation in interpretation is regressive and even betrays the process of becoming. Change in interpretation is good when it serves *creative* transformation. Creative transformation must encourage optimal becoming, including manifesting "openness to other sources of meaning without abandoning previous sources, thereby resulting in an enlargement of perspective."[28] As John Cobb says, "Rather than seeking an essential form of faith identical with that witnesses to in the Scriptures, we must seek to discern the present movement of the spirit that is continuous with a movement begun in primitive Christianity."[29]

Preachers interpreting passages from the Bible (or passages from any other literature) can never be completely aware of the effect of the material in the historic route of the occasion on their processes of interpretation because so many of the effects are shadowy and dim. But through exegesis

25. Farmer, *Beyond the Impasse*, 113.

26. Farmer, *Beyond the Impasse*, 113.

27. Cobb, "Trajectories and Historic Routes," 94–95, cited in Farmer, *Beyond the Impasse*, 113.

28. Farmer, *Beyond the Impasse*, 116

29. Cobb, "Authority of the Bible," 201.

and conversation with the community of interpreters and a range of voices beyond that, the preacher can achieve some degree of awareness of it and can reflect critically on the degree to which it contributes to creative transformation.

Draw on Familiar Exegetical Methods

As noted at the outset of this chapter, the preacher does not need to learn an entirely new array of exegetical skills and methods to work with the Bible and other topics in a process mode.[30] The preacher can draw on exegetical perspectives and approaches learned in virtually all schools of theological education but bring them into the service of a process way of thinking about the biblical text (or the topic) and its relationship to the sermon. Biblical scholars have made an industry of developing different methods for exegesis.[31] Process preachers usually draw on some combination of the following approaches.[32]

- Establish responsible starting and ending points for the text. The text should be a natural unit of meaning that honors the otherness of the text and not a selection the preacher has cut and pasted to remove

30. I cut my exegetical teeth on the historical critical method and continue to believe that, along with literary criticism and theological criticism, it gives the preacher the best chance to honor the otherness of the biblical material. I respect other modes of exegesis, especially those that come from social positions of injustice and suffering. But while preachers in any method can interpret texts so that the texts reflect the images and desires of the preachers, historical criticism does seek to minimize this tendency even while recognizing that the historical critic's lens is always tinted (per Farmer above).

31. The following resources are among guides to various aspects of biblical interpretation. Of course, the exegetical and theological perspectives vary from author to author. Pregeant, *Engaging the New Testament*, 13–41 overviews a wide range of interpretive perspectives with a process touch. Additionally: Hayes and Holliday, *Biblical Exegesis*; Gorman, *Elements of Biblical Exegesis*; Stuart, *Old Testament Exegesis*; Fee, *New Testament Exegesis*; Knight, *Methods of Biblical Interpretation*; O. W. Allen in *Reading the Synoptic Gospels* presents a model easily adaptable to other kinds of biblical literature; Tiffany and Ringe, *Biblical Interpretation*; McKenzie and Haynes, *To Each Its Own Meanings*; McKenzie and Kaltner, *New Meanings for Ancient Texts*; Green, *Hearing the New Testament*; Adam, *Handbook of Postmodern Biblical Interpretation*; Soulen, *Handbook of Biblical Criticism*; Malherbe, "Task and Methods of Exegesis." The preacher can adapt many of these methods to identifying what sources outside the Bible invited people to believe and do.

32. Some of these elements overlap in their concerns, purposes, and methods.

difficult ideas or to get the Scripture reading to appear to say something it does not really say in order to serve the preacher's own agenda.[33]

- Read the text aloud, perhaps with different vocal inflections. Conversely, listen to the text by playing it on an electronic recording or by hearing another person read it. Note how different vocal emphases in reading and hearing can affect the preacher's sense of the text.[34] The same words in different tonalities can take on quite different characteristics.

- Describe the historical context of the community that received text in the expression in which we have it as well as the purpose of the text for the community in that setting.

- Identify the literary/rhetorical genre of the text, the function the text was intended to have in the ancient congregation, and how the genre was designed to achieve this function.

- Place the text in its larger literary contexts (e.g., the biblical book in which it is found, and/or body of work of the author/authoring community).

- Explore the meanings of the important words in the text, particularly what they do in the passage, in the biblical book as a whole, and in the larger works associated with the author or community. For instance, one might study a word in the text, in the book of Romans, and then in the Pauline corpus.

- Determine social and cultural assumptions the ancient listeners would have assumed that may be different from assumptions today.

- Note other observations about the text or its interpretation that may fall outside the previous categories or that particularly catch the interpreter's attention. These observations might include questions for further exegetical, theological, or hermeneutical exploration.

- Consider the possibility that elements of the text resonate with elements of process understandings of the world, human existence, and God's presence and power. As noted above, however, the preacher should be cautious when making these explorations.

33. The Revised Common Lectionary is infamous for slicing and dicing texts so that theologically problematic sections will not be read in public worship. The RCL is particularly egregious in the ways in which it cuts up individual psalms for public reading. See R. J. Allen, *Sermon Treks*, 33–62.

34. On the importance of oral-aural engagement with a text, see our discussion of Whitehead's penetrating discussion of sound and hearing in chapter 8.

In short, the preacher aims to understand the text in its ancient world-view in a way that honors Otherness of the text in light of its historical, literary, and theological settings. In this way, the preacher has a good chance of articulating the invitation(s) offered through the text to people in antiquity.

Of course, the preacher's task is complicated by the fact that scholars often put forward different, even contradictory views, concerning how to reconstruct the historical situation, how the literary elements of the text work together, and how to understand the theological and ethical claims of the text. When confronted by contradictory exegetical conclusions, the preacher must choose the one that makes the most sense *in light of the probabilities from history.* I italicize the preceding phrase because many preachers choose exegetical perspectives that are closest to their own theologies without giving adequate attention to what might have been more or less plausible from the standpoint of ancient assumptions. Preachers often want the authority of the Bible behind them. However, from the conversational point of view in dialogue with process in this book, the preacher does not *need* the authority of the Bible. Indeed, a text that presents a problematic perspective might very well be text that launches a significant conversation.

KEY QUESTIONS

Using perspectives generated by exegesis, the preacher can ask a short series of key questions of the text. These questions are intended to help the preacher enter into theological conversation with the text.

1. What does the text or topic invite its listeners to believe in the way of theological interpretation of the situation of the community to whom the text is addressed?[35]

2. What does the text or topic invite its listeners to believe about God and God's purposes in and for the circumstances of the listening community?

3. What does text or topic invite its listeners to believe God could really do in the circumstances?

4. How does the text or topic invite listeners to respond?

With responses to these questions in mind, the preacher can then be in a position to bring those invitations into homiletical conversation with other invitations from tradition, theology, and other arenas of life.

35. The response to question 1 sometimes overlaps with responses to the other questions.

SURFACE INVITATIONS AND
DEEPER INVITATIONS IN TEXTS

The work of exegesis would seem to be fairly straightforward. However, it is sometimes complicated, from a process point of view, because texts often issue invitations in both *surface* invitations and "basal lures." Since meaning of the phrase "basal lure" is not immediately accessible to many preachers, I usually refer to it as a "deep invitation." The basal lure or deep invitation is "the fundamental disposition [of the text] towards reality itself."[36] As Farmer notes, these "lures operate below the surface of the text at the presuppositional level; that is, they reflect the author's assumptions or presuppositions and so typically are implied rather than stated."[37] The surface level of the text is typically cast in the language and immediate presuppositions of the worldview within which the text is embedded. The deeper invitation is often framed in language or less precise awareness that transcends the immediate cultural expression of the surface invitation.

In addition, the deep invitation sometimes has a subcategory called the "undercurrent." The undercurrent invitation is an "implicit metaphysical understanding" that is "at odds with a straightforward reading of the surface lures."[38] The undercurrent invitation articulates the deep concern of the author. The surface invitation voices a means of moving towards that deep concern but does so in a way that is out of character with the deep concern itself. To take an example, many people have a deep concern for world peace with nations living together so that people and goods can pass freely from one to another and so that the things that make for security are shared among all peoples. A surface invitation, promoted by the arms industries, is that security comes about through massive military presence,

---

36. Pregeant, *Christology beyond Dogma*, 44; cf. 105–28. I have long used the language of "surface meaning" and "deeper meaning" for two similar modes of interpretation, though with less precision, e.g., Williamson and R. J. Allen, *Credible and Timely Word*, 96–101 and R. J. Allen, *Interpreting the Gospel*, 88–91. The two broad strokes of this approach (surface current and deep current) are similar in structure to Rudolf Bultmann's program of demythologizing which (1) recognizes the mythical world pictures in which a text is cast but (2) seeks to restate the purpose of the text in non-mythological contemporary terms, especially existentialist philosophy and theology. Bultmann, however, essentially sought to translate the text from an ancient worldview to a contemporary one. Bultmann, "New Testament and Mythology," 128.

37. Farmer, *Process Theology and Biblical Interpretation*, 22.

38. Farmer, *Process Theology and Biblical Interpretation*, 22; Farmer, *Beyond the Impasse*, 108; Cf. Pregeant, *Christology beyond Dogma*, 105–28, and Pregeant, "Where Is the Meaning?" esp. the case study, 117–24. In *Beyond the Impasse*, Farmer explains the language of "undercurrent" (105–6) and illustrates it through interpreting Revelation 4–5 (135–61). These notions also permeate his *Revelation*.

which includes threat of killing and being killed. Many financial and human resources that could go into promoting human community go into preparing for mutual destruction.

These notions have a family relationship with Whitehead's twofold notion of perception and language. We often perceive the surface invitation in the mode of presentational immediacy, and we become aware of the deeper invitation through causal efficacy. Awareness in presentational immediacy is precise but limited; we often use steno-language to discuss the surface level of the text, that is, what we perceive in presentational immediacy. Perception in causal awareness is dim but deep; we often use tensive language to discuss the deeper invitation of the text, that is, what we perceive in causal efficacy.

The surface current of invitation is what the text invited people to believe in light of the particular ancient worldview of the text. This invitation is typically straightforward from the perspective the immediate worldview of the text. By doing a little exegetical spadework, we can speak about it in steno-language. The surface current sometimes offers an invitation that the contemporary preacher can embrace. For instance, 1 John 3:11 declares, "For this is the message you have heard from the beginning, that we should love one another." Of course, the preacher needs to ascertain the meaning of love, to explore why the author was moved to write this directive, and to consider who is included in "one another." But, while the surface invitation to love one another may have nuances particular to the Johannine community, the invitation itself does not come with a surprising undercurrent.

However, a good many surface currents contain elements that are problematic to thinkers in the process tradition, and also to many others. For example, many texts assume pre-scientific worldviews. An easy-to-see example is a Hebrew assumption that existence is comprised of three stories—heaven above, the earth in the middle, and an underworld below Another example is the presence of demons, especially in the Gospels and Letters. From a scientific point of view, the three-story worldview is simply not true. In the world of the first century, many people believed that demons existed as personal spirits who could inhabit people and communities (and even objects) and could exert a significant measure of control over the ones they inhabited. This direct phenomenon is outside of the experience of most of the communities to whom I relate. Some texts portray God directly acting—or authorizing others to act—in ways that violate inclusive well-being, as, for instance, when God infamously drowns Pharaoh's army. Such activities seem to be contrary to the idea of a God who seeks the optimum becoming of all.

In comparison, as already said, the deeper intention is not typically tied to ancient worldviews. The deeper invitation can reveal the text's "fundamental disposition toward reality itself."[39] The deep invitation can reveal a deep concern for optimal becoming, pointing to things like mutual support in community, love, justice, and provision. Even when a surface level of a text invited people to believe something today's preacher regards as problematic, the undercurrent can point towards something more positive. The surface invitation of the Deuteronomic theology, for instance, is to believe that God blesses the obedient and curses the disobedient. If a community experiences blessing, then it must be obedient. If a community lives in conditions associated with curse, it must be disobedient. Real life experience, however, undercuts this simple formula.

At the undercurrent level, the deep concern of the Deuteronomic theologians is to invite the members of the community to live together in the ways of mutual support as described in the covenant. The Deuteronomic thinking has community in view. When a community accepts the invitation to cooperate with the covenant, the tendency is towards a life of blessing. When a community does not accept the invitation to cooperate with the covenant, then the tendency is towards tension and disarray either in the present or down the road.

NAMING INVITATIONS IN TEXTS

The preacher typically has a fairly easy route to identifying the surface invitation. The preacher simply follows the questions and methods articulated above in "Draw on Familiar Methods" (above).

Russell Pregeant notes that to identify the deep invitation, including an undercurrent, "The interpreter must work through the discursive implications of the text back to the complex of feelings towards which it lures the reader."[40] However, as Langer and others note, such feelings are often hard to describe because they occur in a trans-verbal mode of awareness. Nevertheless. As we saw in chapter 3, William Beardslee and his colleagues point to a way of trying to identify—insofar as one can—the feelings out of which a text comes.[41] The preacher can name the emotions stirred by the text and explore possible relationships between the emotions and the broader and deeper network of feeling that the emotion may signal. A feeling is more

39. Pregeant, *Christology beyond Dogma*, 44.

40. Pregeant, *Christology beyond Dogma*, 44. Pregeant's guidelines also applies to considering invitations that come from other sources.

41. Beardslee, et. al. *Biblical Preaching on the Death pf Jesus*, 60–64. @

than an emotion; but the presence of emotion may be a clue to the nature of the feeling in the depth. Emotion may also be a response to things happening in the preacher's world that are not connected to the text. So, in this matter as in so many, critical reflection and circumspection are important on the preacher's part.

Deep invitations, including undercurrents, are sometimes fairly easy to identify. For example, the Sages seek to learn from experience. Much of the wisdom literature draws proverbs and other admonitions from observation of experience to show individuals, households, and the larger community how to live in personal security, how to live in harmony with one another, and how to make sense of the meaning of life. Such texts seek to promote well-being. Other pieces of wisdom literature are actually undercurrents, that is, they challenge dominant themes in wisdom. The book of Ecclesiastes, for instance, invites the community to think that the direct prescriptions of the typical sage for the good life are not true to the experience of the author of Ecclesiastes. This book does not offer a replacement vision for the meaning of life, it but invites the community to probe more deeply in a way that recognizes, the pain and futility of real existence.

Deep invitations are sometimes hard to identify because the feelings that empower them come to the preacher in the mode of causal efficacy and the preacher must struggle to name them. Long ago Barry Woodbridge observed that the deeper invitation "is not usually a conceptual construct that is consciously pondered. It is felt at a much deeper level than conscious experience, even though feeling it may, in human experience, become involved on an intellectual level."[42] Similarly, J. Gerald Janzen paraphrases Whitehead. "We experience more than we know; and we know more than we can think; and we think more than we can say; and language therefore lags behind the intuitions of immediate experience."[43]

In the spirit of Woodbridge and Janzen, preachers often have the sense that they are more aware of things going on in texts—and especially in their responses to texts—than they can articulate fully. This phenomenon is especially true of deeper invitations, including undercurrents. As an interpreter, I am often dimly aware of something happening in my trans verbal awareness. I can feel it. I know it. In process language, I prehend it. As a person, this grasp contributes to my sense of self and my orientation to the world, but I do not report it in a direct and easy way.

While such events of awareness enrich me, as a preacher I cannot simply stand in the pulpit and feel. I cannot just gesture or make a sound. I

---

42. Woodbridge, "Process Hermeneutic," 80.

43. Janzen, "Old Testament in 'Process' Perspective," 492.

need to try to name such intuitions as carefully as I can. I need to use words, recognizing as Janzen says, that "Language lags behind experience."[44] This is a point at which being a member of a community of interpreters engaged in conversation can be quite helpful. In such a community preachers have opportunities to try out how they name their intuitive understandings of the invitations of texts, and preachers have opportunities to listen to how other preachers prehend the deep invitations of texts.[45] Others among the cadre of interpreters might hear things the preacher misses. Still others in the conversation might see things amiss in the preacher's report.

Working along these lines can be quite risky for the preacher. For the tendency here—as elsewhere in exegesis—is to interpret the things that come to the preacher through the life of intuition in ways that serve the preacher's self-interest without giving due consideration to the possibility that the feelings edging into awareness actually challenge aspects of the preacher's understanding. When the community of interpreters is in a social location similar to the preacher, the conversation may not move beyond perceptions and values already present in the community. But these risks come with the territory.

Two considerations come into play when working with deep feelings that are hard to verbalize. For one, the preacher should have the humility to signal the congregation that preacher's formulation of the invitation has a certain tentativeness. For the other consideration, a preacher can always take heart from the conviction that, according to this process perspective on sermon preparation, when errors of interpretation occur, God offers additional opportunities for the invitation to come into focus for the preacher and congregation.

Every text, then, contains invitations. These lures can be located in both the surface current and the undercurrent. But every lure does not invite creative transformation in the optimum way. Some proposals effectively result in stagnation or even in regression. Some invitations would actually

---

44. Janzen, "Old Testament in 'Process' Perspective," 499. Of course, a preacher can employ nonverbal media in the sermon to bring intuitive awareness into expression in the sermon, e.g., dance, body movement, music, drama, visual media. There may be occasions when such expressions constitute the whole sermon. But listeners receive such expressions in their own ways. Sooner or later, the preacher must *name* what is going on theologically so as to create as much opportunity as possible for the community to have a commonly acknowledged understanding recognizing that these uses of words may fall short of the depth meaning of the awareness.

45. As examples of communities of interpreters, scholars who are present in the conversation through commentaries and other published works, other clergy who meet together in colleague groups, as well as laypeople who meet with the preacher to consider upcoming sermons.

lower the quality of life for some members of the community—and perhaps even for the community itself—if pursued. Consequently, preacher and congregation want as complete an understanding of the invitation(s) as they can get.

Because authority in process perspective derives from conversation between tradition (including and especially the Bible) and experience, the preacher has the freedom to let the text be the text without imposing the process voice on it. Sometimes these determinations come quickly and neatly, but sometimes they are difficult, time-consuming, and messy because historical, literary, and theological factors can sometimes be interpreted in different ways. In any event, even when a text puts forward perspectives that resonate with process thought, the preacher should not rush immediately to the sermon, but should bring the proposals of the text into conversation with other proposals in search of wider, deeper understanding.

A CASE STUDY: MATT 25:14–30

We turn now to a case study of identifying the invitations in the parable of the talents in Matt 25:14–30. This text occurs in the Revised Common Lectionary on the 25th Sunday after Pentecost (Proper 28).[46] The case study begins with identifying some of my pre-associations with the text and then follows the outline of exegetical steps in "Draw from Familiar Methods" (above) with the goal answering the four Key Questions (also above). Because of limitations of space, I give condensed exegetical perspectives.

- *Preassociations*. I have many preassociations with this text. Among them: I typically hear this passage interpreted as a basis for financial stewardship when the congregation is raising the budget and the preachers urges us to be talent givers. I also hear this passage as a call to use my other gifts and abilities to the church. I have heard preachers use this text as justification for capitalism: each slave was responsible for making his own money. Some preachers read this emphasis through the lens of a prosperity gospel. With a negative twist, I hear the story used to exhort people to use their abilities to the utmost in the pursuit of success in life. "Use it or lose it," said one preacher. I also recollect hearing that the servants represent Jews and gentiles. I

---

46. Pregeant, *Matthew*, 173–84 offers brilliant process reflection on Matt 24:1— 25:46, especially on themes of "preparedness," the apocalypse, divine power, and especially on "reward, punishment, and the action of God." I take up his theological suggestions in connection with the case study in chapter 6 which moves from exegesis to theological reflection.

innately identify with the five-talent slave. I will keep these in mind for possible use in the sermon.

- *Natural unit of meaning*. The passage is a natural unit of meaning.

- *Read aloud*. I read the passage aloud several times, using several intonations, especially in regard to the tones of voice of the third servant and of the master. For example, I read the third servant in 25:24–25 as afraid, as embarrassed, and as defiant. I read the master in 25:26–30 as angry, as disappointed, and as incredulous. The outcome of the exegesis will determine the inflection I give the passage when I read it in public worship just before preaching.

- *Historical setting of Matthew*. I take the First Gospel to be written about 80–90 CE from an apocalyptic worldview. The author regards Jesus as God's agent through whom God is replacing the present world, which has so much evil, with the coming Realm of God. Whereas Mark is shot through with the belief that the apocalypse will come soon, Matthew has come to believe that the apocalypse is delayed. Many in the community are in danger of drifting away—perhaps drifting back to traditional Pharisaism. The congregation, which was likely comprised of both Jewish people and gentiles is conflicted over how to bring gentiles into the community. Authority is a central issue for the community. Matthew lifts up the authority of Jesus as the authentic interpreter of the Jewish tradition in light of the coming cosmic transforming and undermines the authority of traditional Pharisees.

- *Literary genre*. While we casually refer to the text as a parable, it is more accurate to say that for Matthew, the story is a soft allegory in which the characters in the story resemble people in Mark's world. These identifications should not be pushed too literally. They are similarities and not one-to-one detailed allegorical elements. The master resembles Jesus while the slaves resemble attitudes within the Matthean community. The master going on a protracted journey is similar to Jesus ascending and waiting for a long time before returning. The assignments to the slaves—to multiply the master's money—compares with the assignments to Matthew's church to embody the qualities of the Realm in its own life and to witness to the Realm publicly, especially by inviting gentiles to become a part of the movement towards the Realm.

- *Larger literary context*. The story is part of Jesus' fifth and final teaching discourse (Matt 24:1—25:46). The purpose of this discourse is (a) to persuade listeners that the apocalypse, while delayed, is still ahead

(Matt 24:144), and (b) to urge listeners to be prepared for the coming
of the apocalypse and the final judgment (Matt 24:45—25:46). The
parable of the faithful and unfaithful servants (Matt 24:45–51) urges
the congregation to continue living faithfully. The parable of the ten
bridesmaids (Matt 25:1–13) admonishes the congregation to maintain
the oil necessary to keep their lamps lit. The parable of the talents
(Matt 25:14–30) implores the congregation, even in its season of conflict, and delays to continue its active witness to the Realm. The parable
of the sheep and the goats (Matt 25:31–46) brings the discourse to a
bracing conclusion by emphasizing that those who have been faithful,
who kept their lamps lit, who multiplied their witness, and who cared
for the hungry, thirsty, stranger, naked, sick, or imprisoned will join
the righteous in the realm while others will be condemned to eternal
punishment.

- **Important words.** The "talent" is an incredible sum of money, perhaps
  worth as much as fifteen years of wages. The saying describing the
  master, "you were a harsh [*skleros*] person," is not a direct description
  of God but a way of heightening the drama of the story. The outer
  darkness and the weeping and gnashing of teeth refer to hell, a place of
  punishment where those consigned to it live forever.

- **Social and cultural elements.** It was commonplace in antiquity for
  masters to go away and to leave responsible slaves managing many of
  the masters' affairs. While burying the talent may seem odd to people
  today, it was a common practice in the absence of banks in the ancient world as a way of protecting resources from thieves and invading
  armies.

- **Other observations.** The characters in the text, like members of Matthew's community, have different abilities. O. Wesley Allen Jr. reminds
  us that this detail indicates that participants in the church are not
  all expected to do the same things in the same way, but according to
  distinctive aptitudes. Allen makes a further key theological point. For
  Matthew, "The ethical Christian life [i.e., the use of our talents in wit-
  ness] is not a test for which we ae rewarded; the ethical Christian life is
  the reward. The more we give, the more we get."[47]

- **Elements that resonate with process thought.** At least on the surface,
  most elements of the story itself seem less to resonate with process
  values and more to conflict with them. The idea of the master being
  altogether absent is contrary to one of my most cherished process

47. O. W. Allen, *Matthew*, 246–47.

convictions. The master-slave relationship is hierarchical and exploit-ative. The master does not participate with the slaves in carrying out their responsibilities. At the end of the story, the master actively con-signs the first servant to eternal punishment, thus again conflicting with the conviction that God would never directly inflict suffering. However, O. Wesley Allen's comment just above—the more we give in the way of discipleship, the fuller our life—is consistent with a process notion of becoming. So is the implication that the slaves are agents in actively creating their own futures as they cooperate, or do not cooper-ate, with the values and practices of the Realm.

Key Questions

We are now in a position to respond to the key questions posed above. The purpose now is to identify how the First Gospel offers answers to these questions with respect to its own situation in history. At this point, I am articulating surface invitations of the text. We return to these questions, to the parable of the talents, and to its deeper invitations in chapter 6.

1. What does the text or topic invite its listeners to believe in the way of theological interpretation of the situation of the community to whom the text is addressed? At the surface level, the text invites members of Matthew's congregation, in the midst of their situation of delay and conflict, to continue to faithfully carry out their mission of embody-ing the Realm, especially welcoming gentiles in the community of the Realm, or to face eternal punishment.

2. What does the text or topic invite its listeners to believe about God and God's purposes in and for the circumstances of the listening com-munity? The response to this question is implied in the response to the preceding one. The text assumes that God is the controlling agent in the Matthean world. God's purpose is to bring the Realm into expres-sion as a social and cosmic reality. God is in absolute control of history and will send Jesus back to the world as part of the apocalypse to trans-form the present world into one in which the qualities of the Realm are manifest at a time of God's choosing; in the meantime, the conflict and suffering of the world continues. After the apocalypse, God will judge people on the basis of the degree to which their attitudes and behavior have been faithful and will welcome some into life in the eternal Realm and consign others to eternal punishment.

3. What does text or topic invite its listeners to believe God could really do in the circumstances? The answers to questions 1 and 2 imply the answer to this one. The text invites listeners to believe that God will bring about the apocalypse and effect the final judgment.

4. How does the text or topic invite listeners to respond? The story invites members of Matthew's community to continue to carry out the mission of the community or face eternal punishment.

5

Bringing the Invitations
of the Text into Conversation
with Other Invitations

In the previous chapter, I surmised that many preachers, at the conscious level, make a two-step movement in sermon preparation. They first explore the invitations of a text in the ancient world and then leap-frog over two thousand years of interpretive history to the second movement of articulating possibilities for today. My impression is that most preachers do consult biblical commentaries and/or other preaching resources (especially online resources).[1] Even with such resources, many preachers prepare sermons as if they are the first expositors since the world of the Bible to interpret the biblical text at the heart of the sermon.

However, other factors are at work in the interpretative situation even when the preacher is not cognizant of them. Per the previous chapter, preachers do not simply take in the text in an objective fashion but always interpret the text through the tint of the lenses we discussed. Moreover, the historic route of living occasions influences the preacher even if the preacher is not cognizant of being in that route.[2]

When preachers jump from the past to the present without considering the intermediate years of interpretation, three things can happen. First,

1. Most online preaching resources offer biblical commentary and hermeneutical possibilities. Some online resources, especially those related to the Revised Common Lectionary, offer additional resources, such as thoughts from theologians, ethicists, and social commentators, as well as worship resources, and even artistic expressions that coordinate with biblical readings, especially those related to the Revised Common Lectionary. While the internet is loaded with preaching resources, the quality is uneven.

2. On "historic routes of living occasions," see above, 93–96.

unrecognized influences from the interpretive route of historic occasions can shape the preacher's interpretation apart from the preacher's awareness. Such influences can be quite powerful, as when the preacher simply assumes an anti-Jewish reading of a text from the Gospels and Letters.[3] Second, preachers can bring ideas and other materials into the homiletical conversation without critically considering whether the materials really belong in the conversation, only to be affected by material that has an extraneous relationship to the developing sermon. The preacher is particularly vulnerable to such incursions when hungry for a sermon. Third, the preacher can overlook voices in Christian tradition (and beyond) who might add spark to the conversation. The sparks can take a range of directions.

- Some sparks might reaffirm the proposal of the text.

- Other sparks could nuance the preacher's perception of the proposal.

- Some sparks might enlarge the direction of the sermon.

- Some sparks might prompt preacher and congregation to look at the proposal from different points of view and see things not previously in view.

- Some sparks can ignite disturbing issues, perhaps even suggesting that preachers and listeners reject the invitation (or aspects of it).

- A preacher may need to resist the urge the extinguish a spark too soon.

Here is one of many points in sermon preparation where the preacher should have Whitehead's dictum hanging on the study wall: "It is more important that a [proposal] be interesting than that it be true."[4]

Of course, human finitude makes it impossible to become aware of *all* the possible invitations around a particular biblical text, biblical theme, theological topic, or social or personal issue. Only God can attend to all such possibilities. But many sermons would benefit from engaging invitations that range more widely than reading the text, consulting biblical and conventional homiletical resources, and turning the sermon over in the imagination.[5]

3. On anti-Judaism as a lens passed down the historic route of living occasions, see Williamson, "Process Hermeneutics," 83–88; Williamson, *Way of Blessing*, 8–10.

4. Whitehead, *Process and Reality*, 259.

5. The Talmud is a vivid example of the value of bringing different invitations related to a text or topic from across time and interpretive viewpoint into immediate proximity. On a subject—such as a passage from Scripture, or one from the Mishnah, or a theological idea or a word—the Talmud frequently presents the views of several rabbi, often interacting with one another across time. The reader thus immediately—and in little time—has access to a wide range of invitations regarding what might be possible

This chapter encourages the preacher to bring the invitations of the text or the topic into conversation with others across time and space. The chapter begins with a focus on invitations from voices in historical theological families, from contemporary theological families, from the life of the congregation, from the preacher's own experience, and from wider sources, such as the arts and the social sciences.[6] Because preachers are sometimes not as familiar with resources for these dimensions of sermon preparation as they are with tools biblical exegesis, I mention some easy-to-use resources at the end of each chapter.

I write as if the categories discussed in this chapter are separated from one another. However, their relationship is not one like grain storage facilities sitting in a row on a farm. Each one is more like a center of gravity with a range of force whose boundaries are permeable and whose forces interact. Most preachers belong to a historical theological family, and to a contemporary theological family.[7] For example, I am a member of the historical Stone-Campbell theological community and the contemporary process theological family. My theological worldview does not exhibit either one in a pure state but draws on elements of both even as it is hesitant about dimensions of both. One of my good friends is a Wesleyan existentialist and another holds a Reformed postliberal position.

The effort in this chapter is to encourage preachers to pay attention to the range of invitations that Christians across the ages have heard in texts and topics. I also hope to support preachers in becoming as awake as can be to the multiple levels of interpretive dynamics at work in the process of

---

to believe and do in relationship to the subject matter.

6. The distinction between "historical theological families" and "contemporary theological families" is arbitrary. For purposes of this discussion, I think of historical theological families as the ones that originated long ago, such as the Orthodox, Roman Catholicism, Lutheranism, the Reformed movement, Anglicanism, Wesleyanism, the Stone-Campbell Movement, Friends, and Pentecostalism. While African American preaching is not univocal, it is quite old and much African American preaching shares characteristics in common. Of course, these families continue into the contemporary era. But for the purposes of this discussion, I think of contemporary theological families less from the standpoint of the time of their origin and more from the standpoint of their attempts to think theologically about issues of recent and current concern. Among contemporary families, I would include evangelical, liberal, neo-orthodox, postliberal, existentialism, Radical Orthodoxy, deconstruction, black liberation, womanist, feminist, Latinx liberation, Mujerista, Asian American, Asian American feminist, Queer, Indigenous People, postcolonial, and of course, process. This taxonomy is developed in miniature in R. J. Allen, *Thinking Theologically*, and is developed in R. J. Allen, editor, *Preaching the Manifold Grace*, 2 vols.

7. For a table coordinating historical and theological families, see R. J. Allen, *Thinking Theologically*, 90; R. J. Allen, *Preaching the Manifold Grace*, vol. 1, 313–314; vol. 2, 306–307.

sermon preparation. The more interpretive possibilities the preacher has on the surface of the brain, the more reflective the preacher can be with respect to those that are more and less helpful.

Considering other voices can have a direct pay-off in a sermon in the conversational spirit. The preacher might compare and contrast some of the invitations from other voices with those of the text and with the inclinations from the process worldview. Naming and describing other viewpoints can sometimes help illuminate the distinctiveness of the perspectives of process thought, especially as refracted through the preacher's particular appropriation of it. Helping the congregation see comparison and contrast in a mode of theological reflection can often be an effective way to help the community understand what is at stake, as well as gains and losses with adopting a process view.

INVITATIONS FROM HISTORICAL THEOLOGICAL FAMILIES

The expression "historical theological families" here refers here to the many Christian voices with their multiple and sometimes differing interpretations of Christian faith from the many different times and places in which the church has lived from the biblical period to the edge of today.[8] Voices in Christian history and tradition are even more diverse than those in the Bible.[9]

For centuries, when Eurocentric preachers and scholars thought of Christian history and tradition, they had in mind Christian developments in and around Europe (and, for the last six hundred years, the Eurocentric stream in North America). Year by year, and with increasing force, however, Christian communities are becoming ever more aware of the limitations of this Eurocentric focus and of the importance of considering invitations offered by Christian groups in other times, places, and cultural situations.

Like many others, I lament the biblical illiteracy of so many Christian communities today, but the problem is deeper than biblical illiteracy.[10] The problem includes historical amnesia and theological illiteracy, that is, lack

---

8. On the importance of conversation with theologians from the past, see Suchocki, *Whispered Word*, 39–53.

9. Roger Carstensen, former President of the Christian College of George, often characterized the Bible as "not a book, but a library." For a recent survey of theological families from history with attention to preaching, see R. J. Allen, *Preaching the Manifold Grace*, vol. 1. For briefer consideration, see R. J. Allen, *Thinking Theologically*, 322.

10. The explicit historical memories of many current Christian communities extend no longer than the most recent generation, indeed.

of awareness of Christian history and lack of familiarity with the resources and methods for thinking theologically about life and its possibilities. In meetings at every level of the church—congregation middle judicatory, upper judicatory—I am struck with how few members and leaders know how to draw on resources from the past, and even the present, in carefully thinking through an issue for today.[11] Theological method often amounts to little more than citing the latest slogan on the issue at hand. Even when such rallying cries are theologically sound, it is important to know why they are sound.

These problems are especially important since, as Delwin Brown points out, traditions can have long-lasting effects even when a community no longer remembers the specific content of its traditions.[12] Barry Woodbridge points out, further, that the preacher does not simply encounter "the text" but through internal relationship with the past, the tradition of interpreting the text between the world of the Bible and today. It follows that the more conscious the preacher can be of the interpreting tradition, the more the preacher can be critical of it—drawing on its expanding dimensions and turning away from its limiting dimensions.[13]

By bringing such voices into the sermon, the preacher helps people locate themselves in relationship to how other communities have interpreted God's purposes in contexts ranging from those that are analogous to the congregation's immediate situation to those that are in radically different contexts. Resources from history and tradition prompt the contemporary listening community to consider both the degree to which it can—and cannot—affirm what prior voices have said, and to ponder how prior churches have reflected on issues in ways that range from models to anti-models.

When consulting voices from the Christian past, one of the preacher's temptations is similar to one that confronts the preacher when working with the Bible: the temptation to "proof text," that is, to use a sentence or two that makes the preacher's point (positively or negatively) but without taking account of the historical and literary contexts of the statement. When attending to an invitation from Christian history and tradition, the preacher should do so in the manner suggested by Hans-Georg Gadamer.

> A person who seeks to understand must question what lies behind what is said. [That person] must understand it [what is

11. The problem is illustrated by a layperson who, in an unguarded moment, once said in a Bible study group, "If I hear it [on a particular religious broadcast that sets forth a truncated idea of Christian faith], I believe it."

12. Brown, *Boundaries of our Habitation*, 77–82.

13. Woodbridge, "Process Hermeneutics," 79–82.

> said] as an answer to a question. If we go back behind what is
> said, then we inevitably ask questions beyond what is said . . .
> Thus, the meaning of a sentence is relative to the question to
> which it is a reply.[14]

The preacher needs an exegetical understanding of statements from church history much like the preacher needs an exegetical understanding of a text from the Bible. Fortunately, preachers are typically prepared for such explorations through the church history and historical theology they took in seminary.

Since preachers are finite beings, they may find it overwhelming to think of listening for invitations in vast and diverse Christian history and tradition.[15] Moreover, a preacher has limited time for sermon preparation and needs to focus that time as meaningfully as possible (while allowing for spontaneity of discovery and free play of the imagination).

Two practical suggestions can help preachers bring conversation with voices in into the regular pattern of sermon preparation, one focusing on one ecclesial movement from history or on one theological family. Turning to one movement or one voice may seem like a small sample of the history of interpretation, but even one sample of listening to a voice between the time of the Bible and the time of today's sermon would help the preacher take more account of the interpretive traditions between the Bible and today than many patterns of sermon preparation that jump immediately from the world of the Bible to the world of today's listening community. In the optimum situation the preacher can locate specific references to the text in relationship to which the sermon is growing. Such references might be in biblical commentaries, sermons, doctrinal statements, or other church documents. Lutherans and preachers in the Reformed movement have the easiest way forward, perhaps, because Luther and Calvin both generated biblical commentaries.

For the preachers going this route, the preacher's own denomination or movement may be a good choice, as might a figure within that movement.[16] Preachers should already have in mind the basic outlines of its theology and its tendencies in interpreting biblical materials, and, if available, could easily become acquainted with resources that enable the preacher to

14. Gadamer, *Truth and Method*, 333.

15. In my view, the preacher would look at such interpretive material less for its exegetical insights and more for the theological perspectives of the voices reported in the commentaries.

16. For the sake of expanding the preacher's contact with otherness, the preacher might attend to a movement or theological figure beyond the preacher's familiar theological and ecclesial worlds.

find interpretation of specific texts. The preacher might pick a particular figure from that movement as a conversation partner for the sermon, such as Augustine, Julian of Norwich, John Wesley, Barton W. Stone, or Sojourner Truth.

If the material from the past does not contain references to the biblical text at the center of the preaching conversation, the preacher can likely extrapolate from the basic theological convictions and doctrinal affirmations and theological method of the ecclesial movement how the person or movement would hear the invitation of the text.

The other practical suggestion for bringing the preacher into conversation with the path is to locate resources that bring several voices onto one place where the preacher can easily hear them, as when studying the Talmud. Preachers now have the advantage of a small but growing number of resources that trace the history of interpretation of particular biblical texts across church history.[17] Here is a brief, representative annotated list of some resources can be helpful.

- The series *Ancient Christian Commentary on Scripture* covers the period from the Gospels and Letters to 750 CE.[18] Each volume follows biblical texts in the manner of a biblical commentary. For each biblical text, the series overviews a variety of theological perspectives.

- The *Reformation Commentary on Scripture* follows the same format as the *Ancient Christian Commentary* but focuses on Reformation theologians.[19]

- For preachers working with theological topics, or to theological themes that connect to biblical texts, Marjorie Suchocki points to Reinhold Seeberg, *The History of Doctrines*.[20] The detailed index of this book allows the reader to identify readily the perspectives of Christian theologians into the nineteenth century on a wide range of themes.[21]

---

17. Works are now appearing that offer explicitly theological readings of biblical texts. While some of these works attend to readings through history, most of them focus on more contemporary theological perspectives so I list them in connection with the text section.

18. Oden, *Ancient Christian Commentary on Scripture*, 29 vols.

19. George, *Reformation Commentary on Scripture*. This series is projected to comprise twenty-eight volumes.

20. Suchocki, *Whispered Word*, 45.

21. Seeberg, *History of Doctrines*, is now published as two volumes in one. For the index to vol. 1, see 438–52. For the index to vol. 2, see 467–92.

INVITATIONS FROM CONTEMPORARY
THEOLOGICAL FAMILIES

Invitations from contemporary theological families can be quite provocative. For they come from people who typically share significant parts of contemporary life but who see key aspects quite differently. Because all perception contains interpretive elements, we cannot say that all these theologians "share the same experience." They tend to have many things in common—such as the same time, the same earth (although sometimes quite different parts of it), similar dwellings, similar patterns of household living, making a living—but different communities can perceive these things in quite different ways.

Although contemporaries, an evangelical worldview can be quite different from a process worldview, and both can be quite different from the worldviews of the liberation theological families. One of the important themes of postmodernity is the way in which encounters with others can help us to recognize the relativities of our own positions and to discern possibilities for life that we may not have considered. Engaging other voices directly can help guard against the temptation to caricature others, presenting them in stilted or incomplete perspectives in an effort to win the assent of listeners. Furthermore, encountering others can help us see things we have not seen before.[22] They can also help us understand *why* others experience the world as they do, and why we find our interpretation of the world to be adequate.

As noted above, by "contemporary theology," I have in mind voices in current and recent generation(s) who think theologically about life today from the points of view of ideas and social dynamics and other matters that at work in today's setting.[23] Some of these theological families originated fairly recently. Others began to come to expression a century ago, while others go back to the Enlightenment. They are contemporary not simply because they were born in the last generation or two, but because they are living theological options that seek to formulate their understandings of the world and of Christian faith in ways that they regard particularly suitable to the early twenty-first century. Contemporary theologies seek to respond

22. Postmodernists sometimes idealize such encounters, as if they always result in happy discoveries. While this is often the case, coming face-to-face with others can sometimes be difficult. These encounters may enlarge us, but they can be quite painful.

23. For distinction between "historical" and "contemporary" theological families in this volume, see note 6 above (p. 111). A guide to many major contemporary theological families and their implications for preaching is R. J. Allen, *Preaching the Manifold Grace*, vol. 2. R. J. Allen, *Thinking Theologically*, offers briefer characterizations.

to issues emerging in the current postmodern ethos. These responses range from hearty embrace to deep skepticism and even rejection.

Preachers are sometimes a little confused when they come across the expression "modern theology," thinking that phrase is a synonym for "contemporary theology." While there can be overlap between the two, "modern theology" typically has the technical meaning of efforts to rethink Christian theology in light of the issues raised by the Enlightenment.[24] Some modern theologies are contemporary in that some theological communities are still continuing to formulate a faith in modern terms.

Like voices from the Bible and Christian history, the voices in contemporary theology are remarkably diverse. One way of organizing the diversity of contemporary theology is to think in terms of categories of response to the Enlightenment (modern) point of view.[25] The preacher is not interested in labels as such. Indeed, the use of labels can too quickly lead to caricature and can obscure points at which communities and points of view could be in dialogue. Nonetheless, brief descriptions can help preachers identify what is important to different theological families as well as how they compare and contrast.

- Some contemporary theologies explicitly reject significant aspects of the attempt to reformulate Christian faith in modern terms, such as fundamentalism, evangelicalism, and post-liberalism.

---

24. We may speak imprecisely of three great periods of theology in many of the Eurocentric parts of the church: premodern, modern, and postmodern. The premodern period lasted until the Enlightenment. The modern period began with the Enlightenment, peaked in the mid-twentieth century, and is now declining in influence. The postmodern period began in the late twentieth century and is becoming a view of the world held by ever more people, even when they do not recognize the name "postmodern." See, e.g., R. J. Allen, *Preaching and the Other*, 7–27. It is important to note that premodern and modern perspectives continue in world and church in the twenty-first century. While some preachers and laypeople claim that these designations have little to do with the typical congregation today, I have noticed in Bible study groups across dozens of congregations of different sizes and denominations that many laypeople hold "folk versions" of these ideas.

25. O. Wesley Allen, Jr., suggested this approach to me as the organizing principle for *Thinking Theologically*. Wesley Allen and I offer a taxonomy of categories based on their apologetic and nonapologetic natures in the language of neighborhoods, mainly in Eurocentric churches in *The Sermon without End*: the Hatfields and McCoys (evangelicals who fight modernity), apartment dwellers (liberals who inhabit the modern building and pay rent to modernity), gated community (postliberals who view the church as its own culture without reference to modernity), and post-apologetic neighborhood (conversational theologies) (1–88).

- Other families, such as the permutations of liberalism, still seek to create a faith that preserves distinctive aspects of Christian conviction while also being at home in the modern house.

- Still others aim to move beyond modernity into a postmodern frame of reference. Much thought associated with postmodernity is deconstructive, that is, it seeks to expose points at which the modern worldview has failed and, especially, points at which the modern world is implicated in multiple forms of exploitation and abuse.

- More and more contemporary theological movements are disinterested in issues raised by the Enlightenment and, instead, take their cues from social location.

- The many liberation theologies typically take the social location of oppression as one of their starting points.

- Theologians from the mid-twentieth century are still influential in some circles because preachers and others continue to resonate with chords in their theologies. One thinks immediately of Paul Tillich, Karl Barth, and Reinhold Niebuhr.

Some commentators see process theology as nothing more than modernism warmed up in a theological microwave oven.[26] Process theologians themselves tend to see process moving in the direction of postmodern perspective but distinguish between "deconstructive postmodernism" and "constructive postmodernism," and to see process exemplifying the latter.[27] Process respects the gains in modernity even as it criticizes points of vulnerability and seeks to articulate an understanding of life that is truly constructive and that is innately open to reconsideration in light of fresh interpretations. Again, the interest here is not in the label per se but in the preacher getting a sense of the lay of the theological landscape and how the various theologies relate with another.

In seminary, many ministers consciously adopt a theological family (such as process) through which they then interpret life. This approach has the value of helping preachers interpret Christian life through a consistent theological lens. An occasional limitation is that the same lens that provides consistency can also discourage preacher and people from considering some

26. One of my acquaintances, who shall remain nameless, describes process as "the capstone of modernism in theology and simultaneously the death cry of modernism in theology." As early as *Science and the Modern World*, however, Whitehead called attention to cracks in the modern project and was taking initial steps in going beyond the limitations of modernism (*Science and the Modern World*, 271–88).

27. See Griffin, *Varieties of Postmodern Theology*.

possibilities that the lens does not bring into focus. This lens, of course, is tinted. Just as the world looks different when looking through green, light brown, light gray, and light blue lenses, so biblical passages look a little different through different theological lenses.

Preachers have many resources available for finding comments from particular contemporary theological families that relate to specific biblical passages on which the preacher might be developing a sermon. This is because many preachers and scholars who interpret the Bible (and God's purposes) from the standpoint of the social location of their communities also generate biblical commentaries from the perspectives of those communities. In such material, the moves from exegesis to theological reflection and hermeneutical application are often fairly easy because the authors interpret biblical texts to speak in order to the communities in particular social locations. The preacher can thus often easily imagine (or even identify) how the interpreters and often theological families they represent interpret what the text invites people today to believe and do.

A resource with particular value to the preacher approaching the pulpit from a process direction is *Chalice Commentaries for Today,* a biblical commentary series written by scholars oriented to process thought, and who engage that conceptuality with ancient texts with an eye for theological meaning for today.[28]

Here are some representative examples of one-volume commentaries on the whole Bible (or on parts of the Bible) that move in this direction.[29]

- *The Women's Bible Commentary.* 3rd ed. This volume, as the name suggests, calls attention to feminist concerns.[30]

- *Searching the Scriptures* is a feminist commentary in two volumes.[31]

28. See generally the Chalice Commentaries for Today series, edited by Kathleen J. Farmer et al.

29. Many of the growing number of books interpreting the Bible from the perspectives of social locations lucidly set out the context of the interpreting community, identify the goals and methods of interpretation from that location and identify hermeneutical points of contact for today. These works, however, typically discuss limited numbers of biblical texts. An important value of a one-volume commentary for preaching is that it comments systematically on large bodies of biblical material, thus giving the preacher a resource that the preacher can use in sermon preparation when working from one text to another when going week by week. he most notable weakness of a one-volume commentary is brevity of interpretive remarks. A one-volume commentary seldom exposes the preacher to the full range and depth of exegesis the preacher needs for a sermon, but it can offer insight from a specific social/theological setting,

30. Newsome et al., *Women's Bible Commentary.*

31. Schüssler Fiorenza, *Searching the Scriptures.*

- *True to Our Native Land: An African American New Testament Commentary.* As the title implies, this work calls attention to interpretive concerns of African American communities.

- *The Queer Bible Commentary* considers biblical materials from the standpoints of the LGBTQAI+ communities.[32]

- *Postcolonial Commentary on the Old Testament.* The comments focus on key texts in the Torah, Prophets, and Writings from postcolonial points of view.[33]

- *A Postcolonial Commentary on the New Testament Writings.*[34] These authors examine texts in the Gospels and Letters through postcolonial lenses.

- The *Africa Bible Commentary* brings together seventy scholars who interpret biblical materials in light of African cultural assumptions.[35]

- *The Africana Bible* reads the Torah, Prophets, and Writings as well as deuterocanonical and pseudepigraphic works from African and African Diaspora contexts.[36]

- The *South Asia Bible Commentary* takes the whole Bible into account with Asian concerns in view.[37]

- Patte, Daniel, ed. *The Global Bible Commentary.* Scholars read texts through social locations from continent except Antarctica.[38]

- *Latino/a Theology and the Bible* is not a one-volume commentary, but it does reflect on biblical interpretation in light of Hispanic experience.[39]

- *The Jewish Annotated New Testament* looks at texts in the Gospels and Letters from the angle of first century Judaism.[40]

Systematic and constructive theologians sometimes write in the genre of biblical commentary. When using such works, preachers should, of course,

32. Guest et al., *Queer Bible Commentary.*

33. Gossai, *Postcolonial Commentary on the Old Testament.*

34. Segovia and Sugirtharajah, *Postcolonial Commentary on the New Testament Writings.*

35. Adeyamo, *Africa Bible Commentary.*

36. Page, *Africana Bible.*

37. Wintle et al., *South Asia Bible Commentary.*

38. Patte, *Global Bible Commentary.*

39. Lozada and Segovia, *Latino/a Theology and the Bible.*

40. Levine and Brettler, *Jewish Annotated New Testament.*

determine the theological perspective from which the commentator interprets the text. Here are two examples.

- Each volume of *Belief: A Theological Commentary on the Bible*, deals with a biblical book (or books).[41] The theological orientation of the theologians varies as does the degree of traditional exegetical engagement with the biblical text.

- The *Abingdon Theological Companion to the Lectionary* offers theological reflections on the lectionary texts by a systematic or constructive theologian in dialogue with a biblical scholar.[42]

INVITATIONS FROM
THE LIFE OF THE CONGREGATION

Virtually all approaches to preaching today emphasize that the preacher should listen to the congregation so as to develop a thick understanding of what is already going on in the culture of the community—questions, issues, values, ideas, relationships, uncertainties, and other things. These phenomena often function as invitations in that they pose things people can believe and do.[43] While such qualities sometimes rise to the level of consciousness, people often take them for granted without naming them. On the way to the sermon, the preacher should identify invitations present in the congregation on two levels: the general invitations that underly the life of the congregation, and the specific invitations the congregation generates with respect to the biblical text or topic that is the launching pad for the sermonic conversation.

41. Pauw and Placher, *Belief*.

42. Wilson, *Abingdon Theological Companion to the Lectionary*, 3 vols.

43. The expression "thick description" comes from the cultural anthropologist Clifford Geertz and refers to a detailed understanding of multiple dimensions of community life and how they interact with one another. Geertz, *Interpretation of Cultures*, 87–125. Guides that help identify the matrix of conversations within the congregation and beyond include:Tisdale, *Preaching as Local Theology*; Carroll et al., *Handbook for Congregational Studies*; Nieman, *Knowing the Context*; Nieman and Rogers, *Preaching to Every Pew*; Frank, *Soul of the Congregation*; Farris, *Preaching That Matters*, 25–38. The questions for lay people posed in McClure et al., *Listening to Listeners*, 181–82, open windows into the listening culture of the congregation.

Listening to the Congregation as Culture and Subcultures

When beginning to think at the general level about invitations at work in a congregation, the preacher can focus on the congregation as itself a small culture. Certain assumptions, attitudes, expectations, and behaviors prevail across the community. These assumptions include beliefs about God, Christ, and the Spirit as well as about the nature, purpose, and possibilities, of humankind, and attitudes regarding the church, nature, time, and how these things relate.[44]

A single congregation typically contains multiple subcultures that can be quite diverse. The subcultures share some key aspects of the values and behaviors of the larger congregational culture, but they also have their own distinctive nuances with respect to that culture. While such nuances can support the larger culture, they can also be in tension with it.[45] We can sometimes identify subcultures in congregations because we see them in organized groups, e.g., Sunday School classes, Bible studies, fellowship groups, mission teams, and the like. The choir or praise band can even be a subculture. Beyond formal authorization by the congregation, however, subcultures sometimes exist as mindsets shared by several people who do not meet in formal structures but who have dinner together, exchange ideas on social media, or see one another at the meetings of local political parties.[46]

O. Wesley Allen thus describes the congregation as a "matrix of conversations."[47] Insofar as possible, the preacher should be aware of the various conversations taking place in the community, and the dynamics they bring to the ethos in which the minister will stand up or click on the camera to preach.

In a classic work, Nora Tubbs Tisdale identifies several realities at the broad level of congregational life that a preacher needs to interpret in order to have an ear to the ground for the broad invitations at work in the congregation.[48] These are:

44. Tisdale, *Preaching as Local Theology*, 77–86.

45. I know many congregations, for instance, in which progressive pastors and a small subculture of progressive members are in strained and even conflicted relationships with the larger congregational culture.

46. There can be significant differences between the formal and informal invitations to which congregations respond. For example, in a Eurocentric congregation, a formal invitation may be that for members of the congregation to love one another whereas an informal but powerful invitation is for the congregation to extend a real welcome only to Eurocentric people of similar economic class, sexual orientation, and political affiliation.

47. O. W. Allen, *Homiletic of All Believers*, 17–37, esp. 35–37.

48. Tisdale, *Preaching as Local Theology*, 64–90.

- Stories that the congregation tells and interviews with people in the congregation. Tisdale notes that the stories people tell may be exceptionally revealing sources of congregational culture. While a preacher can ask for these stories, a preacher can also pick up many stories by just listening to people in everyday settings. Direct interviews, while time-consuming, can often be informative.

- Archival materials: things revealed about the congregation in newsletters, official minutes, budgets, and similar things that portray the congregation's concerns over the years.

- Demographics: who is part of the community, who is not, and their various characteristics, especially their social locations including gender, race, sexual orientation, theological beliefs, social class, and political commitments.

- Architectural and visual arts: what the building says about how the congregation sees itself and the nature of the visual arts associated with the congregation, especially the worldview and things they legitimize by both their presence and absence

- Rituals: things the congregation lifts up in formal services of worship and in other official demonstrations, as well as things that mark identity unofficially but often forcefully.

- Events and activities: things in which the congregation invests time, fiscal resources, and human power, and things the congregation does not do.

- People: congregations often have people who play particular roles, such as sages who embody much of the congregation's ethos and whose presence can legitimate, calm, or open up possibilities, just as the opposite can also be true.

- Theological convictions at both the formal level (e.g., denominational beliefs, congregational mission statement) and the informal level which is sometimes more powerful for some members than the official convictions of the denomination and the congregation.

As I note in chapter 8, I think it is particularly important that the preacher listen to the associations people have with preachers and with preaching in the past. Thinking in terms of the route of living historic occasions, the experiences of the past often influence (not always consciously) the attitudes towards preacher and sermon when the preacher steps into the preaching space and begins the sermon. People can be more or less receptive to the preaching based, in part, on past experiences. Hence, I would add one more bullet to the list above.

- History with the preacher and with preaching. What are the congregation's associations from the past with preaching and with preachers and how do those associations shape the congregation's present attitudes and receptivity to the preacher and to the sermon?

Preachers with process worldviews who engage in these kinds of analysis can note points at which a congregation is (or might be) sympathetic to process perspectives as well as factors that seem to work against process possibilities.

Preachers need to be aware of these things when standing up or turning on the camera to preach. The congregational culture—and the relationships of the culture and the subcultures—is not a blank screen on which the preacher can speak the sermon as if using voice activated software. The listening environment is already charged when the preacher stands up or the sermon comes on the screen.

Scholars of preaching almost universally suggest that the preacher should try to shape the sermon so that listeners can initially make sympathetic identification with it and then follow the unfolding movement. Paying attention to the broad lines of congregational culture can help the preacher find points of sympathetic identification and avoid antagonizing listeners from the first words of the sermon. The preacher can frequently discern conversations already taking place in the congregation which the sermon can join.

Listening for Specific Interpretations of the Passage in the Congregation

These broad lines of congregational culture will seldom disclose how the congregation hears the invitations of particularly biblical texts. But the culture's values will often suggest how a congregation might hear a text. Beyond projecting how a congregation might interpret a text, a preacher can engage the congregation directly regarding how the congregation—and communities within it—hear what a biblical passage asks them to believe and do.

Over the past generation John S. McClure has inspired many preachers to create feed-forward groups for the sermon.[49] The preacher meets with a small group of lay people as part of sermon preparation. The group

---

49. The classic work here is McClure, *Roundtable Pulpit*.

gives its perspectives on issues pertinent to the biblical text and the preaching conversation, thereby revealing some of their own explicit and implicit proposals. The preacher then has a chance to explore how the invitations at work in the congregation relate to the proposals at work in the development of the sermon.

In a conversational approach to preaching, the preacher is not simply mining the congregation for ideas for the sermon. Nor does the preacher expect the feed-forward group to prepare the sermon. The preacher wants to know how the group members identify the invitations coming through the passage and how to respond. The preacher and the group can then ponder group appraisals theologically and hermeneutically. The preacher may decide to use material from the session in the sermon, but, if so, should be sure the members of the group give their permission.

McClure imagines the group meeting weekly and working in three phases. (1) Reflecting on the previous week's sermon and reporting on feedback from the congregation; (2) engaging the passage from the Bible with respect to its historical context, the meanings of words, its literary form and function and related exegetical matters; (3) talking with one another about their questions, about how they see the text connecting with their worlds, about their different points of view regarding the text.[50] The groups might include members of the different subcultures in the congregation.

Part 3 of the discussion could include a focus on the questions, "What do I hear the text asking me to believe?" And "What do I hear the text asking me to do?" McClure wants the group to get to the "So what?" of the passage. What difference would it make to the feed-forward group to believe the invitations they hear in the text, and to respond accordingly? I think another question is pertinent for many listeners, especially those who cannot embrace all the surface current of the text but who can accept the text when interpreted through the deeper current: What if they partially believe and partially respond, or do not believe the invitation of the text?

While McClure sees such a group meeting weekly, the meetings could be scheduled in other ways. The group could meet once a month with an agenda of four or five passages. The group could meet quarterly for a Friday and Saturday retreat. A preacher might borrow the model of Daily Vacation Bible School with meetings every night for a week. When possible, I prefer gatherings that are in-seat, face-to-face in an immediate physical circle of conversation. But Zoom interactions are better than none.

O. Wesley Allen Jr. thinks actual feed-forward groups are unrealistic from the standpoint of the amount of time the preacher has available to

---

50. McClure, *Round Table Pulpit*, 67–69.

manage the group itself as well as to integrate its outcomes into the sermon in a such a way as to take full advantage of the group work. Instead, Allen suggests "imaginative focus groups," that is, the preacher imagines different people who will likely hear the sermon and ask questions such as, "What word from God does Bonnie need to hear this week?" and "How will Michael hear the message I am intending?"[51]

This approach can easily morph toward the invitations offered by the text and possible responses. What might Bonnie believe about the invitations in the text? What might Michael do in response to what the text invites him to do? The preacher's answers to such questions are necessarily tentative since the preacher does not have direct information from the persons named. But the exercise might spark the preacher to recognize matters that might otherwise have escaped attention.

Apropos of the preceding section on listening to the congregation culture and subcultures, the preacher can notice the specific texts that come up repeatedly in the life of the community and how the community uses those passages. For example, what happens in, around, and to the Christmas and Easter readings each year. What invitations does the congregation hear?

Can the preacher identify passages beyond ones associated with the high liturgical days to which the congregation often refers, or to which the community recurs during crisis and other significant times? Do such associations open windows into how the congregation perceives invitations from biblical materials?

A preacher might also interview people one-on-one or in a household regarding what they hear texts inviting them to believe or do. For example, a preacher might make a pastoral call on one household each week for this purpose.

INVITATIONS FROM THE LIFE OF THE PREACHER

Although I pointed to the life of the preacher as a source of invitations in the previous chapter, I return to it briefly as a reminder of the importance of making this consideration a regular part of sermon preparation. Indeed, contemplating the invitations from the text in and around the life of the preacher can sometimes generate material for the sermon itself.[52]

51. O. W. Allen, *Preaching and the Thirty-Second Commercial*, 46. For Allen's detailed program, see 45–49.

52. On the experience of the preacher as a homiletical source, see R. J. Allen, *Interpreting the Gospel*, 54–62.

The preacher needs to be sensitive to the coloration of the preacher's interpretive lens both to take advantage of ways the lens may help the preacher move towards optimum becoming as well as ways in which the preacher's lens can limit her or his perception of the text. The preacher wants to become aware of, and circumspect about, ways the lens may orient the preacher towards patterns of thinking, feeling, and acting that result in minimal or even regressive becoming.

In the previous chapter we joined the stream of early postmodern scholarship in preaching in emphasizing that preachers approach sermon preparation and preaching from the standpoint of social location which is a thick mix of such things as gender, race, ethnicity, sexual orientation, social class, education, political commitments, theological commitments, as well as the personality of the preacher. The lens of the process interpreter is colored by the work of Whitehead, Hartshorne, Suchocki, Cobb, Keller, and others.

An easy step in identifying invitations in the preacher's life is to recall prior direct and conscious associations with the text. The preacher may recollect things like Bible School classes from childhood, a stained-glass window portraying the passage, a hymn or a praise song containing a phrase alluding to the passage, sermons the preacher has heard—or preached—on the passage, associations from the movies and other electronic media, perhaps even a lecture by a professor from seminary days.

As we noted above, aspects of the preacher's relationship to the text and its invitations can be difficult to discuss and yet can be immensely powerful: the effect of causal efficacy.[53] The preacher feels the biblical material and its invitations. The preacher can have an intuitive awareness of the text that is deep and powerful and yet inarticulate. The preacher feels the feelings but can have difficulty using ordinary language to name the feelings.

In a preaching class, a student preached a sermon that was highly intuitive and impressionistic. The student was charged with feeling and spoke with great and seemingly authentic intensity, but the ideas of the sermon were vague and inchoate. In the sermon feedback group, I pressed the student to clarify the content and purpose of the sermon. After several pushes on my part, the student was not able to do so, and looked at me in frustration and said, "I know that I know that I know." While this instance is extreme, I think it represents a good many preachers in relationship to a good many texts: the preacher knows something the preacher cannot say.

---

53. For a more extensive discussion of feeling in the sermon see above, 41–46 as well as Beardslee et al., *Biblical Preaching*, 60–64.

When commenting on the importance of the sermon itself evoking feeling, the authors of *Biblical Preaching on the Death of Jesus* make a remark from which we could extrapolate a way whereby the preacher might begin to bring feeling into articulation.

> The feelings of which we speak are emotional. The feeling of the idea or image is not as such an emotion, but it is always clothed with emotion. . . . Ideas and images arouse joy and sorrow, hope and despair, guilt and purgation, attraction and revulsion, love and hostility."[54]

The preacher can try to name the emotions stirred by a text in the possibility that these emotions signal the presence of deeper levels of awareness.

The preacher's emotions, of course, can be triggered by any number of things in the preacher's environment or memory. It is important to remember that emotions can change quickly. Moreover, an emotion is not always a signal of a deep feeling. These reasons are why Susanne Langer cautions against casually equating feeling and emotion.[55] Preachers often need to be circumspect in thinking that the roots of a particular emotion extend into the far reaches of causal efficacy. Moreover, preachers can only approximately give voice to the feelings they sense from causal efficacy. But, as Bernard Meland says, such language "may be the best we can hope for."[56]

INVITATIONS FROM VOICES
BEYOND THE CHRISTIAN COMMUNITY

The sources of invitations from beyond the Christian community are too many to catalogue. To name a few: other religions, philosophy, psychology, sociology, political science, the social sciences, the arts, the physical sciences, and social movements. Not to be overlooked are places such as the barbershop or hair styling salon, or the talk with the neighbor across the

54. Beardslee et al., *Biblical Preaching*, 61.

55. Langer, *Philosophy in a New Key*, 152–53. Langer writes, "Everybody knows that language is a very poor medium for expressing our emotional nature. It merely names certain vaguely and crudely conceived states but fails miserably in any attempt to covey the ever-moving patterns, the ambivalences and intricacies of inner experience, the interplay of feelings with thoughts, impressions, memories and echoes of memories, or its mere runic traces, all turned into nameless emotional stuff" (100–101). Nevertheless, spoken language is the primary medium of preaching, and preachers need to go as far as they can in describing what they feel. See further, Meland, *Fallible Forms and Symbols*, 21–33, 43–46, 66–68. According to Whitehead, such language is "incomplete and fragmentary" (*Adventures in Ideas*, 229).

56. Meland, *Fallible Forms and Symbols*, 30.

alley in back of the house. In the second and third decades of the twenty-first century, politicians offer radically different invitations for becoming as individuals and communities. Such sources generate vast numbers of invitations every day. Moreover, through divine omnipresence God offers proposals to everyone all the time.[57]

The sources of such proposals are as broad and deep as life itself. Many homiletical conversations would be more vital if the preacher would take the time to ask, "Where might we find help in understanding the biblical text or the topic from resources outside the Christian community?" When preaching on the theology of the environment, for example, the journey to the pulpit would likely take a better route if the preacher would consider not only the theologies of the Bible but would come abreast of recent and credible research into climate change and its effects.

To be sure, a preacher is finite and cannot consider the full range of proposals that might play into the conversation. But preachers can still make optimum use of their finitude by asking such questions early in the week so they will have the time needed to pursue such sources.

CASE STUDY: MATT 25:14–30
(THE PARABLE OF THE TALENTS)

We turn now to some interpretations of the invitations off the parable of the talents from history, from contemporary theologies, from the life of the congregation, from the preacher's own life, and from resources beyond the Christian community. Because a comprehensive examination of such materials would fill a volume on the parable of the talents alone, we look at example materials.

Invitations from Christian Tradition

Not surprisingly, many voices in Christian history from early church to the late nineteenth century see the parable of the talents as an allegory in which the characters stand for particular things. The master is usually Jesus (or God) and the characters are groups of people whose activity takes place while awaiting the second coming of Jesus. The arrival of the master and the accounting with the three servants is the second coming and the final

---

57. Religion can help people recognize and respond to divinely initiated proposals that occur outside religious contexts. But religion can also discourage people from recognizing and responding to such proposals.

judgment. Interpreters offer radically different allegorical associations with the three slaves and their actions.

One strain of allegorical interpretation sees the parable as a story inviting conversion. The first servant is the conversion of Jewish people, the second servant the conversion of gentiles, and the third servant those who do not convert. Those who do not convert face the fate of the third servant.[58] Another strain of explanation sees the parable as inviting evangelists and teachers to pursue their work with verve or to face the consequences that befell the third servant. The first servant is evangelists and teachers sent to Jewish people, and the second a similar group sent to the gentiles. They both carry out their ministries while the third group of evangelists and teachers do not pursue their missions and are condemned for their failure.[59] Among other strains of exegesis, Gregory the Great invites the church to hear the five talents as the five senses, the two talents as theory and practice (that is, understanding things inwardly and putting them into practice outwardly), and the one talent as theory (understanding) alone.[60] Chrysostom, in line with many preachers across the centuries, sees the talents as the abilities of each person, such as use of money or capacity for teaching.[61]

Some of the Reformers backed away from allegorical interpretation. The young Luther, for instance, interpreted parables allegorically but "did nothing but clever tricks with them." The older Luther sought the "plain sense" of scripture.[62] Luther thinks of the slaves in Luke's parallel parable of the pounds (Luke 19:11–27) bespeaking those who are called and commanded to preach for the salvation of others.[63] Calvin said ,"I acknowledge that I have no liking for any of these interpretations; but we ought to have a deeper reverence for Scripture than to reckon ourselves at liberty to disguise its natural meaning."[64] Calvin regards the talents as gifts from God, including vocations and the gift of the Holy Spirit.[65] Nevertheless, many preachers continued to practice allegorical reading.

The 1888 work of German biblical scholar Adolf Jülicher changed the direction of interpreting the parables for many scholars and preachers. Jülicher argued that a parable is not a pure allegory but a story that makes

58. Snodgrass, Stories with Intent, 528.

59. Snodgrass, Stories with Intent, 528.

60. Simonetti, Matthew 14–28, 221.

61. Simonetti, Matthew 14–28, 222.

62. Luther, Luther's Works, 54:406.

63. Luther, Festival Sermons, 195–96.

64. Calvin, Commentary on a Harmony, 3:63.

65. Calvin, Commentary on a Harmony, 3:103–4.

a point. The parable makes use of materials from everyday life to communicate a basic moral or truth. However, preachers and scholars who applied Jülicher's approach to a given parable came away with a variety of lessons or morals. By way of example, here are five lessons one author draws from the story. (1) "Success is the product of our work." (2) "God always gives us everything we need to do what [God] has called us to do." (3) "We are not all created equal." (4) "We work for [God], not our own selfish purposes." (5) "We will be held accountable."[66]

While the purely allegorical interpretation has fallen out of favor with critical commentators, I continue to hear it from occasional laity in Bible study groups. The preacher may want to acknowledge this allegorical voice in the sermon.

Artists have been drawn to the parable of the talents. I vaguely remember John Milton's poem from literature class because it draws on the poet's inability to see: "When I Consider How My Light Is Spent." Milton, in the manner of the third servant, is anxious about what he imagines as the limited accomplishments of his life.[67] An internet search will quickly turn up visual depictions of the parable by Rembrandt van Rijn, Maatthäus Merian, and Jan Luyken. Such pieces might be projected on the big screen in the worship space.

Invitations from Contemporary Theological Families

To my mind, one of the most important streams in the interpretation of the parables in the last generation is a focus on how the gospel writers use them. My own interpretation of the invitation of Matt 25:14–30, summarized in the previous chapter, implies an analogy between the story of the parable Matthew's congregation. Matthew wanted first-century listeners to believe that God wanted them to multiply their witness to the realm of God and would reward those who did so and hold accountable those who did not.

Similarly in the context of Matt 24:36—25:46, process biblical scholar Russell Pregeant in *Chalice Commentaries for Today* hears the parableof the talents reinforcing Matthew's call to be watchful and prepared.[68] To be prepared—to use one's talents faithfully—is to follow the way of Jesus as articulated in the First Gospel: the way of gentleness, humility, feeding the hungry, avoiding hypocrisy and self-indulgence, doing good works (i.e., the

66. Welchel, "Five Lessons for Our Lives."

67. The text of this poem, which is sometimes known as "On His Blindness," is widely available, e.g., Milton, *Complete Works of John Milton*, 86.

68. Pregeant, *Matthew*, 173–77.

restorative works of the realm of God), and, obeying the commandment to love God and love neighbor.[69] Pregeant sees the talents as responsibilities, things like the ones just articulated for being prepared and faithful. The distinctive contribution of the story to the larger discourse is that it calls attention to the risks involved in doing what the Matthean Jesus asks.[70]

Moving in the same exegetical trajectory, Luise Schottroff takes the Matthean invitation of the story to a specific point in light of the parable of the last judgment in Matt 25:31–46. The activity of the three slaves is feeding the hungry, clothing the naked, etc. "The third slave of the parable of the talents would be among those who ask in astonishment, 'When did we see you hungry?'"[71] Warren Carter finds that prior to Matthew, the story pictures the master "behaving in tyrannical ways that imitate dominant cultural and imperial values." In this earlier rendition, the story was a scathing social criticism. However, Carter sees Matthew co-opting the imperial mindset in order to justify the social position (and wealth) of the elites in the community.[72] Carter believes that Matthew has thus corrupted Jesus' original message which promoted the welfare of the non-elite and took issue with the imperial status quo.

Clarence Jordan, one of the founders of the well-known Koinonia Community in Americus, Georgia, and a scholar of Greek, offers a dynamic equivalence translation of the parable as a business owner leaving town and turning over investments to assistants. At the end, the owner says of the third servant, "As for this useless critter, throw him in the back alley. That'll give him something to moan and groan about."[73] For Jordan, the talents are Jesus' ideas: the realm is on the way, it comes through gradual process, it involves suffering on the part of those who want to be in it as they encounter resistance, and this movement results from and in our dependence on God.[74]

Other scholars and preachers see the parable as a vehicle of social criticism and even as suggesting how exploited people could deal with their oppressors.[75] Working from a postcolonial starting point, B. B. Tumi

69. Pregeant, *Matthew*, 174.

70. Pregeant, *Matthew*, 177. Pregeant also deals with theological issues of existential import to today's church which we take up in Chapter 6.

71. Schottroff, *Parables of Jesus*, 223–24. The theological commentaries I consulted move in the same general vein as Schottroff: Case-Winters, *Matthew*, 277; Bridgeman and Carter, "Proper 28 [33]," 295–300.

72. Carter, *Matthew and the Margins*, 487–88.

73. Jordan and Doulos, *Cotton Patch Parables of Liberation*, 120.

74. Jordan and Doulos, *Cotton Patch Parables of Liberation*, 123.

75. These attempts often focus on a form of the story prior to Matthew's use of it.

Senokoane calls attention to the fact that the Eurocentric people in South Africa read the story so as to justify their capitalistic exploitation of black South Africans (and the exploitation of the working class by the wealthy class worldwide). The master is like the Eurocentric population of South Africa who take advantage of the black community for Eurocentric gain. The church and population need to read such texts with suspicion.[76]

Going a step farther, William Herzog, working under invitation of liberation theology, sees the story as unmasking the exploitation of the workers by the repressive master. The master punishes the third slave because that slave spoke honestly and criticized the master as harsh. The parable thus seeks to encourage solidarity among the oppressed in resisting exploitation and repression.[77]

From the world of art, John Hollander, a contemporary poet, alludes to the parable of the talents in a poem about a parent giving each of four children a dime and what they each did with their money. The poem muses on what happened to the dime the last child let lie in the child's pocket with other coins.[78]

Invitations from the Life of the Congregation

For more than a decade, I led the Wednesday Night Bible Study in the county seat congregation in which my spouse was the minister. At the beginning of the night, we studied this parable, I asked the group (as I did many weeks) to say what they brought with them as the meaning(s) of the story. Their responses resonated with my own preassociations of the parable summarized in the previous chapter. Several summarized the parable as "Use it or lose it" referring to things like natural abilities or opportunities. Several remembered it as a call for financial stewardship while adding, "A talent is more than money. It is also time and abilities." Not surprisingly, given the politically conservative orientation of the county in which the church was located, a couple of members saw the parable emphasizing the importance of hard work and taking care of oneself. No one in the group subscribed to a prosperity gospel, but several seemed well acquainted with the association between the biblical story and that gospel.

However, occasional scholars do see this motif in the First Gospel.

76. Senokoane, "Black Reading."

77. Herzog, *Parables as Subversive Speech*, 150–68.

78. Hollander, *Powers of Thirteen*, 9. Brisman uses Hollander's poem as the starting point for an expansive and imaginative, but disciplined, consideration of the parable in "Parable of Talent," 75–99.

These pre-understandings are consistent with those reported by J. Gertrude Tönsing from a review of a smattering of websites dealing with the parable. Tönsing identifies the invitation to believe in "heavenly reward and blessing for hard work and effort." People use the parable to justify capitalism and to blame poverty in capitalist society on laziness. Some Christians believe the story offers direct financial advice. In finance as in life more generally, to prosper one must take risks and acting despite fear.[79]

Invitations from the Life of the Preacher

The scholar Luise Schottroff illustrates how the life of the preacher can come into exegetical and theological play when she says, "To see this third slave as the embodiment of people who reject God's righteousness and God's Torah is simply unbearable to me."[80] I know other preachers who would say similar things about this text and other texts.

Speaking for myself, I have already named all the invitations that I can remember coming to me at the conscious level for consideration in the section on "Preassociations" in chapter 4 and in the previous section on Invitations on the life of the congregation. I need to be consciously aware of as many of these possibilities as I can prior to the next turn in the journey towards the sermon so that journey will not be hijacked by an inappropriate claim.

When I turn my attention to how I feel the parable and its invitations, I can report something of what happens in my inner life, but I am aware of stirrings that I cannot yet name. I can describe things related to my autobiography as well as my process theological worldview.

I begin with my immediate feelings in response to the story as story. As an only child with older parents who treated me like a little adult, I identify with being given a responsibility in the manner of the responsibilities given to the three slaves. When my parents gave me a responsibility (often a junior version of an adult responsibility that was really needed in our household), I perceived that responsibility as an affirmation that I was capable of carrying it out and as an affirmation of trust that I would do so. I felt proud, affirmed, empowered, and capable.

I transfer these initial feelings to the idea that God wants me and my community to serve the present and coming realm in the way of these servants. Moreover, God affirms me, trusts me, and gives me what I need to do. I am both excited and nervous about this role.

79. Tönsing, "Scolding the 'Wicked, Lazy' Servant," 124.

80. Schottroff, *Parables of Jesus*, 223.

I like to be liked. I am uncomfortable with myself when I disappoint others, and I am uncomfortable with them. I do not want to disappoint others. The idea of being cast out, ostracized from my own community, and thrown into a chaos, on the model of the third slave, gives me an empty feeling inside. I grew up in an upper-middle-class setting in which comfort was important. Air conditioning in the summer. Heat in the winter. Clothes appropriate to each season. Tasteful food. Always new life opportunities that were meaningful and fun. The prospect of the being cast into the outer darkness with the weeping and gnashing of teeth frightens me, especially when I remember that other passages in Matthew add fire to the mix (e.g., Matt 3:10, 12; 5:22; 13:42, 50; esp. 25:41).

When I was growing up, I learned early how to organize my life, especially how to work hard to do the things necessary to avoid ending up with results like the third slave. As an adult I am more determined to avoid third slave outcomes.

I was raised to treat others with respect. As an adult, I made a conscious commitment to regard others with respect except when to do so would cause harm to the wider human community. I am, hence, discomfited by the brutal attitude that I hear in the master's final interaction with the third slave. The master speaks disrespectfully. The slave is reduced to a means for production, without regard for the slave's human qualities.

I am also uneasy with the idea that God might be like the master in the story—going on a journey and leaving me by myself to carry on the work. Indeed, such an absence is not what I feel. I feel the omnipresence of God, the More, in support of the highest possibility available at the moment.

At the same time, I recognize that behavior has consequences. When communities violate the relational mutual support God intends for life, they reap the kind of outcome that befell the third slave. I do not like these outcomes when they happen to me, though I sometimes find them sadly satisfying when they happen to people whose values and behaviors undermine favorable becoming for all.

When push comes to shove, I feel like a two-talent slave. I want to serve the purposes of the realm. I want to multiply the witness to God's unrelenting love and God's ongoing aim for the world to become ever more loving, just, peaceful, and abundant. I feel God's affirmation and empowerment. I want to avoid the fate of the third slave. My question: how to do so?

Invitations from beyond the Christian Community

I am not aware of many associations with the parable of the talents from beyond the Christian community. Octavia Butler's novel *Parable of the Talents* comes to mind.[81] To oversimplify, this science fiction novel provokes the question of whether we use our talents and resources in the exploitative and destructive ways of the politician Andrew Steele Jarret (who wants to "Make America Great Again") or of the Earthseed group seeking to form a new religious community around the notion that God is change. The story, however, acknowledges the difficulties, costs, and ambiguities involved in making such choices.

In a book on employee performance in contemporary organizations Bruce E. Winston devotes a chapter to the parable of the talents, pointing to essential qualities of performance for workers in companies today. These qualities are integrity, credibility, and accountability.[82]

After doing the work of chapters 4 and 5, the preacher is now in the middle of a conversational circle in which invitations with radically possibilities are calling out, "I'm the one." In chapter 6, the preacher uses theological criteria to sort through the possibilities and identify the ones that can help establish the direct of the sermon and the particular conversations it hopes to encourage.

---

81. Butler, *Parable of the Talents*.

82. Winston, *Biblical Principles*, 49–63.

6

Theological Reflection and Formulating a Direction for the Sermon

THROUGH CONVERSATION WITH MANY students and preachers, I have discovered an aspect of my experience of sermon preparation is common to many preachers. There is an exhilarating moment when I have worked exegetically with the text and have identified and begun to ponder other voices from past and present that offer perspectives the text and its invitations. In that moment—which can last anywhere from a part of a second to a day or two—I feel the possibility of a sermon. I am energized by the prospect of working on and helping the congregation join the conversation. Big ideas and stories may come to mind, points of identification with the congregation, and even possibilities for the movement of the sermon. Sometimes I actually feel a rush of anticipation in my mind and body.

But the exhilaration of the moment typically passes into the more sober awareness that I do not yet have a *sermon*. I typically have a lot of homiletical stuff, much of it promising, but I need to think more precisely about my theological relationship with what the biblical text or topic invites in the way of believing and doing, even as I also need to evaluate theologically the invitations of other voices. I need to figure out the nature of the conversation to take place within the sermon itself and the kinds of conversations I hope the sermon prompts in its afterglow.

This chapter seeks to help the preacher take three significant steps beyond that exhilarating moment toward the sermon itself. First, the chapter poses a simple theological method the preacher can use to reflect on the degree to which the invitations of the biblical text or the topic are appropriate to the preacher's deepest theological convictions and are truly believable in light of the preacher's worldview. The preacher can also use this method to evaluate invitations from other voices including tradition, contemporary theologies, the life of the congregation, the preacher's own life, and invitations from beyond the Christian community. Second, with such a theological analysis in hand, the preacher can determine the theological relationship of the preacher and the congregation with the text or the topic and with the other invitations in the sermonic conversation. Third, the chapter considers how the preacher might formulate the direction of the conversation that could take place in and through the sermon, including possible hermeneutical connections with communities today.

At the outset, it is important to acknowledge that these stages of sermon preparation are a little messy for the preacher working in the trajectory of this book, especially when compared to many other paths of sermon preparation that are clearer and more direct. But life itself is messy, and this aspect of sermon preparation can help the preacher keep the sermon close to real life.

THEOLOGICAL REFLECTION ON THE INVITATIONS IN THE CONVERSATION

Sermons, along with other parts of congregational life, are intended to help the congregation make theological sense of the world, the life of the congregation, the lives of the households and individuals in the congregation. The preacher should help the congregation name the invitations in the text or the topic as well as the invitations in other voices in the conversation taking place on the way to the sermon and the preacher seeks. The preacher should also help the community evaluate those invitations regarding the degree to which the invitations promote optimum becoming. The preacher can further help the congregation discern how to respond appropriately to the various invitations, accepting some, turning away from others, and adapting still others.

An overarching goal of preaching is to help the congregation become in the most optimum ways available at the time. Such becoming should enhance the becoming of the larger networks of communities in which the congregation lives. To recall, Marjorie Suchocki describes this goal as "inclusive well-being" for all, for the community of the church and for communities beyond the church.[1] The invitations from God that come to and through the churches are so the ecclesial communities can "manifest

---

1. Suchocki, *Fall to Violence*, 60–61, 66–71.

an actualized love among their members."[2] Such love leads to inclusive well-being within the church.

> But just as the love which is in God cannot be contained, so must the love in these communities go beyond their own borders. The well-being which is within must pour fourth as a directed influence towards the well-being of all, serving the wider society. The boundaries of these communities, like the boundaries of God, are to be open, pouring forth an energy for good beyond themselves. The center of love which forms the core of the communities must influence the creation of goodness among all communities.[3]

Sermons and other modes of ministry are supposed to work together to help the listening community identify responses to the invitations that are more and less promising, and to help the congregation consider how to respond appropriately.

Process theology sets out a theological vision that yields a set of theological values and norms with which the preacher can evaluate invitations and which the preacher can use to interpret life situations. I think of these things as the preacher's "deep convictions about God and the world." Process theology offers preacher and congregation a particular understanding of the nature of the cosmos as a living organism in which all elements are interrelated and affect one another. It envisions a God who is omnipresent and who ever invites the participants in every living occasion to accept invitations that will move towards inclusive well-being within the possibilities available in that occasion for all involved in occasion—human beings, animals, and all other elements of nature. The power of God is not coercive but is relational and operates by invitation or lure. Human beings and other elements of creation (to the degree that they are able) can partner with God to bring about some degree of well-being, or they can refuse to participate with God and thus contribute to the decline of well-being.

The preacher enters the conversation moving towards the sermon with these values and norms in mind and uses them to evaluate how proposals are similar to those values and norms as well as how proposals differ from them. At the same time, a true conversation always contains the possibility that a proposal may prompt the preacher to reformulate aspects of the preacher's deep convictions.

Marjorie Suchocki points that theologians all have criteria by which to work with biblical texts and other materials, whether explicitly or implicitly.

2. Suchocki, *End of Evil*, 129.
3. Suchocki, *End of Evil*, 129.

The criterion for Luther, for example, was his interpretation of justification by grace through faith. The criterion for Walter Rauschenbush was the life and message of Jesus, especially Jesus' "unparalleled example of extending care to marginalized or outcast persons in society" as the principal indication of the character of the Realm of God. For John Cobb, a leading process theologian, the leading idea is creative transformation.[4]

> These various criteria are not necessarily mutually exclusive,
> nor are they exhaustive. But whatever our criteria may be, if we
> intend theological faithfulness in our preaching ministries, we
> must identify our own criteria. How do we organize the symbols
> of Christian faith and practice? Naming this can help us find
> our way through the maze of differences and challenges within
> the texts. It can also help us work responsibly with the symbols
> within the texts we preach.[5]

In Suchocki's spirit of identifying theological criteria, I offer two criteria rooted in process conceptuality that summarize key values and norms that preacher and congregation can use when considering proposals, one criterion emphasizing theological content and the other emphasizing experience—the two nodes of authority in the process worldview. The preacher identifies the invitations in a text: what the text invited people in antiquity to believe and do and evaluates these invitations from the perspective of each criterion. The preacher and community can use these criteria to evaluate the degree to which invitations from other voices promise a becoming that manifests God's purposes of mutually supportive community or works against those purposes.[6]

4. Suchocki, *Whispered Word*, 52–53.

5. Suchocki, *Whispered Word*, 53.

6. For many years I have joined Clark Williamson in articulating three criteria that are similar to these two but are expressed in more traditional theological language. The earlier formulations of the criteria are: (1) appropriateness to the gospel, (2) intelligibility, and (3) moral plausibility. In this earlier approach, the word "gospel" refers not to the literary works of Mark, Matthew, Luke, and John, but to a compact formulation of the community's deepest convictions about God. I join Williamson in formulating these purposes as an ellipse: God's unrelenting love for all and God's unrelenting desire for justice for all. Intelligibility is a way of speaking about believability. To have a claim on the church, a proposal must be intellectually credible in light of a contemporary worldview, and it must be logically consistent with other things that the church has established as appropriate to God's unrelenting love and irrepressible will for justice. Moral plausibility is not a separate criterion from appropriateness to the gospel but a nuancing one that explicitly calls for the community to consider the social consequences of a proposal. Does the text call for all concerned to relate with one another in ways that are loving and just? The preacher and congregation can apply these criteria to any proposal—to any text, personal situation, ecclesial circumstance, or wider

1. *Appropriateness to God's aim for inclusive well-being.* In order for the preacher to endorse it, an invitation should be appropriate to the preacher's deep convictions concerning God's purposes for inclusive well-being. God's ongoing and thoroughgoing aim is for all people and all other things to live together in communities of mutual support. The invitation should invite optimum becoming. God seeks for every element in the universe to experience feeling unrelentingly loved and to live in justice with all other things. God always and everywhere seeks for every element of the universe to become together as an ongoing community of mutual support. God seeks for every person, every animal, and every piece of creation to experience optimum becoming in its own deepest urges and in harmony with its relationships with all other things. Preacher and congregation can employ this criterion by asking of each invitation: is this invitation appropriate to the deep conviction that God relentlessly aims for the world to become a community of inclusive well-being?

When employing the first criterion, the preacher should consider both the invitation floating on the surface current of the text as well as possible invitations in the deeper currents, including undercurrents.[7]

1. *Seriously believing the proposal could happen in the world today.* Is the proposal truly believable? That is, can the congregation realistically expect that the invitation might come to expression in real life? In order for the congregation to endorse it, a proposal should be "seriously believable," that is, the congregation should be able to expect the proposal's possibilities for God and the world to come about.[8] In particular, the preacher looks for the degree to which the invitation assumes that God will act in the process model through invitation or lure and the degree to which the invitation will involve human beings and

---

social movements. As a working preacher I find it helpful to cast them as questions: (1) To what degree is an invitation appropriate to the gospel? (2) To what degree is an invitation intelligible? (3) To what degree is an invitation morally plausible? For my first expositions of these criteria see: Williamson and R. J. Allen, *Credible and Timely Word*, 71–129. They appear frequently, in my work. Broadly on appropriateness and intelligibility (credibility) see Williamson, *Way of Blessing*, 77–90. Since the present book is cast more directly in the language of process conceptuality, I reframe these three criteria slightly in the language of the process world of thought and reduce them to two criteria since becoming according to God's purposes inherently includes the social dimension implied by the criterion of moral plausibility.

7. Surface currents and undercurrents are discussed in chapter 5, 99–101.

8. The phrase "seriously believable" is inspired by David Kelsey who proposes "seriously imaginable" as a criterion for adequacy. *Uses of Scripture*, 172–73.

other participants in ways that are consistent with their possibilities and limitations. Preacher and congregation can employ this criterion by asking: in view of how preacher and community think things happen in the world today, *can the congregation believe that possibilities promised in the proposal can really come to pass?* If the preacher does not believe the proposal can occur as described, then in positive perspective, what *can* the preacher expect to occur?

In the preparation of the conversational sermon in a process mode, these criteria serve as norms by which to gauge the content and prospects of the range of proposals coming into the conversation—from the Bible, from the history of the church, from contemporary theology, from the lives of the congregation and from the preacher.

At the same time, it is important to recognize that these assessments are not always clear and cleanly cut. The preacher must sometimes deal with ambiguity and with degrees of theological adequacy or believability. A text may be more or less adequate. An image that comes to mind is that of the preacher passing a theological measuring device similar to a voltage meter over the appropriateness and imaginability of a text or other voice. Just as the gauge on the voltage meter indicates the voltage in the line over which it is passed, so the theological meter measures the degree to which a text is appropriate to inclusive well-being and being seriously imaginable.

Some Issues that Come Up Repeatedly

When working with these criteria, theologically difficult issues come up repeatedly. At the surface level, many texts contain elements of judgement and condemnation picture God actively causing suffering to human beings either through God's direct action or by God authorizing an intermediate (e.g., other human beings, or elements of nature) to inflict pain on others. It is inappropriate to my deepest conviction about God to think that God would launch actions that would result in agony, even upon those who have caused agony to others. But, at a deeper level, such texts are often based on an act–consequence model: actions have consequences. It is true to my experience that actions that harm others, e.g., through unjust and exploitative attitudes and behaviors, often have the consequence of bringing misery and life disruption to those who engage in the damaging actions.[9] God does

---

9. Such consequences may not be immediate. They may take generations to unfold. The book of Revelation, for instance, depicts God destroying the Roman Empire because of its idolatry, injustice, and violence. The book of Revelation was written about 90–95 CE, but the Roman Empire in the West did not fall until 476 CE amid crisis and

not actively will the damaging result; people bring it on themselves. The lure of the deeper reading of the text, then, is to live together in an ethos of inclusive well-being in order to enhance the becoming of all and to avoid the negative consequences of exploitation.

Another issue that comes onto the screen of my theological mind is the nature and extent of divine power. Many biblical texts picture God acting unilaterally to cause things to happen in and among human beings as well as in the world of nature. At the surface level, some texts emphasize the magnitude of divine power, while most simply assume that God has the ability to act unilaterally even if God does not do so in particular instances. Indeed, for some biblical writers things happen either as a result of God's direct initiative (and corresponding exercise of power) or by God's permission. In the latter case, God could directly cause things to happen, but does not do so. My worldview does not affirm a God who can step directly onto the stage of history and cause things to happen in this one-sided way. At a deeper level, the preacher can sometimes take such a text as an invitation to participate with God in making things happen that promote inclusive well-being and avoiding things that work against such well-being.

Some texts misrepresent others. Indeed, some passages unfairly caricature others for the purpose of discrediting them. This is especially true in the pictures of the Jewish leaders in the four Gospels and the Acts where the Gospel writers, with varying degrees of animosity, paint many Jewish leaders, and sometimes larger bodies of Jewish people, in largely negative terms.

In cases in which texts contain problematic elements, whether at the surface or deeper levels, preachers need to help the congregation (a) clarify what they really believe is appropriate to God's aim for inclusive well-being as well as (b) clarify what they really believe God can do and, also, (c) clarify what it is appropriate and possible to believe what the congregation can do in partnership with God.

Preachers need to remember that awareness of our experience is always relative. We need to be willing to reshape aspects of our theological visions and worldviews when fresh perspective or new data calls for revision. While it does not happen often, preachers may find that the invitations of a text or a fresh experience causes the preacher and congregation to rethink aspects what they believe is appropriate and seriously imaginable.

---

violence. The fate of the Roman Empire illustrates the saying in the book of Revelation, "If you kill with the sword, with the sword you must be killed" (Rev 13:10b). This statement rests on the Jewish principle that people are punished through the very means by which they sin (e.g., Wis 11:16).

CATEGORIES OF RELATIONSHIP BETWEEN THE TEXT AND DEEP THEOLOGICAL CONVICTIONS

My experience in working with texts and topics with an eye towards preaching making use of the criteria of appropriateness and serious imaginability is that the text—or parts of the text—fall into one of the following theological relationships.[10] The preacher should attend to both the surface and deeper currents which can result in a text having one hermeneutical relationship with the congregation at the surface level and another relationship at a deeper level. This relationship helps the preacher make theologically appropriate use of the text in the sermon.

- Some biblical texts prove to be appropriate and seriously imaginable. Such texts exhibit God's concern for inclusive well-being and the congregation can believe that God acts in the ways pictured in the text. It takes little time for the preacher to help the congregation recognize this state of theological affairs and to think about the implications of the invitation at the center of the text. The preacher can "run" with this text.

- Some biblical texts at the center of the sermon are not fully imaginable at the surface level with respect to portraying events that violate the ordinary scientific way of explaining how things work in the world. Miracle stories are prime examples, such as the manna in the wilderness during the exodus or Jesus walking on the water or the resurrection of Jesus from the dead. In this case, the preacher may turn to a deeper sense of the text to find that the text may use the mythological language to speak of an experience that is existentially compelling. Often, I find that such language in a text is a figure or symbol for things that happen in life in less dramatic, miraculous ways. For example, the congregation might not believe that God will literally provide manna in the front yard, but the story of the manna calls attention to manifestations of provision through people, institutions, and feelings through which God helps communities make their way through wilderness situations.

- Some biblical texts present God's statements and actions in ways that are inappropriate to the community's deepest convictions about God's purposes for inclusive well-being. While calling attention to the theological or ethical shortcoming of the picture

10. In the following characterizations, I use the indications of "some biblical texts," "most biblical texts," and "a few biblical texts" on the basis of an unscientific impressions.

of God in the text, the preacher may also find that the undercurrent offers a perspective that honors the difficulty in the text while giving the preacher a perspective that can contribute positively to the congregation's becoming. For example, many texts portray God judging a community and actively, even aggressively, condemning that community to suffer punishment in very painful ways. As noted above, believing that God is unrelenting love who ever offers good to communities, I reject this picture and see it as an inaccurate portrayal of God. God would never, in this frame of reference, actively decree that the Babylonians would destroy Jerusalem and send its leadership in exile in order to punish the community. However, from an undercurrent perspective, we need not regard God as the active agent in such events. Through idolatry, injustice, exploitation, and trust in instruments of violence, communities often set in motion patterns of behavior that cause the kind of rot in community that eventuates in collapse. God does not have to send the Babylonians to destroy Judah. The community brings about its own collapse through violation of covenant.

- A few biblical texts are so problematic at both the surface and undercurrent levels to the degree that the preacher is called to indicate that the text is not authoritative for the congregation. For example, the book of Revelation indicates that all whose names are not written in the Book of Life—especially those who aligned with the beast and the fall prophet (the values and practices of the Roman Empire and the Roman imperial religion that supported it)—will be consigned to a lake of fire where the smoke goes up forever and ever (Rev 20:7–10, esp. 11–15). This notion is completely antagonistic to the idea of God as everlasting love who seeks optimum possibilities for becoming in every situation, no matter how limited. The God of unrelenting love would never settle for such alienation and such painful circumstances. The preacher, then, is called to repeal this picture of God and replace it with one that is more consistent with a God of everlasting love who seeks the experience of love among all creatures.

In many traditional approaches to sermon development, the preacher is obligated to find something in the text that can authorize the direction of the sermon. The categories of relationship between the invitations of the text and the theology of the preacher reveal that this is not always possible. Texts in part and in whole may be theologically problematic. Rather than force their theological preferences onto texts, preachers operating in a process modality bring other voices into the conversation leading to the sermon.

BRINGING MULTIPLE VOICES
INTO CRITICAL CONVERSATION

As proposed in chapter 5, the preaching journey will ordinarily be enriched by listening to voices from Christian history, from contemporary
theological families, from the life of the congregation, from the preacher's
own life, and from sources beyond the congregation. In the same way that
the preacher reflects critically one the text, the preacher should evaluate
the invitations of each voice in the congregation according to the criteria
of appropriateness for inclusive well-being and of being seriously imaginable. Likely the preacher will find that with theological invitations of each
voice will fall into one of the categories of relationship of text and theology
just mentioned. Some will be appropriate and seriously imaginable. Some
will be inappropriate but imaginable, others appropriate but unimaginable.
Some will be inappropriate and unimaginable.

As far as I know, there is no single routine that a preacher should follow
in bringing the voice of the text and the other voices in the congregation.
I often think of each voice sitting in a room for conversation and having a
turn to speak.[11] Figure 1 is a visual representation of such a conversational
setting. Initially, I thought of a diagram of a conversational circle with the
voices represented by smaller circles of equal size arranged in a perfect
circle. I even thought of including a "talking stick," an imaginary stick that
would be passed from voice to voice giving the holder the right to speak and
invoking silence (and, hopefully, listening) on the part of others. However,
that visual representation suggests that all voices in the conversation are
equal, and, in fact, that is seldom the case. Some voices speak with more
force than others.

---

11. Trying to give an especially early twenty-first century feel to this work, I have
tried to think of this interaction taking place in a Zoom room. Each voice occupies a
different place on the screen and has its turn to speak, and time for exchanges among
voices. But the Zoom environment does not allow for the same level of physical nuance
in communication that comes from being person-to-person in the same space. Zoom
does not catch the full extent of presence and body language. There is something about
being in the same space that is irreducibly human. While texts and other representatives of voices are not always human, imagining them in a human setting seems to me
to move them off the page or screen and into a more relational mode.

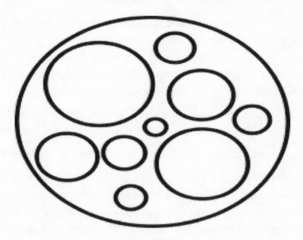

Figure 1: Voices in the Circle of the Preaching Conversation

The outer circle represents the conversation on the way to the sermon, and perhaps within the sermon itself. The inner circles represent voices in the conversation. The inner circles are assorted sizes because different voices in the congregation often speak with different weights in the minds of preacher and congregation. In many such conversations the two largest circles are the invitations of the text and the theology of the preacher and/or congregation. Unfortunately, the diagram does not capture the interaction among the voices that takes place in the preaching conversation. The smaller circles vary a great deal in size as a reminder that voices in the conversation have varying degrees of strength—some much stronger and some much quieter. The degree of strength with which a voice speaks is sometimes the result of the inherent quality of the contribution. Some sources have better information or perspective than others. But the attention a preacher gives a voice is sometimes the result of tint of the preacher's lens or the degree to which a contribution has caught the attention of the preacher. Along the way, preachers can misperceive and overlook important voices.

As in the case of the parable of the talents (Matt 25:14–30), the number of voices in the conversation can be overwhelming. Because of their finitude, preachers must sometimes be selective in the number of interpreters whom they consider.

The preacher listens to each one, evaluates it according to theological content and worldview, and considers how it might affect the sermon.

- Do the invitations in the voice help the preacher think more precisely about inclusive well-being and about the degree to the preacher and congregation can seriously imagine God working in the way described in the text? At one end of the spectrum of helping the preacher think more precisely is the voice that affirms and enlarges process conceptuality. At the other end of the spectrum is the voice with ideas that run against the current of process thinking but that help the preacher think afresh about the values of process approaches.

- Does the voice offer a perspective the preacher needs to take seriously in moving towards the sermon and, perhaps, in the sermon itself?

- Does the voice raise a question the preacher needs to consider?

- Does the preacher, at this point in preparation, think she or he needs to mention the voice in the sermon itself? The preacher may want to mention a voice because doing so strengthens sermon. The preacher may sometimes answer "Yes" because some listeners share the opinion of a resource, and the preacher needs to engage that opinion directly.

After attending to the voices in the conversation, the preacher moves towards formulating a direction for the sermon.

FORMULATING THE DIRECTION OF THE SERMON

In conventional sermon preparation, the preacher identifies what the text invites listeners to believe and do, and then moves immediately to hermeneutics to figure out how to apply those claims in the contemporary world. The preacher can move without further ado to formulate the direction of the sermon.

Scholars of preaching have diverse ways of expressing the animating center of the sermon. Haddon W. Robinson refers to "a big idea," a single theme that controls the entire sermon. It should be "a bullet, not buckshot."[12] Fred Craddock, the most influential teacher of preaching in the latter half of the twentieth century, urges the preacher to state the core of "the message in a simple affirmative statement."[13] Lucy Lind Hogan recommends that the preacher develop "a very brief sentence of what the sermon is all about" while the preacher should remain open to a "flexible focus" that may evolve with the sermon.[14] Paul Scott Wilson, who taught at Emmanuel College in Toronto, calls for a "theme sentence," that is "the sermon in microcosm."[15] For Henry H. Mitchell, long-time Professor of Preaching

---

12. Robinson, *Biblical Preaching*, 17.

13. Craddock, *Preaching*, 155–57.

14. Hogan, *Graceful Speech*, 118–19.

15. Wilson, *Practice of Preaching*, 48, 39–54.

at the Interdenominational Theological Center, the sermon must have a "controlling idea" and a "behavioral purpose."[16] Thomas G. Long who was on the faculty of Candler School of Theology, expands this notion to include both a focus statement and function statement. The focus statement is "a concise description of the central, controlling, and unifying theme of the sermon. In short, this is what the whole sermon will be 'about.'" The function statement describes what the preacher hopes will happen among listeners when they hear the sermon."[17] Samuel D. Proctor, for whom the Samuel D. Proctor School of Theology is named, sees forming the proposition as some of the hardest work in sermon preparation as the proposition sets the direction of the sermon by pointing to what God can bring out of any situation or event.[18] In another context, I have referred to "the sermon in a sentence" and encouraged preachers to identify what they would like for the congregation to think, feel, and do.[19]

Under these umbrellas, the preacher summarizes the big point of the sermon in a sentence or two, considers the purpose of the sermon, and subsequently organizes the material to help the congregation perceive the biblical text or the topic, God, and world from the perspective of the preacher's theology, often in dialogue with the theologies in the congregation.

What Will the Sermon Invite?

A sermon needs an organizing theological focus and a specific purpose. A preacher operating in concert with process theology will often want to articulate such things in specific theological terms to use as a guide for developing the sermon.

As I describe it here, the sermon revolves around invitation, consequently, the language of invitation can help the preacher think clearly about the theological direction and purpose of the sermon as well as provide the principle unifying qualities of the sermon. Preachers takes the invitations they have discovered in the biblical material or the topic and the various voices in the conversation and in an atmosphere of theological reflection and attention to worldview and to what the preacher and congregation believe to be seriously imaginable and formulates the direction of the sermon.

---

16. Mitchell, *Celebration and Experience in Preaching,* 53–56. Frank Thomas makes use of this notion in *They Like to Never Quit,* 97.

17. Long, *Witness of Preaching,* 127; cf. 113–35.

18. Proctor, *Certain Sound of the Trumpet,* 33–34.

19. R. J. Allen, *Interpreting the Gospel,* 148–50, 155–58.

At the risk of suggesting a memorable phrase that does not do justice to the depth of work that leads to it, one might think of this summary as "The Big Invitations of the Sermon." In this light, a preacher might ask three key questions that relate to the main considerations the preacher has been exploring thus far in relationship to the text or topic and the various other voices in the conversation. The preacher seeks to articulate invitations that promise optimal becoming in the current context. Everything in the sermon should help the congregation consider these invitations.

1. What will the sermon invite the congregation to believe about God's purposes for inclusive well-being?

2. What will the sermon invite the congregation to seriously imagine regarding the ways in which God might be present and active in regard to those purposes?

3. What will the sermon invite the congregation to do as a result of participating in this sermon?

Since preaching should be context-specific, the first of these invitations will often refer to God's purposes of well-being in the congregation and in the immediate neighborhood and city. But, since all things are related, the scope of the sermon may extend beyond congregation and nearby community.

The second invitation invites the congregation to imagine God acting in the world in ways that they can truly believe in light of a scientific worldview. The preacher wants the sermon to pose God's activity in which the congregation can be confident.

The third invitation spells out possibilities for the congregation to respond to the particular lure of God towards well-being articulated in the first invitation. The response will often call attention to God's presence with, in, and through the congregation: the congregation does not act by itself but with the omnipresent God alongside. Congregation and God participate together.

Because of the relativity of perception and the everchanging nature of life process, the sermon in this movement is less a pronouncement and more an exploration. Preaching in this mode often has a tentative character. The preacher invites consideration. This preacher is less like an Amazon driver who delivers a package to the door and is more like a player-coach who is both getting the players on and off the field while also being in the middle of the action both on and off the field. The player-coach cannot determine the outcome of the game. The players do that. But the coach is involved, both affecting and being affected. The preacher hopes for a sermon that sets out the invitations clearly and respectfully and that itself invites the congregation to engage the invitations.

The Preacher Helps Facilitate the Conversation

When it comes to formulating the sermon itself, the preacher needs to pay close attention not only to what the text invites people to believe and to do in relationship to the congregation's deep convictions and their assumptions about what is possible in the world. The preacher also needs to pay close attention to the similarities and differences in the preacher's deep convictions and worldview, and those of the congregation.

When the preacher and congregation are on the same page with respect to what they believe and how they understand God to operate in the world, the preacher can create the sermon on those assumptions. By contrast the preacher may need to think carefully about how to try to communicate with the congregation when the preacher and the congregation have different convictions about God's purposes and what is possible and not possible for God to do in the world.

In the sermon, the preacher often needs to explicate the relationship between what the text invites people to believe and to do and the deep convictions and worldview of preacher and congregation. This is particularly true when the invitations of the text differ from thatthose of the preacher. Such an explanation is even more important when the convictions and worldview of the preacher differ from those of the congregation. The preacher wants people in the congregation to be as clear as they can be about the issues and what is at stake.

When exposed to distinctive voices, many people are interested in—even intrigued—by sorting through the differences. They readily join the conversation. Even when congregations as a whole are not ready to participate in a conversation, I have nearly always found a few people in a congregation who are ready to do so. Nearly every congregation has at least a pocket of people with progressive attitudes even if they do not think of themselves in that way. Moreover, many thoughtful conservatives are interested in exploring new or different ideas.

Sometimes, however, members of the congregation are slow to tune into the actual issues being discussed in the sermon. Many congregants tend to hear what they already believe. They tend to understand a biblical text through the tinted lens of their own theology. The same thing is true of the preacher; congregants tend to interpret what the preacher says as if the preacher is doing so in the same theological world as the listener. This tendency is especially present when listeners like the speaker and identify with her or him.

These listener proclivities are among the reasons that listeners will hear a sermon in which the preacher advocates ideas with which people disagree and yet will greet the preacher at the door with a heartfelt, "Good sermon." They are not dishonest. They really have not *heard* what the preacher said.

Consequently, to help the congregation appreciate the distinctiveness of the voices in the conversation, the preacher may need to stress these differences. In doing so preachers may be tempted to caricature or to make fun of viewpoints with which they disagree. I have heard preachers speak of perspectives that are not their own in dismissive and angry tones. I have even heard preachers disrespect persons whose interpretations are unlike those of the preacher. Such modes of expression often create distance between the preacher and those who think along different lines. For example, a student in preaching class preached a sermon in an arrogant tone. Another student responded, "That attitude just closed the door for me. I wouldn't even give that sermon the time of day."

To be sure, a preacher cannot guarantee a hearing, especially among those with contrasting views. But a preacher is usually advised to seek positive identification with the listeners as points of entry into the conversation.

Every Sermon Is not Armageddon

Just as the preacher seeks to empower the freedom of the congregation so a perspective from Ernest T. Campbell can offer the preacher a significant measure of freedom from Sunday to Sunday. Campbell, who was preaching minister at the Riverside Church in New York City, said "Every battle is not Armageddon," for which a homiletical equivalent is, "Every sermon is not Armageddon."[20] Preachers do their best to formulate a sermon that points in the direction of creative transformation. But finitude—on the part of the preacher, the sources of proposals, and the congregation—sometimes conspires in a sermon whose invitations fall short of the highest possibilities for becoming. In such cases, the preacher can be renewed by the fact that another week lies ahead, and with it a fresh opportunity to help the congregation interpret God's aims. Indeed, as we note in the afterword to this book, God is always present to offer the invite preacher and congregation the highest available possibilities in the process of becoming.

20. Campbell, "Every Battle Isn't Armageddon."

CASE STUDY: MATT 25:14–30

We can see an example of listening to the invitations from the biblical text and from various other voices by first recalling what the parable of the talents asked hearers to believe and do and theologically evaluating those invitations. In a next phase, we identify and theologically analyze invitations from history, from contemporary theology, from the life of the congregation, from the preacher's own life, and from voices beyond the Christian community. As this part of the chapter rises to a climax, out of the ongoing congregational mix, we formulate a direction for the sermon using the organizing principles of what (1) the sermon invites the congregation to believe about God's purposes of inclusive well-being for the world, (2) what the sermon invites the congregation to see as a seriously imaginable expression of God's power at work—things we really believe God can do—in seeking to help he world manifest more inclusive well-being, and (3) what the sermon invites the congregation to do in response to God's lure towards more inclusive well-being.

Theological Reflection on
the Invitations of the Text, Matt 25:24–30

In chapter 4, we identify what the parable of the talents in the context of Matthew, invited listeners to believe and do.[21]

1. At the surface level, the parable invites members of Matthew's congregation, in the midst of their situation of delay and conflict, to continue to faithfully carry out their mission of embodying the Realm, including welcoming gentiles in the community of the Realm, or to face eternal punishment.

2. The parable assumes that God is the controlling agent in the Matthean world. God's purpose is to bring the Realm into expression as a social and cosmic reality. God is in absolute control of history and will send Jesus back to the world as part of the apocalypse to transform the present world into one in which the qualities of the Realm are manifest at a time of God's choosing; in the meantime, the conflict and suffering of the world continues. After the apocalypse, God will judge people on the basis of the degree to which their attitudes and behavior have been faithful and will welcome some into life in the eternal Realm and consign others to eternal punishment.

21. See pages 104–108 in this volume.

3. The parable invites listeners to respond by living as a community whose internal life embodies the values and qualities of the Realm of God and whose external life witnesses to those values by inviting gentiles into the movement towards the Realm and by demonstrating the values and practices of the Realm to the Roman Empire and other groups.

Turning to theological analysis, an important aspect of the surface current of the text is appropriate to God's purposes of inclusive well-being as the parable invites the Matthean community to demonstrate the values and practices of the Realm of God (the epitome of inclusive well-being) both within the life of the community and for the sake of enhancing the well-being of the world outside the community by inviting them into. The movement towards the Realm has come to fresh expression through the ministry of Jesus and the church but will not be fully and finally present until a later time.

The evaluation takes a turn when focusing on the question of whether the text is seriously imaginable at the surface level. The idea of the master (God) being altogether absent, as on a long journey, is contrary to one of my most cherished process convictions that God is omnipresent. The master-slave relationship is hierarchical and exploitative. The master does not participate with the slaves in carrying out their responsibilities. Furthermore, the parable assumes that an omnipotent God will bring about the final transformation in a single apocalyptic event. This mode of operation is quite different than process theology's conjecture that God works through invitation. Moreover, the parable pictures the master throwing the third slave into the outer darkness for wailing and gnashing of teeth forever (see Matt 25:46). In my version of process theology, God does not actively cause people to suffer in this way.

With respect to being seriously imaginable, the parable is truer to contemporary experience in portraying the outcome of the story. Those who seek to multiply the demonstration of the Realm of God often experience qualities of the Realm in their everyday worlds. Those who refuse to witness actively and boldly set in motion attitudes and behaviors that lead to diminution of circumstances and even life collapse. God does not have to push a button to activate such results; we bring them on ourselves.

The parable invites listeners to respond in ways that are consistent with inclusive well-being and that are seriously imaginable as the parable urges the Matthean community not only to keep up but to multiply its witness to the Realm in the internal life of its community as well as in its external witness.

On deeper levels, the story resonates with convictions at home in process conceptuality. Though not a process thinker, O. Wesley Allen's comment—that the more we give in the way of discipleship, the fuller our life—is consistent with a process notion of becoming.[22] More the slaves as agents in actively creating their own futures as they cooperate, or do not cooperate, with the values and practices of the Realm is a process perspective.

In terms of the taxonomy of hermeneutical categories above, elements of what the text invites the community to believe about God's purpose for inclusive well-being are appropriate to those purposes (magnifying the reach of the Realm) and others are inappropriate (the punishment of the third slave). I can seriously imagine God present with the church as it witnesses to the Realm in the manner of the servants, but I cannot seriously imagine the larger framework of the parable in the surface current, which is to prepare for the apocalypse. At a deeper level, however, I can imagine how failure to bring the qualities of the Realm into expression can result in age-old issues causing personal and communal affairs to fail.

Theological Reflection on Invitations in Christian Tradition

In light of the exegesis in chapter 4, I note that most of the allegorical interpretations from the period outside the church until the Reformation press the allegorical associations much more precisely than Matthew seems to do. Nothing in the text or in the wider Matthean narrative suggests that the slaves are Jews, gentiles, and unconverted people, nor does anything in the passage or in the wider reading of the first gospel confine the associations to evangelists and teachers, even less as the five senses, theory, and practice. Furthermore, these interpreters assume the theological acceptability of the punishment of the third servant. Casting the third slave into the outer darkness, weeping, and wailing, is not likely to improve the inclusive well-being of the slave.

While scholars today tend to see the parables in more theologically and aesthetically fulsome ways than as simple stories to teach lessons, the latter viewpoint sill occurs, especially among lay people. Seeing the parable as nothing more than a vehicle to carry a lesson is aesthetic and theological reductionism and strips the parable of its narrative power. Moreover, the statement often overlooks important dimensions of meaning in the parable. Some of the lessons lose their theological roots and become just life lessons. The lesson approach often leaves everything up to us and does not always

22. O. W. Allen, *Matthew*, 247.

leave a place for God to play an appropriate role in the parable and its effects, such as being present and offering continuous invitations.

While few of the voices from history do add to the positive perception of the parable, a preacher might mention how people in earlier days interpreted the parable. The preacher might then compare with a contemporary interpretation and appropriation of the parable.

Theological Reflection on Invitations from Contemporary Theological Families

Several interpretations from contemporary scholars and preachers raise issues that a preacher could take seriously. Building on the insight that interpretation of the parable in the Eurocentric Western church has, until recently, tended to interpret the parable of the talents in ways that either support Western ways of life, including capitalism, a stream of interpretation, represented by scholars such as B. B. Tumi Senokoane and William Herzog see the parable of the talents as a criticism of economic and social exploitation and as encouraging resistance to such practices. This approach is concerned with well-being especially on the part of those whose well-being has been diminished on the part of the repressive classes. Even if preachers like me cannot subscribe to the specific exegetical tenets of such interpretations, these ways of thinking remind preachers that the concern for well-being includes the whole of life.

My own exegetical reading of the story, summarized just above, has family similarity with that of Russell Pregeant, Luise Schottroff, Warren Carter, and Clarence Jordan.[23] While I have given theological consideration to the invitations of the parable of the talents in this broad stream of interpretation, Russell Pregeant, a biblical scholar who subscribes to process theology, deepens that consideration. Pregeant notes that God's goal is a world of "peace, justice, love" and that "Mere vengeance against evildoers would do nothing to reconcile the world to God."[24] Furthermore, God's judgment (as on the third slave) linked to a system of reward and punishment assumes God's ability to act unilaterally. Pregeant uses these ideas as touchstones for rethinking God and judgement in more significant ways than I have done so far.

---

23. For my reading, see chapter 4, 104–108. For Pregeant, Schottroff, Carter and Jordan, see earlier in this chapter.

24. Pregeant, *Matthew*, 181; cf. 33–36. Suchocki rises to poetic as well as theological heights when considering these issues in *The End of Evil* and *The Fall to Violence*.

> According to process theology . . . God's judgement takes place
> not in the world or in human history but in God's own life. That
> is to say, God's judgement consists of receiving everything that
> happens in the world for precisely what it is, whether good or
> evil. However, God also redeems what happens in the world by
> always providing for a new future. This means, on the one hand,
> that God does in fact in order to affirm the moral base of the
> universe, but it also means, on the other, that such action does
> not take the form of retribution. Thus, in the end, the "reward"
> for performing acts of mercy is nothing other than this—that
> such actions live on in God precisely as acts of mercy. Converse-
> ly, the only punishment there is for acts of oppression is that
> these actions too live on for precisely what they are.[25]

Going a step farther, "If process thought holds that God receives all actions
in the world for what they are, it also contends that God redeems such actions by always providing new futures in which there is a new potential for
overcoming what is negative."[26] With the literal notion of a *final* judgment,
"we actually draw a limit on God's grace."[27] Some biblical impulses coincide
with the preacher's intuition towards the eventual redemption of all things
in God.[28]

Theological Reflection on Invitations
from the Life of the Congregation

The members of the Wednesday night Bible Study Group who summarized
the lesson of the parable as "Use it or lose it" typically think of the admoni-
tion applying to natural abilities, opportunities, and in general ways to life.
"Use that musical gift or lose it." This can be a useful principle. God certainly
favors all things that add to inclusive well-being, including such things as
making beautiful music. But in the First Gospel, the focus is specifically
on acting in witness to the Realm of God, that is, on behalf of inclusive
well-being.

The parable is a part of the stock in trade in campaigns to raise the
church budget, often under the banner of stewardship. Many congregations
lengthen the banner to include not just money but time, talent, and other
resources. The parable can serve such occasions if the preacher's vision

25. Pregeant, *Matthew*, 183.

26. Pregeant, *Matthew*, 183.

27. Pregeant, *Matthew*, 184.

28. Pregeant, *Matthew*, 184.

extends beyond mere institutional maintenance and aims towards the congregation as a community of witness to truly inclusive well-being. Indeed, through financial and other means, the congregation can be in solidarity with people in desperate situations (e.g., natural disaster) with communities in other parts of the world.

While no one in the Bible Study group in the congregation on the night we studied this story heard the parable through the ears of the prosperity gospel, this interpretation is well known, and I suspect some in the congregation may subscribe to it. It does set forth a vision of financial and material well-being but at the levels of the individual and the household with insignificant attention to *inclusive* well-being. Moreover, the prosperity gospel assumes a gumball machine picture of God: put in the coin of hard work as prescribed by the prosperity gospel and out comes reward. The parable is not an attack on the laziness (a charge with which capitalists often attack certain members of society) but an indictment on lack of imagination.

There is nothing in the parable itself or in the assumptions of its world that providing a basis for capitalism. Indeed, the Gospel of Matthew sets out the Realm of God as the social vision for which God is working. The Realm is a community eschewing the kind of cut-throat competition self-serving focus of capitalism and seeking instead relationships of love, justice, peace, and abundance for all.

Preachers can use their familiarity with the local situation to gauge the degree to which it is important to bring such things into the sermon itself. A preacher might especially want to add such material to the sermon if members of the listening community hold such views, or if they encounter others at the coffee shop who subscribe to such perspectives.

Theological Reflection on Invitations from the Life of the Preacher

As I read over the "Invitations from the Life of the Preacher" that I set out in chapter 5, I realize that subsequent theological deliberation has resolved many of the issues expressed in the earlier section.

One of the most important principles for public communication is identification between speaker and hearer. The listener typically needs to feel points of contact with the speaker. I am reminded that other people in my theological world, including the congregation, raise some of the questions and issues about the parable similar to—and sometimes the same as—many of the ones I have here. Much of the material here might help create identification with listeners of kindred spirit. Of course, there are limits to both the amount and kind of autobiographical material a preacher can use in the sermon, so if I contemplate doing so, I need to be circumspect.

Theological Reflections on Invitations from beyond the Christian Community

As noted in chapter 5, I am not aware of many invitations associated with the parable of the talents from beyond the Christian community. While the main theme of Octavia Butler's *Parable of the Talents* concerns well-being, it seems a stretch to me to bring science fiction into the theologically complicated world of preaching on the parable. However, at this point I may have a two-talent imagination and a preacher with five-talent imagination could create a conversation bringing together the parable, the listeners, and the science fiction of the novel.

DESCRIPTION OF WHAT THE SERMON WILL INVITE THE CONGREGATION TO BELIEVE AND DO

With the foregoing thoughts in hand, it is possible to set out the broad lines of what the sermon will invite the congregation to believe and do. These ideas bubbled up—as they often do—from the previous phases of sermon preparation. In these invitations, I take account of some elements of the exegesis of the parable as well as. This statement is not the sermon-in-miniature. There will be some additional material as part of the sermon itself that is not mentioned here but that serves the invitations of the sermon. I have to admit that these themes are beginning to sound repetitive.

1. *What will the sermon invite the congregation to believe about God's purposes for inclusive well-being?*

    - The sermon will invite the congregation to believe that God aims for the congregation—both as community and as individuals and households within it—to multiply their witness to inclusive well-being even in seasons when the life of the congregation and the larger social world (like the congregation and setting to whom Matthew wrote) is unsettled and even chaotic.

    - The sermon will invite the congregation to believe that the witness includes both enhancing the internal life of the congregation as itself a community of well-being as well as acting in the larger world to promote inclusive well-being.

- The sermon will invite the congregation to believe—as O. Wesley Allen says—the more we engage in working for inclusive well-being, "the fuller our life."

2. *What will the sermon invite the congregation to seriously imagine regarding how God might be present and active in regard to those purposes?*

- The sermon will invite the congregation to believe that God is unrelentingly present and partnering with the congregation as it seeks to witness.

- The sermon will invite the congregation to believe that God does not directly initiate punishment.

- The sermon will nevertheless invite the congregation to believe that failing to act on behalf of inclusive well-being has the consequence of contributing to the dissipation of genuine community, whether immediately or in the long run.

3. *What will the sermon invite the congregation to do as a result of hearing these invitations?*

- The sermon will invite the congregation to name resources the congregation has available for making such a witness and to imagine how they might use these resources.

7

Shaping the Sermon in Ways That Facilitate Conversation

WHEN THE PREACHER HAS much of the exegesis in hand, has listened to the voices in the conversation, and formulated a direction for the sermon, the preacher can move towards creating the sermon itself. Scholars in preaching often refer to this aspect of preparation as "shaping" the sermon, that is, creating a movement for the sermon that gives the congregation a good opportunity to engage the message. To be sure, the form of expression is not simply the container of meaning; the way the preacher says something contributes to the significance of what the preacher says.[1]

The styles of expression that are most theologically congenial with preaching in a *processus modus operandi* are organic, that is, they arise from the preachers themselves out of the interplay of preacher, text, congregation, and sermonic purpose.[2] Organic sermon patterns are more closely related

---

1. See pages 43–51 of this volume.

2. More than seventy years ago, H. Grady Davis called for organic sermon forms, *Design for Preaching*, 139–62. While Davis was not a process theologian, his organic approach to preaching has some resonance with process themes that go beyond recalling that process was once called "philosophy of organism." The organic sermon grows afresh out of the living and evolving relationship of preacher, text, congregation, context, and the purpose of the sermon. Ideally, every sermon has its own design that rises organically from the life of preparation, Richard Park locates Davis' work in a stream flowing from that of Samuel Taylor Coleridge and stresses that the organic forms intermingle and mediate thought and intuition (Park, *Organic Homiletic*, 9–66). The form is not the container of content in the same way that the milk carton contains milk. Form, thought, and feeling mix together in organic shape more like the milk and eggs mix together in scrambled eggs. Park comments, "Davis emphasizes that sermon form should grow from within the preacher—organically—rather than strictly using the rhetorical templates for form which preachers of [Davis's] time typically 'imported' from outside

to the organic quality of process theology than more wooden sermon structures. The organic sermon intermixes thought and feeling in a wholistic way and touches the listener/conversation partner on multiple levels of awareness.

Ideally, a fresh shape unique to preacher and sermon would bubble up from sermon preparation each week. But the preacher lives "east of Eden" with respect to sermon preparation: preachers sometimes struggle with the shape of the sermon. At such times, in the language of Thomas G. Long, the preacher might look in the stockroom of sermon patterns and use one that comes close to fitting the text, context, purpose, and preacher.[3] Moreover, the preacher can set out essential perspectives of process thought in almost any sermon form.

The question of shape becomes a little more complicated when process theology takes flight in a conversational approach to the sermon. As we observed in chapter 3, Much conversational preaching is monological in form but conversational in character. Some shapes more easily accommodate a conversational ethos than others. When shaping the sermon in a conversational mode in concert with process theology, the preacher seeks a shape that encourages the congregation participate in the conversation and to consider implications of the conversation.

The sermon itself is an event like other events. The preacher hopes to shape the sermon so that the moment of preaching will be sensitive to causal efficacy, can embrace the evolving character of the moment, and offer invitations in ways that are appropriate to the context and that promise a future of inclusive well-being.

This chapter first takes into account considerations of process theology and conversational preaching with respect to shaping the sermon. The chapter then looks at several approaches to shaping the sermon that have organic qualities and are amenable to a conversational character. In chapters 4, 5, and 6, case studies involving the parable of the talents (Matt 25:14–30) appear at the ends of the chapters. In the current chapter, I use the same parable as the chapter unfolds as a case study for several sermonic shapes.

---

of themselves. For Davis, an appreciation of organic form means that effective sermon form might vary from preacher to preacher and from sermon to sermon. Such an approach embraces the possibility of using a multiplicity of sermon forms" (Park, *Organic Homiletic*, 2). These themes were later developed and magnified in the New Homiletic.

3. Long, *Witness of Preaching*, 188.

PROCESS THEOLOGY, CONVERSATION,
AND THE SHAPE OF THE SERMON

The preacher can usually make use of process theology without referring to the technical language of the process movement by expressing
process concepts and theological moves in clear and accessible language.
As someone once said, the sermon needs to be in lay-speak. But, from time
to time, a preacher may need to explain aspects of process thought that are
germane to the conversation at the heart of the sermon.[4] The purpose of the
sermon is not to introduce people to process theology per se but to invite
the congregation to consider interpreting life through a process tint. Having a grasp of key perspectives may make it easier for the congregation to
consider this possibility.

When preaching in settings in which process ways of interpreting the
world are not familiar—which is most congregational settings—I often find
it helpful to use a simple autobiographical narrative for dealing with important aspects. "(1) I once thought this way . . . (2) but these questions and
issues nagged me . . . so that (3) eventually I came to think . . . with the result
that(4) this is why I am compelled to this way of thinking . . . and (5) here
is how it is beneficial . . ."[5] Listeners are often able to identify with such a
story. Even if they do not themselves embrace the new manner of thinking,
listeners often come away with a sympathetic understanding of why it is
compelling to me.

Insofar as possible, when shaping the sermon the preacher also needs
to consider the presence of causal efficacy. Causal efficacy is the powerful
but dim and often intuitive awareness existing at the level of feeling that
does not come to complete expression in conventional modes of thought
or language. Some of the force of causal efficacy is revealed in the congregational culture we noted above.[6] The sermon will stir associations from
causal efficacy whether or not the preacher intends to do so. Consequently,
preachers need to do their best to recognize causal efficacy and work with it.

Insofar as possible, the preacher can try to imagine the how causal efficacy is present in the congregation with respect to the direction of the sermon. The congregation is not a *tabula rasa*. The participation of the sermon

4. In passing, I note that preachers in other theological traditions may need to do
something similar. In addition, theological illiteracy is so pervasive that preachers
across all theological families should routinely explain theological terms, even basic
ones like love, peace, justice, salvation, justification, and sanctification.

5. These five steps could help deal with a concept within a sermon or they could
shape an entire sermon.

6. See 122–124.

in the congregation is inherently informed by the causal efficacy that is moving, often unconsciously, in individuals, households, and the congregation. On a spectrum of disposition, causal efficacy can contribute to the congregation being predisposed towards the direction of the sermon positively (at one end) or negatively (at the other end) or anywhere in between.[7]

The preacher can try to evoke aspects of causal efficacy that work with the invitations in the message and to frame the sermon in ways that recognize resistance and invite creative transformation. Because the life of feeling is so intuitive, non-linear, imprecise, and trans-rational, a preacher cannot evoke or speak of causal efficacy as precisely as in the language of presentational immediacy. However, the preacher can often use well-placed stories and other forms of imaginative language to help the congregation feel the presence of causal efficacy. Along this line, my rule of thumb is that every sermon could contain at least one story charged with the emotions and complications of real life.

IDENTIFYING A SHAPE FOR THE SERMON

When moving towards identifying a shape for the sermon, the preacher should not just default to a shape the preacher likes but should consider the factors that are at work in the living occasion that is the sermon. The preacher can then embrace a shape that has a good opportunity of facilitating a meaningful conversation with the congregation regarding the invitations at the heart of the message. Towards this end, a preacher can often ask three questions.

- What do we need to consider as a community to have a responsible conversation around the invitations in the sermon?

- How can I shape this sermon so that the congregation can adequately perceive the invitation(s) of the sermon and have believable opportunities to respond to the invitation(s) of the sermon?

- How can I put this sermon together so that the listeners have maximum opportunities to understand the concepts in the proposals, and to feel the larger realities connected with invitations of the sermon?

The preacher aims to arrange the sermon so the congregation can identify with the conversation and participate in its give and take.

7. For a range of congregational dispositions, see R. J. Allen, *Interpreting the Gospel*, 153–55.

For a generation in the late twentieth century and early twenty-first century, the literature related to shaping the sermon was dominated by scholars who advocated particular systems of arranging the sermon. To oversimplify, the preacher put the sermon together following a formula.[8] However, for the process preacher who seeks an organic shape there is no single process way to form sermons.

A key process insight at this juncture is that a sermon is an event, and each event comes to life in its own way, depending upon the proposals, persons, and forces that feed into the moment and the preacher's response in the moment. The preacher is not bound by pre-existing patterns of movement for the sermon but can shape the sermon according to the nature and purposes of each message in its particular context. Indeed, a preacher can shape sermons in as many ways as life has events, and expressions have forms. To reiterate something from earlier, process philosophy was once called "philosophy of organism," a reminder that each sermon could have a form that is organic to its living moment.

A guiding principle is that the shape of the sermon should be consistent with the invitation(s) that the sermon offers the congregation. Fred Craddock speaks for many in the preaching community today. "*How* one communicates comes across to the hearers as *what* one communicates. . . . There is no avoiding the fact that the medium is a message, if not the message."[9] A preacher speaking out of the process-relational world seeks consistency between the experience of life (especially the experiences of discovery and insight) and the experience of hearing the sermon.

8. The early work of Fred Craddock, the most influential figure in preaching in the second half of the twentieth century, pointed to inductive movement as a basic pattern for preaching. My teachers and friends, Edmund Steimle, Charles Rice, and Morris Niedenthal, think of the sermon as story (*Preaching the Story*). Eugene L. Lowry used the provocative words "oops," "ugh," "aha," "whee," and "yeah" to designation a literary pattern that moved from upsetting the equilibrium of the congregation through resolution, experiencing the gospel, and pointing to the future (*Homiletical Plot*). David Buttrick conceives of the sermon as a plot that progresses through a series of carefully articulated moves (*Homiletic*). Thomas G. Long introduces the provocative notion of the literary function and form of the text suggesting a function and form for the sermon (*Preaching and the Literary Forms*). Paul Scott Wilson sees the sermon as four pages— Page 1: bad news in back of the text, Page 2: bad news in our world, Page 3: good news in the text, Page 4: good news in our world (*Four Pages of the Sermon*). Thomas H. Troeger conceives of the sermon as movement of images (*Imagining a Sermon*). Of course, all of these scholars acknowledge that communication can take place in a variety of styles. Craddock, *Preaching*, 176–81, and Long, *Witness of Preaching*, 136–95 make this point explicit.

9. Craddock, *As One Without Authority*, 114. Craddock's emphasis. While Craddock is not Whiteheadean his early work shows acquaintance with Whitehead: *As One Without Authority*, 49nn13–14.

Another guiding principle is that the congregation should be able to follow the sermon. I mention this factor because each year I hear sermons that wander aimlessly without a real starting point, or discernible things to consider along the way, or a real ending. The preacher stops speaking, but it is as if the preacher has stepped off a cliff and is suspended in the air, neither falling nor rising. The worst of such sermons are streams of consciousness in which the stream does not seem to serve a larger purpose than immediate self-expression on the part of the preacher.

Nevertheless, for a preacher who is disciplined in developing a sermon around a coherent set of invitations the formulation of the sermon can be a moment of creative transformation. Indeed, in the communication climate of the early twenty-first century, the preacher is free—even encouraged—to transgress any number of rules and patterns for preaching and to launch into fresh modes of expression.

SOME SHAPES FOR THE SERMON
IN THE STOCKROOM

Although the preacher has great freedom when creating the sermon, preachers sometimes find it helpful to have some models for bringing together content and sermonic form in ways that could foster a conversational ethos. The preacher brings a sermon out of "the stockroom." The next section of the chapter describes several approaches to sermon form on the shelves of the stockroom.[10] A preacher might find some of these possibilities directly useful but might also adapt them or find that they serve as launching pads for developing fresh homiletical expressions.

It should go without saying by now that just as conversations can have different tones and feelings, so do sermons. The preacher seeks a shape that is appropriate to the sermon.

I have remarked several times on conversational sermons having a dialogical feel but typically being monological in voice. Nevertheless, actual mouth-to-ear conversations can take place in the pulpit and with the congregation whether in the church building or on Zoom.[11] Along the way,

---

10. Most of the models discussed here, and additional models, can be found in R. J. Allen, *Patterns for Preaching*; O. W. Allen, *Determining the Form*; Elliot, *Creative Styles of Preaching*; and Long and Plantinga, *Chorus of Witnesses*. O. W. Allen and R. J. Allen, *Sermon without End*, mention several patterns that can have a conversational character, especially the sermon as "panel discussion" and the sermon as movement from question to question (133–35). Nearly every introductory textbook on preaching contains a chapter on sermon shapes.

11. Still interesting as a starter in this regard: Bond, *Interactive Preaching*.

I mention some possibilities involving multiple people speaking aloud in the conversation. I use the parable of the talents to illustrate some of these forms. This discussion is illustrative and not exhaustive. Moreover, the boundaries between some of these forms are not clear and firm. Some of the approaches overlap.

Scholars of preaching often distinguish between deductive and inductive approaches to the movement of the sermon. In deductive models, the preacher announces the thesis (or the major invitations) of the sermon at the outset of the message and then develops those invitations in the body of the sermon. In the inductive approaches, the preacher leads the congregation on a journey to the major destinations. Scholars of preaching associated with the historic churches, especially those who subscribe to the New Homiletic, show a preference for inductive preaching while acknowledging that deductive preaching can have a supplementary place.[12] The very names "process" theology and "conversational approach to preaching" suggest preferences for inductive approaches. At the end, however, I do turn to deductive approaches and indicate how they can not only explain process theology but do so with a certain conversational ambiance.

Development of the Sermon Taking on a Life of Its Own

I hesitate to begin with this approach because a reader could take it to undercut the other approaches that are more systematic. But after a lifetime of hearing sermons, I observe that this approach is quite widely practiced. Many times in clergy colleague groups I have asked preachers who are receiving feedback on sermons they have presented, "When you began to piece this sermon together, what was your plan?" The preacher often answers, "I really didn't have a plan or a structure. I had some ideas. And I kind of knew where I wanted to go, but I just pulled out the keyboard, and started typing and pretty soon the sermon was kind of developing itself."

I mention this approach here because I think it is more widespread than we commonly acknowledge. Preachers in feedback groups are often chagrined to admit what they are doing. In contrast, I want to legitimate it as an expression of organic development, and to suggest some things preachers in the process tradition might do to take advantage of its strengths and to minimize its dangers.

This mode of preparation is similar to writing a novel.[13] Novelists often say that when they have a sense of setting, characters, and plot, and begin

12. O. W. Allen, *Re-Newal of Preaching*.

13. For insight for preaching from writers, see McKenzie, *Novel Preaching*.

to write the novel, the story takes on a life of its own. As the writer clicks the keys, surprising things can appear in the setting. Characters sometimes develop unexpectedly. The plot twists and turns in ways the author did not originally intend.

Similar things are often true of preparing sermons. At the desk, things begin to happen on the screen that I did not have in mind when I sat down. The evolving sermon grows out of listening to the text, to the other voices in the conversation, to the theological reflection and to hermeneutical considerations. The sermon invites the congregation towards believing and doing what the preacher had earlier articulated in seriously imaginable ways. But the pattern of the sermon takes on a life of its own.

This approach draws its inspiration from living occasions: things happen that feed into the next things that happen that feed into the next things that happen. In the happenings the preachers sometimes hear things from recent study in fresh ways or feel things from causal efficacy that they had not felt. Preachers' fresh moments of awareness and connection as the sermon comes into view in the mind or on the screen. The preacher needs to be open to such things, even when they appear to intrude on the immediate direction the preacher is going. That's the way life is. A message pops up on a cell phone and it rearranges the day. Indeed, the divine lure can come to expression in such ways.

At the same time, when working in this mode, the preacher needs to have time-outs to step outside the immediate creative process and ask, "Is the homily developing in a theologically appropriate and seriously imaginable way? Is the homily developing coherently around a significant invitation or could it easily lose focus? Does it offer connections to the listening community? Is a process perspective discernible in the way the sermon is coming to life?"

When I tried a limited version of this exercise with the parable of the talents, I pondered the setting and the characters, and began to wonder how the story appears from the point of view of the two-talent slave. I mentioned earlier that I think of myself as a two-talent person, but I had never considered the parable from that point of view. How does it feel to be a five-talent witness in a cultural setting that splashes ten-talent people all over the media? How does it feel to be a one-talent person when the five-talent person living across the street has so many more resources? What are the five-talent levels of resources that can be used in the service of the Realm? How does that witness to the Realm become a source of encouragement and energy for us? And what is my attitude—and responsibility—to the one-talent person?

Of course, the magic of self-preparation does not happen as often as I wish. Some Sundays, a sermon pattern in the stock room offers a communicative way to organize the message.

Flying a Plane

A preacher could take Whitehead's model of flying an airplane as a model for preaching. According to Whitehead, making a discovery is often "like the flight of an aeroplane. It starts from the ground of particular observation; it takes flight in the thin air of imaginative observation; and it lands again for renewed observation."[14] Writing about what happens when learning takes place, Whitehead approaches particular observation, flight in thin air, and landing again in the language of romance, precision, and generalization.[15] These three moments could form three moments in the movement of a sermon.[16]

- *Romance.* By "romance," Whitehead means "fascination." People are often naively fascinated by observation of the particular bits and pieces of a subject. People can be drawn to the subject even without understanding it. Indeed, the fascination can spark the desire to learn more about the subject.

  A preacher might call attention to questions raised by the text or the topic, or to incongruities between aspects of the text or topic and our experience. What does this naive encounter with the text or topic seem to invite the congregation to believe, feel, or do? This part of the sermon invites people into the conversation.

  With respect to the parable of the talents, the preacher might highlight aspects of the story that pose issues for the congregation. For example, why did the third slave bury the one talent? Is the verdict on the third servant really fair? Matthew tells the parable to reinforce witness to prepare for the coming apocalypse, but can we really continue to believe such an event will occur? The preacher might mention voices that offer provocative interpretations of the parable here, including preassociations the congregation brings with them into the sermon.

- *Precision.* We could easily misunderstand Whitehead's reference to the "thin air of imaginative observation" as meaning thin in the sense

14. Whitehead, *Process and Reality*, 5. For elaboration, see Sigmon, "Preaching from the Perspective," 273–290..

15. Whitehead, *Aims of Education*, 17–20.

16. Whitehead, *Aims of Education*, 17–20.

of insubstantial. Whitehead, of course, means just the opposite. The learner seeks more precise understandings of subject as the subject needs to be understood. This perception takes place in "thin air," that is, in air that is as little clouded as possible by misperceptions that limit imaginative discovery.

A preacher could help people seek a more precise apprehension of the text through exegesis and through other research and reflection. The preacher might present and evaluate different interpretive possibilities. The preacher identifies the specific issues out of which the text arose and sets out the invitation of the text. "What does a mature understanding of the text or topic invite the congregation to believe and do?" This part of the sermon typically includes conversation among the invitations of the text and other possible proposals for theologically interpreting the subject of the sermon. The preacher invites the congregation to think about the proposals that have come to expression in light of the criteria of appropriateness to God's aims for becoming as well as the degree to which the congregation can believe that the invitation can actually come to life.

With respect to the parable of the talents, the sermon might shed light on the preacher's exegesis of the text, highlighting the context for which Matthew wrote and the invitations in the parable, comparing this interpretation with those of other voices.

- *Generalization.* In learning, people generalize on the relationship between the discoveries gained from the moment of precision and other moments or other data in life. In the flight analogy, "renewed observation" means to look again at elements of life through the lens of the discoveries made in the "thin air of imaginative observation." Where and how do these discoveries play out?

The preacher helps the congregation generalize from the particular invitations generated in the phase of precision to particular invitations generated for today's world. What might it mean to the congregation to believe the major invitation(s) of the sermon and to act on them? The preacher invites the community to imagine how its life might unfold if it embraces the major invitation(s) that have come to light.

With respect to the parable of the talents, the conversation might help the congregation identify threats to inclusive well-being. The conversation might further explore how the possibilities of inclusive well-being are manifest in the congregation's world and the resources (talents) available to the congregation to point towards and facilitate increased well-being.

This pattern of preaching has the advantage of being modeled on the way in which people often encounter new phenomena, learn about those phenomena, and decide how to respond to them. When our five children were small, I often watched them come upon something unfamiliar that captured their attention, focus on it to see more clearly what was there, and then to decide whether they wanted to engage it, and, if so, how to do so.[17]

Telling the Story of the Preacher's Interaction with the Text

This way of preaching is inspired by two sources: (1) TED Talks and stories on the Moth Story Hour on National Public Radio and (2) the practice of giving testimony in some churches. To be sure, these sources have their distinctive characteristic, but they share the common element of coming from the speaker's personal experience.[18]

TED Talks and stories on The Moth Radio Hour each have their own nuances. The TED Talk originated with short talks in which speakers brought their best of their insight in winsome ways on technology, entertainment, and design. The field of interest is much broader now, embracing topics from science, culture, politics, matters related to the human condition and academic concerns. The purpose of the talks is rather general. "TED is dedicated to researching and sharing knowledge that matters through short talks and presentations. Our goal is to inform and educate global audiences in an accessible way."[19] The talks feature "Ideas Worth Spreading" that are typically new and innovative. The speakers present these ideas in arresting ways, usually framing them in a narrative that tells the story of the speakers' interactions with the topic as the speaker came to new insight.[20]

---

17. A church leader could also use this pattern for structuring many kinds of educational events. The occasion might begin with ideas and activities to engage the participants and point them in the direction of the study, then identify the topic itself and its importance, and move towards a full-bodied consideration that would include identifying how the phenomenon becomes manifest in the congregation's experience and delineate possible outcomes and how such outcomes might benefit or disbenefit the congregation and the wider community.

18. The New Homiletic has placed great emphasis upon the sermon as creating experience. Of the many discussions of this phenomenon, I still find illuminating Reid et al., "Preaching as the Creation of Experience," 1–9.

19. "TED Talks," para. 1.

20. Both The Moth approach and TED Talks share common ground with the various paths of narrative preaching. See R. J. Allen, "Theology Undergirding Narrative

Akash Karia, who studies these talks, identifies the "magic ingredi-ent" as the storytelling.[21] Karia has deduced twenty-three storytelling quali-ties from TED Talks that give the stories their engaging quality. Among them: dive right into the story,[22] take the listeners on a journey that con-tains conflict,[23] draw on one's own personal thoughts and feelings,[24] draw the characters fully and with sensitivity.[25] Karia encourages the storyteller to create mental motion pictures crisp and evocative sensory description (sight, sound, touch, smell, taste).[26] Using specific details from one's own story adds to internal credibility and positive stories have greater long-lasting effect then negative ones.[27] The "spark"—the thing that moved the speaker, especially something that allowed the speaker to deal with the conflict—is key.[28] The talk reveals the change in the speak and names the takeaways.[29]

The purpose of The Moth is "to promote the art and craft of storytell-ing and to honor and celebrate the diversity and commonality of human experience."[30] The Moth stories actually occurred and report the story-teller's experience on a theme assigned for a particular storytelling event. The storyteller has a stake in the event—something to gain or lose. The storyteller usually begins with "a great first line that sets up the stakes and grabs attention." It comes from the storyteller's own life and community; the storyteller does not speak about some other person or some other com-munity. The instructions are:

> Make us care about you. Paint the scene. Clearly state your fears, your desires, the dilemma. Make us invested in the outcome. Introduce the conflict. Make us worried for you. Impress us with

Preaching," 27–29. Eugene Lowry offers four designs for narrative sermons: running the story, delaying the story, suspending the story, and alternating the story (Lowry, *How to Preach a Parable*, 42–160). Of these I note that running the story and alternating the story are especially amenable to conversational approaches as the "running" and the "alternating" offer opportunities for the preacher to step outside the story itself and to bring other voices into the sermon.

21. Karia, *TED Talks Storytelling*, 7–8.

22. Karia, *TED Talks Storytelling*, 7.

23. Karia, *TED Talks Storytelling*, 11–14.

24. Karia, *TED Talks Storytelling*, 14.

25. Karia, *TED Talks Storytelling*, 17–18.

26. Karia, *TED Talks Storytelling*, 21–25.

27. Karia, *TED Talks Storytelling*, 27–35.

28. Karia, *TED Talks Storytelling*, 37–38.

29. Karia, *TED Talks Storytelling*, 38–42.

30. Moth, "About the Moth," para. 1.

observations that are uniquely yours. Rope us into the moment when it all goes down. Conclude as a different person. Trium-phant? Defeated? Befuddled? Enlightened? . . . changed.[31]

The sermon, of course, should not be focused on the preacher per se. But preachers could refract theological experience in the spirit of The Moth through their own stories.

It might appear the TED Talk differs from The Moth in that the former introduces listeners to a particular content while the stories in The Moth focus on an aspect of the speaker's own immediate experience. However, Gilead Church in Chicago welcomes The Moth's style of storytelling with a theological focus in worship. Sermons at Gilead often follow a Moth-like narrative movement into which the preachers weave their experience with the scriptural text.[32]

The stories in The Moth are reminiscent of the practice of testimony in some congregations. When giving testimony, people bear theological wit-ness to something important that comes out of their experience.[33]

Both TED Talks and The Moth suggest elements for moving from the personal element to the pulpit. The preacher can tell the story of the preach-er's interaction with the text or topic. Here is a sketch of one approach.

- The preacher begins with something in the text or topic that attracted the preacher's attention. This impetus could be anything ranging from a question to a surprising observation to an experience to the preacher's awareness of a feeling. It raises an issue about which the preacher wants more. Where and how does the text or the topic hook the preacher?

- The preacher recounts the story of how he or she studied or examined the topic. What questions came up initially, and then emerged while working on the text? What did exegetical study turn up with respect to the historical setting, including the originating feelings, with respect to the literary qualities of the text, and what it asked people to believe and do?

- The preacher might then recall what she or he did after the initial surge of interaction with the text. For example, a preacher might report on

31. See Moth, "Moth on Tumblr."

32. Kennel-Shank, "At Gilead Church in Chicago."

33. For an approach to preaching centered in a critically considered notion of testi-mony, see the insightful work of Florence, *Preaching as Testimony*. Lillian Daniel hopes to reclaim the power of testimony in preaching and throughout the life of the church in *Tell It Like It Is*, as does Thomas G. Long, *Testimony*.

following the text and its issues through some of the major voices in church history and contemporary theology, highlighting points of difference and perhaps conflict. What do these different voices invite the congregation to believe and do with respect to what the text invited? And what are the points of comparison and contrast? What do the various voices offer? What are the drawbacks of the different proposals?

- The preacher could bring the criteria of appropriateness to the divine purposes and believability into the conversation. This could occur earlier and continue along the way in connection with each voice, or it might come in a single part of the sermon as the preacher considers the welter of proposals that that have come into view.

- The preacher would ordinarily indicate both what she or he has come to believe, and what she or he should do in response, and why the preacher has come to these places.

- As a final move, the preacher might articulate take-aways that result from accepting the invitation that has emerged in the conversation with the text and with others. The sermon might also move suggest that the congregation include consider.

While the preacher might tell the story in the first person, at its best the "I" of the sermon is not limited to the individual person of the preacher but functions representatively for the congregation. In the tone of the talk, the preacher might invite the congregation to find themselves in the story. As the preacher unfolds the story, for instance, the preacher might directly ask listeners to consider points at which their own experience resonates with—or differs from—that of the preacher or others in the world of the sermon.

The Contrast Sermon

The literature of preaching contains several similar types of preaching that contain a threefold movement reminiscent (in different ways) to the famous Hegelian dialectic that begins with a thesis, identifies the antithesis, and then offers a synthesis. Whitehead acknowledges a debt to the Hegelian model in conceiving of romance, precision, and generalization, but seeks to go beyond it.[34] Samuel D. Proctor points to the possibility of variation on this movement, suggesting that some sermons might rearrange the parts, for example, beginning with the antithesis (the problem the sermon

---

34. Whitehead, *Aims of Education*, 17.

addresses) as the introduction, and then moving to the thesis (the proposition giving focus and direction to the sermon) with the body of the sermon as the synthesis (the outcome of the thesis interacting with the antithesis).[35] My honored colleague Frank A. Thomas thinks of the sermon beginning with a situation, recognizing complications, revealing assurance, and ending in celebration.[36] Preachers are often drawn to Paul Ricoeur's three-phase hermeneutical movement: (1) encounter the text in first naiveté, (2) reflect critically on the text, (3) return to the text, informed by critical reflection in second naiveté.[37]

Process theology's hermeneutical movement of contrast belongs to this general family of three-movement patterns of consideration. Process theologians use the notion of "contrast" in a particular way, as Ronald L. Farmer describes.

> A contrast is the unity had by the many components in a complex datum (for example, holding many colors together in a unified pattern as in a kaleidoscope, as opposed to a single color). Contrast is the opposite of incompatibility, for incompatibility results in the exclusion of one or more elements to achieve (a more trivial) harmony. The more a subject holds the items of its experience in contrasts and in contrasts of contrasts, the more it elicits depth and intensity of experience.[38]

Farmer makes a crucial addition.

> In order to achieve the unity of a contrast, the interpreter must discern a novel, more inclusive pattern which can contain the discordant propositions in such a manner that the contrast between them contributes to the intensity of the whole. When this occurs, the interpreter experiences creative transformation.[39]

I find that creative transformation most often takes place when I look at the text first on the surface current and then took another look at the text in the deeper currents. The interaction of these two currents often opens up a third theological current that is appropriate to inclusive well-being while being seriously imaginable.

From this approach, we can see a three-step model for the sermon.

---

35. Proctor, *Certain Sound of the Trumpet*, 53–130.
36. Thomas, *They Like to Never Quit*, 88–102.
37. E.g., R. J. Allen, *Contemporary Biblical Interpretation for Preaching*, 131–37.
38. Farmer, *Beyond the Impasse*, 187; cf. 115.
39. Farmer, *Beyond the Impasse*, 187; cf. 115–16.

- Initial Invitation: The preacher sets out the initial invitation of the text. The preacher often considers the text on the surface current here. The parable of the talents invites listeners to believe that if they do not witness aggressively to the presence and coming of the Realm of God, they will be cast into eternal torture.

- Contrasting Invitation. The preacher sets out an alternative invitation, often prompted by interaction with the initial invitation and often taking issue with the initial invitation. With the parable of the talents, this invitation is to reject the idea that a God of inclusive well-being would (or could) cast people into the ultimate state of suffering-being for eternity.

- Creative Transformation. The preacher helps the congregation retain key aspects of the initial invitation while generating a new invitation that enlarges the community's perspective. In the case of the parable of the talents, one aspect of transformation is to think that while failure to witness to the Realm may not result in divine punishment, it does undermine community and lead eventually toward community collapse.

On the one hand, this strategy enables process preachers to make positive use of many difficult texts. On the other hand, as Farmer avers, a process approach cannot bring all invitations into contrasts that are harmonious. Nor is every interaction between among invitations a creative transformation because such a transformation "must manifest openness towards the insights of new propositions without abandoning the insights of old propositions, thereby resulting in an enlargement of perspective."[40] Some biblical passages are simply inappropriate to inclusive well-being, are not seriously imaginable, and cannot be harmonized (in the process way) with other invitations. The sermon must critique such invitations and offer alternative theological visions that promote inclusive well-being and that the congregation can seriously imagine.

Panel Discussion

A panel brings together several people who have their own viewpoints to the subject at the center of the discussion. Members contribute their own perspectives to the panel, and they interact with others. Thinking of a panel discussion as a model for preaching, two possibilities come to mind. For

---

40. Farmer, *Beyond the Impasse*, 187; cf. 115–16.

one, the preacher could actually convene a panel of different people who would contribute to the sermon. The participants could express their own perceptions of the topic and could interact with one another through such things as asking for clarification, raising questions, suggesting criticisms, or seeking amplification.

For the other, the preacher could structure the sermon for one person so that its different parts function like different individuals on a panel. In this case, the preacher would set out different perspectives, The sermon might look something like this:

- Introducing the subject. The minister might explain the nature of the sermon and provide background on the parable of the talents and on its various interpretations.

- Panelist (or viewpoint) number one. This panelist might review popular interpretations of the parable.

- Panelist (or viewpoint) number two. This panelist might present the interpretation of the parable that sees it as a protest against injustice.

- Panelist (or viewpoint) number three. This panelist might offer the interpretation that regards the parable as Matthew's encouragement to the congregation to multiply their witness in a time of uncertainty and conflict.

- Summary of discussion and pointing towards next steps. The minister might seek to deal with the contrasts in interpretation in the model just above. Or the minister might encourage the congregation to identify the interpretation that makes the most sense and consider its implications.

The general approach of a panel discussion also applies to preaching in the form of a theological quadrilateral,[41] a three-legged stool,[42] as well as the elimination sermon,[43] and the faceting sermon.[44]

41. One might think of the so-called "Wesleyan Quadrilateral" as a kind of "panel" approach to conversational preaching. I follow others in adapting the quadrilateral so it might better be called a "Theological Quadrilateral" since it redefines some of the ideas Wesley had in mind. The sermon turns sequentially to four voices as resources for interpreting Christian faith. The preacher could present these voices, or a panel of speakers could speak to them: (1) the Bible, (2) tradition, (3) experience, and (4) reason. The theological quadrilateral gives the preacher influenced by process a natural window to bring the process approach to interpreting experience into the sermon.

Wesleyan scholars point out that this approach functions in traditional Wesleyanism in a kind of exegesis-application manner. Preachers see the four sources working together to enhance Christian life. Preachers identify what the biblical witness invites them to believe and do, and then clarify and expand their understanding of that witness through Christian tradition, identify the verification or amplification through experience, and use reason to summarize and apply the result.

However, a preacher can take the model in a conversational direction. A preacher can listen to what the biblical component proposes and then turn to tradition and experience not only to clarify, amplify, and verify, but also to question and to reflect critically. Within each category the preacher may highlight different points of view. In the end, the preacher can use reason to sort through a way of believing and doing that makes sense in light of the various voices in the congregation.

In this revised use of the model, preachers often pay attention to the degree to which contemporary interpretation of experience coheres with or differs from voices in the Bible and tradition. A preacher may conclude that experience confirms the claims of Scripture and tradition, but a preacher may also conclude that with respect to the subject of the sermon, experience has more authority than parts of the Bible or tradition. The four sources give the preacher a natural structure with which to arrange the conversation.

While the flow from Bible to tradition to experience to reason is a natural one, the four elements could be arranged in a different flow. For example, tradition may raise a question for which the sermon turns to biblical resources considered under the operation of reason with an eye towards how the result of the conversation plays out in experience. On the history of the quadrilateral, see Gunter et al., *Wesley and the Quadrilateral.*

42. A preacher could make a conversational adaptation of the Anglican/Episcopal "three-legged stool" as a model of authority which considers the Bible, tradition, and reason.

43. Elimination and faceting as approaches to organizing a sermonic conversation are similar in movement but are different in function. They are similar in that each involves considering an aspect of the sermon and then moving to another aspect. But they differ in the function of those individual foci.

In the elimination sermon, the preacher presents an issue, perhaps regarding how to make sense of a biblical text or a theological topic, and then goes through a series of different ways of interpreting the issue, critiquing each one and showing why it is not satisfactory until arriving at a possibility that more satisfactorily frames the issue that others.

44. A riff on the elimination sermon can be adapted for conversational preaching

A caution. In a situation in which live panelists are live and speaking in the worship space or on Zoom, it would be easy for a panel discussion that involves three or four actual people to go beyond the length of the sermon-time to which a congregation is socialized. The congregation could begin to think about the length of the sermon rather than its content. If the sermon involves multiple people, the chair of the panel—perhaps the preacher—would need to keep an eye on the clock to keep the sermon at a reasonable length. If the sermon involves one voice but different viewpoints, the preacher might speak one perspective from one place, another voice in another place, and the other voice in still another place so that the congregation's visual focus changes slightly as it would when watching an actual panel.

Dialogue in the Pulpit

I think of dialogue in the pulpit as involving two (or more) people in an actual give-and-take conversation about the biblical text and its interpretation.[45] The congregation overhears the conversation taking place between or among the speakers. The speakers sometimes address the congregation directly. Speakers might ask for the congregation itself to add to the conversation by speaking aloud to the whole assembly or in small groups with one another.

It may be helpful at this point to recall David Tracy's characterization of conversation. These traits should appear in the dialogue sermon with this caveat. Tracy's tone seems to be for academic settings and to presuppose a level of directness that is respectful but also somewhat hard-nosed, especially in the case of the "hard rules" below. In congregational settings the preacher may want to frame such matters with softer edges, not relinquishing content but phrasing it in ways that are more typical of everyday speech and are less confrontive.

> Conversation in its primary form is an exploration of possibilities in the search for truth. In following the track of any

---

from the faceting approach advocated by W. E. Sangster. In the same way that someone can help up a jewel to the light and turn it so as to admire its many different facets, so a preacher could help up voices from the Bible and from other sources, and look at the text from different points of view (Sangster, *Craft of Preaching*, 87–92). Whereas the elimination sermon calls attention to deficiencies in interpretation, the faceting preacher listens for how each facet (each voice in the conversation) adds to the community's understanding of the jewel (the text).

45. More than two people might be in the pulpit or other preaching space—perhaps three or four.

question, we must allow for difference and otherness. At the same time, as the question takes over, we notice that to attend to the other as other, the different as different, is also to understand the different *as* possible.[46]

A main purpose of the dialogue sermon to encourage the congregation to consider the possibilities offered by the text and by experience and to find points of similarity and points of difference. On the one hand, the speakers put their understandings at risk by allowing the text and the other participants in the conversation to question those preunderstandings.[47] In this role, the Christian source might offer the preacher enriching ways of viewing the world. On the other hand, the speakers (and perhaps congregants) also put questions to the text and to the other speakers and the congregation to ascertain the degree to which text is appropriate to their core beliefs about God and the understandings of experience.

Tracy points out that conversation comes "with some hard rules."

> Say only what you mean; say it as accurately as you can; listen to and respect what the other says, however different or other; be willing to correct or defend your opinions if challenged by the conversation partner; be willing to argue, if necessary, to confront if demanded, to endure necessary conflict, to change your mind if the evidence suggests it.[48]

While these rules apply in give-and-take with another person, they also apply in conversation that takes place in groups. They apply not only conversation with people, but also with the biblical text and other voices in the conversation.

Preachers can approach dialogue sermons in one of two ways (or a combination thereof). One way is to script the dialogue so that the speakers know exactly what is coming, in the same way the NPR teams read the news at the beginning of each hour. Each reporter knows what the other is going to say. This approach makes sure the sermon touches on the issues that the preachers regard as essential to the conversation. It gives the preachers the confidence of knowing what they will say. It also calls on the preachers to speak the script with the verve of actual conversation. I sometimes hear speakers essentially read such scripts with minimal vocal expression and eye contact, which dampens the interactivity of the moment.

46. Tracy, *Plurality and Ambiguity*, 20.
47. Tracy, *Plurality and Ambiguity*, 16.
48. Tracy, *Plurality and Ambiguity*, 19.

A second approach to the dialogical sermon is to have a list of is-sues the preachers would like to cover in the sermon but not to develop a manuscript. The speakers would have a sense of how the conversation will flow, but the conversation takes shape and comes alive in the moment. In real conversations, insights and questions are often sparked by the give-and-take. If this sermon goes well, it will feel like a real-in-the-moment conversation and the speakers can bring the fresh perspectives into it. The congregation itself may make provocative additions to the sermon. Indeed, creative transformation can take place as the sermon unfolds. On the other hand, this sermon can run aground on the shoals of inadequate preparation, and inopportune interruptions of thought.

Turning to the parable of the talents, preachers might pose the dia-logue sermon around several key issues raised by the parable and its inter-pretation. I refer here to "the speakers," but the speakers could also invite the congregation to talk aloud during the sermon.

- How the speakers have heard the parable used in the past.

- What the speakers learned while studying the parable.

- Questions the study of the parable (exegesis) raise for the speakers.

- Possible responses to the questions, including a perspective from pro-cess theology.

- How the speakers see the outcome of the conversation. Perhaps may the speakers agree on the outcome. Perhaps they differ.

- Implications for moving forward. What might the congregation do in response to the outcome(s) of the congregation. If the speakers have come to different outcomes, do the differences point to different things the congregation can do?

World Café

The World Café has emerged as a popular model for bringing people to-gether in small groups to discuss important topics.

> A world café is a structured conversational process for knowl-edge sharing in which groups of people discuss a topic at several small tables like those in a café. Some degree of formality may be retained to make sure that everyone gets a chance to speak. Although pre-defined questions have been agreed upon at the beginning, outcomes or solutions are not decided in advance.

The assumption is that collective discussion can shift people's conceptions and encourage collective action.[49]

The preacher could adapt this model for an actual out-loud conversational interaction during the time designated for the sermon.

The café conversation would typically center on a biblical text. The preacher could launch the conversation by providing important background information on the text and its interpretation. The preacher would also formulate the "pre-defined questions" for discussion. The preacher would serve as the guide for the conversations, keeping the participants moving from question to question. The preacher might ask for reports from the small groups to the plenary congregation after each question or at the end of the conversation. For example, the preacher might ask, "What are the most important things that came out of your discussion?" At the end, the preacher might ask the groups to report, "What are the most important take-aways from this conversation?"

Ideally, such an event could take place in a space with tables or in a worship space with moveable chairs. I have witnessed such an approach in a sanctuary with pews, and many people found it awkward to have extended dialogue in the inflexible seating designed to face everyone in one direction. Also ideally, the time for the sermon would allow adequate time for the small group conversations to explore the questions. However, in a setting with relatively brief time available, the preacher could choose perhaps one or two questions and monitor the time carefully so that people maintain interest in the discussion and do not begin to be restive.

I have seen such events in which the discussion in the small groups were led by leaders who had some preparation and others in which the small groups functioned on their own. The former seem to get the conversations going much faster and to keep the comments from wandering too far afield. Of course, leaders sometimes let suggestive possibilities die in the group.

When holding a World Café on the parable of the talents questions for discussion might include some of the following.

- How do you see the situation of our church and culture as similar or dissimilar to that of the congregation to whom Matthew wrote?

- Matthew sees God at work through Jesus manifesting the Realm of God, which is God's desire for all people to experience inclusive well-being. Where do you see God at work for inclusive well-being today?

- With which slaves do you identify in the story? What prompts you towards that identification?

49. See "World Café (Conversation)." This website gives important further reading.

- What resources do you have personally and in your household—and what resources do we have as a congregation—with which we can increase our witness for inclusive well-being?

- How can we join God in working for inclusive well-being in the world?

However, this possibility for conversational preaching does come with a significant reservation. I have been in many World Café conversations in congregations, middle judicatory, and upper judicatory levels of the church. The level of exegetical and theological discrimination is often minimal. A good many people have insufficient biblical, historical, and mature theological resources to participate meaningfully. Indeed, I have been at some Café tables at which people did little more than exchange religious platitudes garnered from religious media or voice their preexisting opinions without really being open to hearing others. People often go away having expressed themselves but not having truly interacted with others. Preachers who go this route need to do as much as they can to provide participants with the resources the participants need.

Puritan Plain Style

I think of the Puritan Plain Style as the rescue dog of preaching because I have frequently come to the end of the week with ideas about a text, various proposals popping in my head, some juicy quotes from systematic theology, and a story or two, but I do not have a sermon. When the pieces have not quite come together, the Puritan Plain Style often offers a structure.

While preachers using the Puritan Plain Style usually do so in the exegesis-application model, the preacher can easily nuance this style so that it is more conversational. With the latter perspective in view, I sketch parts of the Puritan Plain Style with approximate percentages that each part contributes to the sermon.

- Introduction. The preacher seeks to engage the congregation's interest in the text or topic. The preacher may not so much "introduce" the text or topic as much as help the congregation connect its experience with the text or topic. Indeed, the sermon will often be part of conversations that are already alive in the community (5–10 percent of the sermon).

- Indication of the Direction of the Sermon. This part of the sermon is quite brief—a sentence or two, at most a short paragraph. The preacher typically indicates in an explicit way what the conversation is about. Occasionally the preacher may preview the major invitation of the sermon.

- Exegesis of the Biblical Text. The preacher articulates the proposal(s) put forward by the text or by the church's typical understanding of the topic. Per the previous points, the preacher helps the congregation recognize what the text invited people in antiquity to believe about God and the world as well as how to respond (15–20 percent of the sermon).

- Theological Conversation about the Proposal in the Text. The preacher helps the congregation reflect theologically on the proposals in the text. This may involve bringing the invitation of the passage into dialogue with other proposals on the subject. It should certainly include evaluating the text—and other proposals—in light of the two criteria named above—appropriateness to God's purpose for becoming as well as believability (15–20 percent of the sermon).

- Implications of the Conversation. The preacher helps the community identify what might happen if they say "Yes" to what the conversation has identified as possibilities for believing and acting that are appropriate and believable (15–20 percent of the sermon).

- Transition from the Sermon into Life. Although this part of the sermon is sometimes called the "conclusion," something more is involved. The preacher really wants to end the sermon in such a way that the community will continue to consider its invitation in the rest of the service and in broader life. Hence, I have come to think of this part of the sermon as "transition from the sermon into life" (5–10 percent of the sermon).

The Puritan Plain Style is easy to use because it gives the preacher a form into which to pour content. The parts of the sermon are clearly defined so preachers know exactly where they are in sermon preparation. Of course, when used week after week it becomes predictable and even anesthetic, as does any approached repeated Sunday after Sunday.

DEDUCTIVE POSSIBILITIES

When preaching deductively, the preacher makes the big point at the beginning of the sermon and then develops it.[50] The great strength of this style of

---

50. In the classical deductive sermon, the preacher communicates a summary of the invitation at the heart of the sermon. The preacher states plain what the preacher

preaching is that the congregation knows very early in the sermon what it is about. The great danger, of course, is that when so alerted, the congregation can immediately lose interest. In any event, a preacher on a process wavelength could easily employ a deductive sermon form to communicate a process approach to a biblical text or a doctrine or a Christian practice or a personal or social issue. Even more obviously, the preacher could use such a sermon form to introduce or expand on aspects of process theology.

Without much mental effort, a preacher can also add a conversational element to virtually all deductive forms. Within the process of deduction, the preacher can site how other voices might relate to the subject matter.

There are different ways of developing sermons deductively.[51] Haddon Robinson offers a helpful discussion of three modes of deductive preaching that could serve this purpose.

- Under the rubric of "the idea to be explained," the preacher explains an idea and indicates its significance for the congregation.[52] The preacher can add a conversational element here by comparing and contrasting the idea to be explained with other perspectives on the idea. A preacher might set out a process understanding of the nature and extent of divine power.

- As the title implies, "a proposition to be proved" is a sermon in which the preacher identifies an important idea that the preacher wants the congregation to believe. The preacher shows why the congregation can believe the big idea.[53] The preacher can add a conversational element here by citing voices that speak against the proposition. For example, I might develop a sermon that seeks to persuade the congregation that there is a transcendent power (which our tradition calls God) at the center of existence.

- "A principle to be applied" is a self-interpreting designation. The preacher states a principle and asks the question, "So what? What

would like for the congregation to believe and do. In a modified form of deductivism, the preacher might state clearly the subject of the sermon without revealing the particular theological claim that the sermon will develop. As an example of the former, the preacher might say, "Marjorie Suchocki asks, 'How do we *know* that prayer is communication with God?' (Suchocki, *In God's Presence*, 2). I want to make the case that it is reasonable to believe that when we pray, we commune with God." As an example of the modified approach: "This morning, I want to think with you about the subject of prayer."

51. See, e.g., O. W. Allen, *Determining the Form*, esp. the "propositional lesson" (21–28).

52. Robinson, *Biblical Preaching*, 78–82.

53. Robinson, *Biblical Preaching*, 82–84.

difference does this idea make?" The preacher can add a conversational element here by citing voices that question the principle or that offer different ways of applying it. Working with a process interpretation of the parable of the talents, a minister could articulate the principle that we are in partnership with one another and with God to work toward inclusive well-being and apply that principle to the setting of the congregation.[54]

The preacher might also use a deductive model in which the preacher gives voice to the major claim of the sermon and then makes points or otherwise sets the sermon up with divisions that are structurally similar to points. The crucial factor is that each point or division relates directly and logically to the invitation that the preacher has stated deductively at the beginning.

Preachers sometimes chuckle at the idea of a sermon as "three points and a poem." On the one hand, three is an arbitrary number. On the other hand, three points are usually about the right number for a fifteen-minute sermon when it comes to having enough time to name and give some orientation to each point. Here are some examples of possible categories that a preacher might use to develop points or other divisions.

- Lessons from the major invitation for the congregation

- Implications of the major invitation at the level of the individual, the congregation, the wider community

- Aspects of the invitation from the past, in the present, for the future. (This approach has a natural affinity to process in that it recalls what happens in living occasions)

- How we experience the invitation as young people, in middle age, as seniors.

Whatever the organizing principle, the preacher needs to make the sermon interesting. Many deductive sermons struggle less because of the pattern of movement and more because the ideas are dull.

Over the last fifty years, preachers have become quite self-conscious about the form of the sermon. Thinking with a friend of mine about the burning bush through which Exodus pictures God calling Moses, a laywoman whose name I do not know said of God calling people today, "Any old bush will do." I would not go so far as to say "any old form will do" for

---

54. Robinson, *Biblical Preaching*, 84–85. Robinson also develops "semi-inductive arrangements": "a subject to be completed" (85–86) and "induction-deduction" (87), as well as inductive arrangements (87–96).

the sermon. The preacher wants a form that will serve the purposes of the sermon. But having lived through this period, my observation is that the congregation's existential participation with the sermon has less to do with form per se than it does with the degree to which the preacher connects with the experience of the congregation in a way that is theologically life-giving.

8

Embodying the Sermon
in Ways That Invite Conversation

A SERMON IS NOT fully a sermon until it comes to life through the preacher
speaking with the congregation in the same physical space or through electronic media. This aspect of the sermon is sometimes called "delivery" but
today is more fully referred to as "embodiment."[1] In contemporary North
American context, people often have associations with "delivery" that are
too limited to describe what happens in preaching. Several times a week a
truck stops in front of our house and a uniformed driver dashes across the
yard, places a package on our screened-in porch, and dashes back to the
truck. This kind of delivery is little more than transferring the package from
the warehouse to the truck to our porch. The person in the uniform has a
very low intensity relationship with the package and with me.

By contrast, the preacher does not simply transfer the sermon from
the study to the pulpit where the preacher places it in the mind of the congregation. Preachers literally embody the sermon, that is, they bring the
sermon to life through their bodies. There is no sermon until the preacher
speaks (except insofar as preachers speak to themselves). This way of thinking about embodiment is now commonplace in books, articles, conferences,
and the wider lore of preaching.[2]

1. Wilson, "Preaching, Performance," 60.

2. This perspective comes with two caveats. (1) Congregants and preachers can
encounter sermons via print. While people can be deeply touched through print,
Whitehead's theory of the priority of speaking and hearing in communication (below)
suggests that the effect could be even more powerful through oral-aural exchange. (2)
Preachers can embody sermons in ways that distract the congregation from giving optimum attention to the content of the sermon. For example, listeners can be anesthetized

In this chapter we first consider proclamatory and conversational approaches in the pulpit and then turn to the most important element in the embodiment of the sermon: the relationship of preacher and community. We focus on the process perspective on what happens when the preacher speaks aloud and the congregation listens. The chapter then notices how the preacher's expression in body, voice, gesture, and presence can invite the congregation into participating in the sermon or can diminish the congregation's conscious interest. The chapter pauses to emphasize the importance of reading the scripture passage(s) meaningfully. We meditate on silence as a medium of awareness and also as one of the preacher's best friends. The benediction of the chapter comes from Marjorie Suchocki's proverb: the preacher must let the sermon go.[3]

PROCLAMATORY AND CONVERSATIONAL APPROACHES IN THE PULPIT

A longtime teacher of preaching with an emphasis on bringing the sermon to life in the pulpit, Charles Bartow, makes a helpful distinction between "declamatory" and "conversational" styles of preaching.[4] Style, of course, is often related to content as is the case of these two approaches to embodiment. While these approaches pertain to the physical ways of speaking, they also pertain to theological representation, subject matter, and tone.

Leaning towards caricature, Bartow captures the spirit of proclamation. "The declamatory style assumes that those doing the talking somehow are in possession of truths that their listeners, for one reason or another, do not possess. . . . Declaimers, therefore, simply announce to people what they have on their minds."[5] This model "can be impressive, dramatic, celebrative and convincing."[6] The proclamatory style is a top-down approach to theology and preaching. The declamatory tone can be found in wooden and

---

by lifeless embodiment. As someone said, "The preacher does not even appear to be interested in the sermon." Another said, "Why does the preacher just read the sermon? If I wanted to read it, I could get a copy and read it for myself." For another example, listeners can be so caught up in idiosyncratic mannerisms they focus on the mannerisms and not the message. As someone said, "I counted eight-seven 'uhs' in that sermon." However, some listeners do connect with the content even through distracting embodiment.

3. Suchocki, *Whispered Word*, 55–68,

4. Bartow, *Preaching Moment*, 63–65. Bartow's "declamatory" is functionally similar to my "proclamatory."

5. Bartow *Preaching Moment*, 64.

6. Bartow, *Preaching Moment*, 64.

stone pulpits high above the floor in traditional church buildings, in simple speaking stands on the same level as the congregation, and on the stages of contemporary worship spaces that are much like theaters or auditoriums.

At one time, a great deal of proclamatory preaching was heavy-handed. Oftentimes it still has that quality, but the heavy-handed declamation style is not as widespread as it once was. But declamatory theological inclinations linger in many pulpits. Though expressed in ways that are less stuffy and self-important, declamation is sometimes veiled behind contemporary touches such as storytelling, the use of images, and rhetorical questions (in distinction from real questions). Proclamation can even take place through inductive preaching.

When I first imagined a conversational style in the pulpit, the initial image that came to mind was a host in electronic media welcoming guests to the show. This person often talks in moderate tones, speaks in modest vocal patterns, and establishes a casual ambiance. While that approach may fit particular moments and contexts, it is not a universal pattern for preaching in a conversational medium.[7] Actual conversation, which is the model for a conversational embodiment, contains a range of moments including such things as quiet interactions, questions asked with more and less degrees of energy, outbursts of enthusiasm, occasional eruptions of anger and silences—some meaningful, others awkward. One moment in a conversation can be quite dramatic and loud while another will generate the heat of passion while still another can invoke a silence that is almost too fragile to break. The different effects are natural demonstrations of what is happening as the conversation explores the text or the topic.

A conversational approach in embodiment is characterized by a certain feel: that of the preacher wanting to share with the congregation ideas, possibilities, and emotions that could support inclusive well-being. Nearly all preachers have default positions for their bodies, arms, postures, and vocal tones. The default embodiment position for many conversational preachers is relatively low-key, with modest gestures and a moderated voice. The preacher often starts in default but departs from it for emphasis at various points of the sermon and returns to default for less emphatic parts of conversation.

This approach is consistent with the way in which Marjorie Suchocki conceives of God usually presenting the initial invitation in a quiet way. Indeed, she describes it as a "whisper."[8] Of course, some invitations come in much larger ways. The Black Lives Matter movement that expressed itself in

7. Bartow sketches qualities of conversational style in *Preaching Moment*, 64–68.

8. Suchocki, *Whispered Word*, 1–12.

the streets in many places in the summer of 2020 seemed to me an invitation writ as large as a cultural movement.

The preacher may need to adjust voice and gesture for the requirements of sound and space. In order to be heard and seen in a large worship space, preachers will likely need to project their voices more fully than when being involved in a conversation with twelve people around a circular table. The same thing is true of hand movements and other gestures. The small motions that can communicate quite effectively when people are ten feet apart in a circle of interaction are sometimes lost in a large worship space in which some of the seating can be hundreds of feet away. On the broad chancel or stage of the worship space, the preacher often needs to be move in ways that are bigger than ordinary movements in order to appear as big as life.

ONE OF THE MOST IMPORTANT ELEMENTS IN EMBODIMENT: A SENSE OF RELATIONSHIP

The most important element in the embodiment of the sermon is not the preacher's use of the voice, or the preacher's gestures, or whether the preacher relies on notes or leaves the pulpit to roam around the worship space while preaching. One of the most important elements in embodiment is the congregation's perception of the preacher's relationship with the community.[9] From process perspective, of course, the preacher is inherently related to the congregation since all things are related. Relational dynamics will be at work whether or not the preacher pays attention to them.

How the congregation perceives the nature of the preacher-congregation relationship often plays a role in the degree to which members of the community are willing to participate in the sermonic conversation. A congregation will be more likely to engage the conversation if they experience the preacher and the congregation as seeking mutual well-being. The listening congregation is less likely to join the conversation when they experience

9. I say "one of" the most important dimensions of embodiment because for some people, a sense of relationship with the preacher is secondary to the actual content of the sermon and/or to the feelings generated by the sermon. Aristotle argued that a persuasive speaker brought *ethos*, *logos*, and *pathos* to the speaking situation, that is, people respond to the speaker through their sense of the preacher's character and their sense of relationship with the preacher (*ethos*), through the content of the sermon (*logos*), and through the feelings generated by the sermon (*pathos*). Nearly all listeners respond favorably when these things are present. However, a study of people who listen to sermons found that some people primarily listen to the sermon through one of those categories. Even so, many listeners place a premium on *ethos*. See R. J. Allen, *Hearing the Sermon*, 18–96.

the congregation—and the relationship with the preacher—as threatening mutual well-being.

One of the most important things the preacher can do to encourage congregational participation in the sermon on Saturday night or Sunday morning is to be an agent of inclusive well-being from Monday through Saturday.

The congregation tends to have a positive disposition to the preacher when these things are present in the preacher and in the sermon. The preacher enhances the innate relationship with the congregation by living with integrity, respecting other persons, and speaking honestly.[10] The preacher builds trust by preparing thoughtful messages that deal with ideas that are significant for the congregation.[11] The preacher proves reliable by honoring authentic feelings, empathizing with the congregation, and avoiding emotional manipulation.[12]

The preacher enhances the congregation's sense of relationship with the preacher when the preacher is a responsible member of the community who lives ethically, who speaks thoughtfully, and who is empathetic. When these characteristics are present, the congregation tends to look forward to the preacher stepping into the preaching space, but the inverse is true when such marks are absent.

Other factors also play important roles in the degree to which congregants will accept the invitation to join the sermon. Some listeners may not be interested in the subject matter. Others may be distracted by small children or lower back pain or the fact that they can feel the chilly air from the air conditioner vent blowing across them.

Writing from a Whiteheadian view of language, Stephen Franklin puts the matter this way. "The hearer's judgment of the source of the sounds has a . . . basic role to play in the linguistic context. The hearer's judgment as to the source of the sounds often—perhaps always—affects the nature of the propositional prehension Associated with those sounds."[13] The hearer's perception of the preacher depends not just on what the congregant sees in the moment in presentational immediacy but is touched by "realities given by means of causal efficacy."[14]

This phenomenon helps explain why parishioners are sometimes inordinately excited by a particular sermon or seemingly explicably resistant to

10. R. J. Allen, *Hearing the Sermon*, 18–41.

11. R. J. Allen, *Hearing the Sermon*, 42–69.

12. R. J. Allen, *Hearing the Sermon*, 70–96.

13. Franklin, *Speaking from the Depths*, 232.

14. Franklin, *Speaking from the Depths*, 232.

another. The hearer's response may be less prompted by the actual preacher and the actual sermon than by some deep connection in causal efficacy, now lost to consciousness but still a live point of contact.

As far as possible, a preacher should try to identify associations of the congregation with their histories with preachers—positive and negative—that continue to come into play. A preacher can try to build on positive associations and to avoid negative associations that may not be connected with the preacher of the moment but that irrupt because of preachers and preaching from earlier times. One way the preacher can make such discoveries is by focusing on the history of preaching in the congregation as part of the preacher's exegesis of the congregation.[15] A preacher might convene a conversation group for this purpose. And, of course, a preacher who has ears to hear can pick up a lot just by listening to what people say about their previous preachers and by asking respectful follow-up questions.

SPEECH COMES FROM AND TOUCHES DEEP LEVELS OF THE SELF

Speaking is central to the act of preaching. In *Modes of Thought*, Whitehead notes that expression for communication by means of sound emerged among human beings before sight.[16] While gesticulation may have preceded sound, "the weak point of gesticulation is that one cannot do much else while indulging in it."[17] When producing sound, the limbs are free to do other things.

> But there is a deeper reason for the unconscious recourse to sound production. Hands and arms constitute the more unnecessary parts of the body. We can do without them. They do not excite the intimacies of bodily existence. Whereas in the production of sound, the lungs and throat are brought into play. So that in speech, while a superficial, manageable expression is diffused, yet the sense of the vague intimacies of organic existence is also excited. Thus, voice-produced sound is a natural symbol for the deep experiences of organic existence.[18]

---

15. For exegesis of the congregation, see 121–125..

16. Whitehead, *Modes of Thought*, 31.

17. Whitehead, *Modes of Thought*, 31.

18. Whitehead, *Modes of Thought*, 32.

Sound (including speech) is the most natural expression for the deep aspects of life and can be the purest representation of the self. Indeed, "Speech is human nature itself, with none of the artificiality of written language."[19]

Speech is always immediately contextual. The sounds of speech "indicate by the very means of their presentation, important physical and emotional connections with concrete circumstances."[20] Furthermore, as Lyman Lundeen says, "Speech maintains the organic connection between explicit detail and context, which is so important for definite communication."[21]

On the side of the speaker, Stephen Franklin finds a connection between the body creating sound and perception in the deep mode of causal efficacy. "The production of the spoken word evokes in the speaker feelings of causal efficacy—feelings of that power whereby our reality emerges and gives us our identity. In short, the spoken word reinforces the speaker's sense of being an efficacious agent in a world of efficacious agents."[22]

On the side of the listener, Whitehead notes that spoken communication elicits invitations.

> Spoken language is merely a series of squeaks. Its function is
> (α) to arouse in the prehending subject some physical feeling
> indicative of the logical subjects of the proposition (β), to arouse
> in the prehending subject some physical feeling which plays the
> part of the "physical recognition" (γ), to promote the sublima-
> tion of the "physical recognition" into the conceptual "predictive
> feeling" (δ), to promote the integration of the indicative feeling
> and the predicative feeling into the required propositional [in-
> vitational] feeling.[23]

The interrelated functions of language are thus to arouse and to promote invitations.

The preacher is stirred by awareness arising from causal efficacy and brings as much as possible to expression in speech. The sermon itself becomes a form of feeling. In a similar way, listeners are stirred by receiving the speech sound from the preacher. The preacher's act of speaking produces sound waves that pass through the air and physically touch the eardrums of

19. Whitehead, *Modes of Thought*, 37. "Writing as a factor in human experience is comparable to the steam engine. It is important, modern, and artificial. Speech is as old as human nature itself. It is one of the primary factors constituting human nature" (*Modes of Thought*, 37). On the fusion of speaking and reading from print, see our comments below on the importance of expressively reading the Bible aloud.

20. Lundeen, *Risk and Rhetoric in Religion*, 49.

21. Lundeen, *Risk and Rhetoric in Religion*, 49–50.

22. Franklin, *Speaking from the Depths*, 237.

23. Whitehead, *Process and Reality*, 264.

the listeners. The sound waves—while invisible—have a material compo-nent. Sound waves are constituted by quite a lot of physical movement of molecules in the air. When they reach the eardrum of the listener, the ear-drum physically moves, along with the in the ear canal. The physical bodies of both the speaker and the listener become directly involved generating and in processing the words that strike the ear. The preacher's words can touch the deepest recesses of the life of feeling in the congregation.

As we have already indicated, most sermons should contain a certain amount of basic information about the world of the Bible, along with other data from history, contemporary theology, and other sources. This informa-tion may initially appear to be steno-language (language in the mode of presentational immediacy). But such information is seldom stenographic in the limited sense. Such material is seldom simply hard packages of data that pass from the shelf in the mind of the preacher to the shelves in the minds of the listener. When the sermon becomes through sound, it connects with a significant range of perception on the part of the listeners. Even when unintended, the spoken word sometimes elicits a deep response.

As he ends his probing *Speaking from the Depths*, Stephen Franklin calls attention to a key theological implication of these views of language for preaching. Franklin points out that language and experience exist in re-lationship: experience elicits language which then elicits experience which then elicits language. Language invites each new occasion to new possibili-ties. The community's response to that invitation creates the circumstance for another invitation. Franklin thus reflects that language can aid God in creating and recreating the world.

> The spoken word reinforces the preacher's sense of being an efficacious agent in a world of efficacious agents. By giving all entities their initial aim at the first stage of concrescence, God is working at the very depths of actuality. Thus, it is significant that the Bible uses the analogy of God *speaking* [the] word and, thereby, creating the universe.[24]

The preacher who *speaks* thus becomes a partner with God in offering the possibility of inclusive well-being to all.[25]

24. Franklin, *Speaking from the Depths*, 379. Franklin implies that specifically Christian language has these effects and that the best place to learn Christian language is the Christian community (*Speaking from the Depths*, 376–78). While certain noting that Christian language can have transformative effect, many process theologians—in-cluding me—would not limit such language to that spoken by the church.

25. Walter Ong, a preeminent scholar of orality and literacy acknowledges a debt to Whitehead (among others) as he launches his foundational work identifying leading qualities of sound and speech in oral culture (Ong, *Presence of the Word*, 17). Some

EXPRESSION THROUGH THE BODY

While speech and sound may be the primary element in expressing and receiving the sermon, the preacher in the pulpit is more than a speech engine. The preacher is a complete body, and the body as a whole plays a significant part in public communication. Listeners are stirred not only by the speech irrupting from the preacher's mouth, but by the minister's entire self in the moment of preaching.[26] When human beings are in the same space, they feel one another and thus affect one another even when such influence does not register as a distinct line of conscious recognition. The preacher should pay attention to the full range of bodily expression to maximize the opportunity for invitations to take hold in the congregation and to minimize interference.

The preacher's embodiment should be consistent with the tone of the invitation in the sermon. The vocal tones, the gestures, the preacher's posture, and movement should represent the content of the message.[27] For example, when the conversation focuses on joy, the preacher should usually speak and move in ways that are themselves joyful. If the sermon is more somber, then the preacher should be more somber in vocalization and actions. The content of the sermon and the embodiment are mutually reinforcing when they work together. By contrast listeners tend to disengage from the conversation when the content and the embodiment take place on different channels, perhaps even working at cross purposes. When I think of the latter, I remember a preacher during my seminary days (the time of

---

of these qualities are not as vivid in today's media-oriented cultures as in oral-aural settings. But these qualities are still resident in the congregation by means of causal efficacy.

These are some of the qualities Ong identifies. Speaking from person to person puts the people in the moment and is thus especially existential (111–12). Words are powerful. Indeed, words can have direct effects in the same ways as weapons or tools (112–13). Sound comes from the deep interior of the self, and they are received in the deep interior of the self. This phenomenon is similar to the notion of internal relationship albeit it is more explicit (117). Hearing the same sound—being touched by the same sound—creates a remarkable sense of connection and community among people (123). Sound surrounds people in a way that visual media do not (except in venues with 360° visuals) (129), Ong seems to echo Whitehead when he says, "Although . . . sound perishes each instant that it lives, the instant that it does live is rich. Through sound we can become present to a totality which is a fullness, a plenitude" (130).

For Ong's analysis of what happened in the transition from oral-aural to literate and thence technological cultures, see his still valuable *Orality and Literacy*.

26. Susanne K. Langer notes how the self is stirred through a variety of media in *Philosophy in a New Key* and especially in *Feeling and Form*.

27. Brown, *Delivering the Sermon*, 512.

the war in Vietnam) who spoke so angrily about the need for peace his face turned as red as if he had been on the beach all day without sunscreen.

Not only do I tend to disengage from such preaching, but I tend to question its trustworthiness. When the preacher speaks about joy in an angry manner, for instance, I wonder whether the preacher truly understands joy, and more importantly, I wonder whether the message about joy is true.

Speak Fully and Expressively

With respect to the preacher's body in preaching, several things come to mind.[28] First, at the most basic level, the preacher needs to speak loudly enough so the congregation can really hear the sermon. The sound waves need to reach the ear drum with full force if the voice is to have maximum effect. Moreover, listeners who struggle to make out the preacher's words may disengage from the sermon. Even in these days when worship spaces are equipped with ever more sophisticated electronic amplification, preachers sometimes fail to use the technology to full advantage with the result that hearers are frustrated, and some tune out of the sermon altogether.

Furthermore, the preacher should speak in vocal tones that are consistent with his or her typical ways of speaking. Preachers sometimes speak with artificial vocal emphases, sometimes characterized as stained-glass voice, or they speak in machine-gun style, blasting people from the pulpit with rapid-fire voice bullets. Artificial qualities in the way the voice sounds can suggest a certain artificiality to the preacher and to the content of the sermon. Of course, preachers sometimes need to speak with more volume in order to be heard, but preachers can do so while maintaining their own vocal rhythm. And preachers may put on a particular voice for the sake of emphasis.

Eye Contact

While speech is typically the most powerful element of embodiment in preaching, serious contact from eye to eye often creates a sense of connection that goes deep into the self. One cannot see the soul of another person, as a former President of the United States said of looking into the eyes of another world leader. But in a context of mutual understanding eyes can indicate insight, raise questions, affirm, laugh, signal anger, weep, disapprove,

---

28. For an excellent guide to practical matters of embodiment, including exercises, see Brown, *Delivering the Sermon*. See similarly, Schlafer, *Your Way with God's Word*.

invite, give permission, indicate importance, attest understanding, under-line resolve, and communicate any number of other things. Indeed, worlds can flash between two sets of eyes in a fraction of a second.

But when the preacher's eyes are locked on a manuscript much of the nuance that passes from eye to eye (in the larger context of embodiment) is lost. Having noticed the eyes in sermons for many years, I notice that eye contact is most important at key moments in the sermon. I also notice that in ordinary conversation, we do not always look people in the eye. In fact, there are some things—often tender or embarrassing or just odd—when we look at the floor or out the window or up the ceiling. A preacher does not need to drill into the eyes of the congregation every minute. But, when preachers look at the congregation, they need to look into the eyes. I know a number of preachers whose faces are up from the pulpit but instead of look-ing into the eyes of the congregation, they focus their eyes over the heads of people and, essentially look at the wall.

Move Physically with the Content of the Sermon

Preachers should stand and move in the pulpit in ways that are natural to the preacher's usual ways of moving in the world. The preacher needs to stand up, be erect, and not slouch (except for occasional effect). A slouch-ing preacher who hangs over the pulpit or the speaker's stand like a drip rag communicates slothfulness, regardless of whether that is intended. A preacher who stands in the pulpit like a fence post—unmoving except for a slightly talking head—appears to represent the idea that life is stiff and inflexible, effectively denying that life is continuously evolving process.

Preachers differ in the degree of animation that is natural to who they are. But every preacher should develop the freedom to use face and hands in gestures that coordinate with the content of the sermon so that what the congregation sees reinforces what the preacher is saying. Preachers some-times use gestures that are stilted. Instead of serving to accent the message, such movements can call attention to themselves and prompt the congrega-tion to focus on an issue such as, "Has our pastor pulled a muscle? Is she in pain?"

I find that reserved embodiment, even stiffness in the pulpit, is one of points at which students often struggle. They are self-conscious and nervous and will not let go. The two things I have found that help preachers try to get past this phenomenon are to offer the preachers images of other preachers who speak and move naturally in the pulpit and to say to the struggling preachers that they simply must force themselves to move hands, arms, and feet, even though such efforts initially seem artificial and even fearful.

Preachers sometimes need to grow into the freedom to be themselves. They need to discover the patterns of movement that can be consistent with who they are and with the conversation that is the heart of the sermon.

Preachers who move away from the pulpit often do so to be free of the physical barrier of the pulpit itself so the congregation can feel closer to them (and so they can feel closer to the congregation). They have more freedom to use their bodies in dramatizing important elements of the sermon. But, as preachers move away from the pulpit, the movement itself sometimes becomes distracting. The preacher sometimes roams around the sanctuary or the platform like a lost dog sniffing at every tree and fence post and fire hydrant. Where the preacher wants the movement to suggest the freedom of the gospel and to improve communication between preacher and listener, the effect of random movement is to embody a directionless movement that seems not to be going anywhere (unless the preacher uses it to make a point).

For preachers who seek freedom of movement away from the pulpit, I suggest plotting the movement like a director plots the movement of the characters in a stage play so that the preacher has four or five places to move for particular moments of the sermon. To use an imperfect image, when I was in school in New Jersey and rode the train into New York City, the train made stops along the way. Each stop was different. Similarly, the preacher could "make a stop" for two or three minutes at one place at the beginning of the sermon, then the preacher could make other stops along the way. This approach embodies the sense that the sermon is a living event with motion that is constructive and purposeful. Along the way, of course, the preacher can build in the physical representations of things like "on the one hand . . . on the other hand" . . . "my thought reversed itself" . . . "I was frozen in place."

Embodiment and Authenticity

When the preacher's embodiment seems affected, I tend to doubt the authenticity of the sermon. In comparison, when the preacher's body in the act of preaching is consistent with the way the preacher moves and acts in other parts of life, the sermon seems more likely to be authentic. When I am not distracted by the preacher's embodiment, I am more likely to open myself to the conversation.

Process theology hinges on the notion of life as constant process. In the pulpit, the preacher should be as animated as life. The preacher who is animated in ways that are appropriate to the message subtly suggests the integrity of the message as well as its believability. A preacher whose embodiment is inappropriately stiff, stilted, or subdued subtly suggests lack of integrity in the message and, thereby, calls into question the trustworthiness of the message.

Practice in the Worship Space

For many preachers, the best way to prepare for preaching is to go to the worship space and practice the sermon. The results are even better when I can get a visual recording (or at least an audio recording) of the practice sessions. I get a feel for the sermon in the space. I discover ways to stand, what to do with my hands given the nature of the pulpit or the speaker's stand or standing away from the pulpit. By going over the sermon several times out loud, it becomes better fixed in my memory. I use a technique that, I think, came from the old Dale Carnegie Course in public speaking which is to associate things in the worship space with different parts of the sermon. Thus, when I look at the stained-glass window with the picture of Jesus in Gethsemane, I remember the introduction. When I look at the clock hanging from the balcony, I think of the exegesis, etc.

To Preach with or without Notes

One perennial discussion is whether the preacher uses a manuscript (or notes) or preaches without paper, iPhone, or iPad. From the process perspective, the preacher's sense of *presence* with the congregation is more important than the question of "Do you preach with or without manuscript notes?" The feeling of presence has to do with the degree to which the preacher is authentically connecting with the congregation as a living member of the community.

I regularly hear preachers who stand in the preaching space and read the manuscript, eyes down, officious voice, with furtive glances up from the manuscript simulating eye contact. This preacher usually comes across as similar to the driver who jumped out of the sermon truck and ran the package into the pulpit and is ready to run back to the truck. The feeling of presence is minimal, even when the content of the manuscript is conversational. I also hear preachers who step into the middle of the chancel or stage, microphone in hand and placed just an inch from the mouth, who want to appear to be present with congregation but whose sermon never quite connects because much of what could have been existential content is somewhere else. Not long ago, I heard a sermon that was essentially a soliloquy in which the preacher implied, "Come emote with me," but the purpose of such emotiveness never came into focus. My spouse said afterwards, "Beautiful images. But what did I see?"

The point is that the use or non-use of written material does not determine the degree to which a preacher is present. The question is how the preacher uses supportive material or how the preacher develops the content of the sermon so it can engage listeners.

The preacher who uses a manuscript as a way to achieve focus and direction can be more fully in conversation with the listeners than the preacher who speaks without notes but whose sermon might generously be called "stream of consciousness." The reverse is true, and so is every approach in between. The preacher can carry the notes across the pulpit like a slug carrying a load of dirt. A preacher can speak a sermon without notes in the most eloquent, evocative way. The issue is how the preacher uses such material.

EXPRESSIVELY READ THE SCRIPTURES IN WORSHIP

I pause briefly over the public reading of the Bible in worship because it is so important and because it is often so poorly done. Indeed, the reading of Scripture can be boring. Readers sometimes step up to the reading desk without having looked at the passage previously. They sometimes mispronounce words and fail to see how the parts of the reading are grammatically connected. Their lack of preparation signals the congregation, albeit inadvertently, that the Bible is not very important.

Whitehead notices that speech is usually embedded in a particular context whereas books for reading are removed from their generative contexts. While this phenomenon has the virtue of making a literary expression available to any reader any time, it loses the immediacy and dynamic of the originating context.

In the last generation, scholars have gone farther than at any time since the Enlightenment in recovering the oral-aural contexts in which the biblical materials came to expression. Significant parts of the Bible were written down less as "books" in the way we think of them and more as "scripts" or "prompts" for oral performance. By treating the materials in the Bible as books many preachers and scholars lose at least some feel for the dynamic properties of speech identified in this chapter.

Whitehead calls attention to a way whereby speech and silent reading can be reconnected.

> Spoken language is immersed in the immediacy of social inter-course. Written language lies hidden in a volume, to be opened and read at diverse times and in diverse places, in abstraction from insistent surroundings. But a book can be read aloud. Here we find an instance of the fusion of writing and speech. Read-ing aloud is an art, and the reader makes a great difference. The immediacy of the environment then enters into the abstraction of writing.[29]

One immediate implication, as we noted in chapter 4, is that the preacher should read the text aloud and listen to it as part of sermon preparation.[30]

Another immediate implication is that the person who reads the Bible in public worship (sometimes called a lector) should bring the passage alive in the manner of a truly spoken word.[31] At the simplest level, this makes the reading of Scriptures interesting and suggests the importance of the Bible. More importantly for the sermon, such a presentation helps the congrega-tion hear the passage itself. Such reading often helps the congregation begin to recognize differences in what they might have assumed the passage says and what it actually says.

Of course, all reading aloud is interpretation. The sermon is usually best served by reading the Bible with inflection and tone consistent with the direction of the sermon.[32] A reader who has not talked with the preacher to get the direction of the sermon sometimes reads the Bible passage with emphases that differ from those of the sermon, thus creating confusion in the minds of listeners.

This discussion raises the question of who should read the passage aloud in worship. The older I get the more I am convinced the preacher should read the biblical text immediately prior to the sermon. The preacher's

---

29. Whitehead, *Modes of Thought*, 39.

30. See 97.

31. One of the best guides for such reading is Ward, *Speaking of the Holy.* Going beyond expressive reading of the text to performing it, see Ward and Trobisch, *Bringing the Word to Life.* Cf. Rhoads, "What Is Performance Criticism?" The Network of Biblical Storytellers provides many resources. Phil Ruge-Jones recounts how he learns a story in Ruge-Jones, "Preparing to Perform."

32. For as broader discussion of enhancing the place of the Bible in worship, see Allen and Williamson, *Adventures of the Spirit,* 113–15.

oral interpretation is thereby consistent with the direction of the sermon and the passage is freshly in the minds of the congregation.

On one aspect of this subject, I am something of an outlier among scholars of preaching. I strongly believe people should bring their Bibles to worship and follow along with the public reading of the text and refer to the text in the Bible during the sermon. Biblical illiteracy is so profound that the church should take every measure to help. Scholars and preachers who emphasize orality and performance often want people to keep their eyes and ears on the lector during the performance of the text. My personal report is that I can both be present to the performance and check the wording of the text (which is consistent with Whitehead's observation that people can speak, hear, and do other things at the same time). If listeners attend only to the oral event, then I hope they soon return to the written text to note how the performance may have enriched their perception of the text.

THE FULLNESS OF SILENCE

Silence is a phenomenon that does not always receive adequate attention from preachers and worship planners. Many North Americans today fill their everyday lives with sounds from radio, television, smartphone, computers, and constant chatting. Sometimes people become numb to the particular sounds that are running in the background. Such a flood of indiscriminate sound can serve as a barrier to awareness of the deeper things in life.

Bernard Meland explains why pastors and worship should honor the value of silence in the service of worship and in the preaching moment.

> It does not follow . . . that the realities of these lived experi-
> ences lay dormant or unexpressed, except as they can break
> forth verbally in language. Nor is living with integrity, with style
> and beauty, always, or necessarily, the fruition of language em-
> ployed instructively, testimonially, or with moral direction or
> insistence. *Presence*, sheer presence in and of itself is a mode of
> communicating.[33]

Indeed, "there is language in silences."[34]

In silence we can become aware of the depths of reality in ways that we cannot fully express in words or even in the arts. The preacher who honors silence by being silent, from time to time may help the congregation become aware of God as sheer presence. The internal relationship between God and

33. Meland, *Fallible Forms and Symbols*, 30.
34. Meland, *Fallible Forms and Symbols*, 30.

community means that God is ever affecting that relationship, but silence often opens a little more window for preacher and congregation to be more fully attentive to the currents passing through the wires of that relationship, as well as the currents passing through the wires of the congregations and networks with one another.

The Pause: One of the Preacher's Best Friends

Preachers and worship planners may enhance both sermon and service by the judicious use of silence. Some years ago, I coined the little saying, "The pause can be a preacher's best friend." It may not always be the preacher's *best* friend, but a pause at the right moment of a sermon can give time for part of the message to soak in. A moment of silence can highlight what the preacher has just said. It can resonate with the self. When asking a real question, for instance, the preacher might pause long enough for people to consider the question and the possibilities of response.

Yet, preachers and other worship leaders are often uncomfortable with silence in the sermon and in the service. When a preacher is in front of the congregation, silence can feel very threatening. The urge is often to fill the void with sound. To honor silence, preachers often need to invoke the personal discipline to persevere through what seems like a long time of silence. With experience, reluctant preachers can gradually become comfortable with silence, especially as they sense the congregation being stirred in the silence.

LETTING THE SERMON GO

Preachers who step into the preaching space need to be prepared to follow Marjorie Suchocki's sage advice to let the sermon go.[35] She recalls an experience of sitting in a sanctuary when some words came to her for a book she was writing. She arose to return home.

> I needed to keep the words inside my head until I could write them down, and my image [walking home] was to keep my head absolutely upright lest the words should tumble out of my ears and be gone. I had to keep the words until I could give them away! But once they were written, they were no longer exactly

35. Suchocki, *Whispered Word*, 55–68.

my words anymore. They belonged to whomever read the book. They were mine only to give away.[36]

The preacher is in a similar position. The words of the sermon come through the preacher, but once we speak, the words take on a life in the congregation.

Nevertheless, Suchocki elevates every preacher's self-image by adding the stunning observation that the preacher not only offers the sermon to the congregation but also to the universe. "This is not just a fanciful statement. We exist in so thoroughly a relational creation that everything affects everything else."[37] She does caution, "Oh, the effect may not be at all what we like to think about as fame or notoriety."[38] But there will be some effect. Suchocki continues her counsel: "You will give your sermon away whether you want to or not, so you might as well do so intentionally."[39]

But, regardless of the preacher's intentionality, people respond out of the multiple dynamics that are at work in them and in their circumstances.[40] Indeed, the distinctiveness of each congregant means that, to at least a certain degree, each listener will hear a different sermon.[41] Will Beardslee and colleagues note that this can be a good thing when listeners refract the sermon through the points at which it helps them become in ways that promote growth towards well-being.[42] Nevertheless, as a preacher, I sometimes find this hard to accept. I want them to get my point and to respond accordingly. Sometimes this happens, but not with the regularity and public demonstration I would like. However, I have gradually learned that letting the sermon go can be an act of grace for me in that it helps release me from making an idol of my own preaching.

The congregation receives the invitations of the sermon as initial aims; the members of the community, and the community itself, makes their own responses.[43] As we point out in the afterword, God is present in those moments to work with the congregation in light of the congregation's

36. Suchocki, *Whispered Word*, 57.

37. Suchocki, *Whispered Word*, 57.

38. Suchocki, *Whispered Word*, 57.

39. Suchocki, *Whispered Word*, 58.

40. While not writing as a process theologian, Marianne Gaarden points to a "third room in preaching" where the sermon meets the experience of the listener, and the listener typically comes away with a new meaning that reproduces neither the preacher's state purpose nor the listener's prior experience. See Gaarden, *Third Room of Preaching*.

41. Marianne Gaarden explains how this happens in *Third Room of Preaching*, 55–106.

42. For their full discussion, see Beardslee et al., *Biblical Preaching*, 64–72.

43. Suchocki, *Whispered Word*, 59.

orientations. If the people make less than optimum responses to the invitations, then God works with those responses to offer the highest available move towards inclusive well-being.

9

Sample Sermon
The Parable of the Talents: Matt 25:14–30

THE FOLLOWING SERMON COMES out of the conversation in the book with
the parable of the talents (Matt 25:14–30). The steps of discovery that lead
to the direction of the sermon and the invitations it offers appear in the case
studies at the ends of chapters 4, 5, and 6. I shape the sermon according to
the Puritan Plain Style. I use this shape because the Plain Style is especially
clear in the way in which it sets out the different voices in the conversation
and the way in which it calls attention to the pathway to coming to theological clarity and to thinking about the implications of the conversation
for today. As noted in chapter 7, the plain style consists of six parts: (1)
introduction, (2) indication of the direction of the sermon, (3) exegesis of
the biblical text, (4) theological conversation about the invitation in the text,
(5) implications of the conversation, (6) and transition from the sermon
into life. In this case, however, I have omitted the indication of the direction
of the sermon in order to maintain a little bit of suspense—and hence, hopefully, to sustain congregational interest.

The sermon is annotated to identify what I hope will happen in
each section. The annotations appear in italics immediately prior to the
paragraph(s) to which they refer.

I prepared this sermon for a service of worship in a congregation of
the Christian Church (Disciples of Christ) in a a county seat in the Mid-
west. The congregation is Eurocentric, middle-class, well-educated, and has
a progressive element.

The sermon is not held out as a sterling model for others to emulate. It
appears here as a plainspoken sample of one way to bring process theology

and a homiletic of conversation into expression in an old and reliable form of preaching.

INTRODUCTION

The introduction seeks to establish identification between the preacher and the congregation by drawing on an everyday life experience.

I'll bet you have the experience of looking at something you have known about for a long time, but then coming to see it in a new light.

I remember one time when my spouse's parents came from their home in another state to visit us when we had a four-year-old at home. I had been around her all her life. Changed her diapers. Did my share of driving her back and forth to preschool. Read stories to her at night. Or, perhaps I should say I read stories to her as long as I could stay awake. But we had four older children, and I have to say that much of the time I was only vaguely aware of her as a small shape moving around our house.

So, we had dinner with my spouse's parents. A lot of stories. A lot of laughter. As desert was coming to an end, my father-in-law said he was pleased by how much our four-year-old had developed a sense of humor.

Sense of humor? I had not noticed that she had a sense of humor. I noticed that she constantly wanted to kick the soccer ball, needed rides to her friends, and kept me awake past my bedtime reading stories. Sense of humor? But then I saw it once . . . and again . . . and then again . . . and I began to realize she really does have a natural and neverending sense for humor.

INDICATION OF THE DIRECTION
OF THE SERMON

The indication of the direction of the sermon is brief. It acknowledges a familiar interpretation of the story which I hope the congregation will recognize while suggesting a fresh perspective. Sometimes the indication of the direction of the sermon reveals the specific invitation(s) of the sermon, but, again, I give a general indication without revealing the specific invitation of the sermon in the hope of sustaining interest.

I've been around the parable of the talents all my life, especially during stewardship season. How can I persuade people to give their time, talents, and money to the church? Maybe you've heard that sermon. But getting ready for this morning, I had the experience of seeing things in the parable of the talents I have not seen before.

EXEGESIS OF THE BIBLICAL TEXT

The exegesis starts with abbreviating retelling of the parable with a contemporary touch with pertinent commentary. The exegesis moves to the setting of the text in context of Matthew as a means to identifying "what I have not seen before." Along the way, the exegesis reveals some of the invitations of the text.

According to Matthew, Jesus' major work was to manifest the Realm of God through preaching, teaching, and healing. (Matt 4:23). That is, Jesus announces the coming of the Realm of God, invites people to join the movement toward it, interprets it, and demonstrates it. The Realm of God is a coming world of love, justice, peace, and abundance. I like Marjorie Suchocki's phrase for it: "inclusive well-being."[1]

But, from Matthew's point of view, there is a problem. Although Jesus worked some of the signs of the Realm, the final coming of the Realm of God is delayed. In Matt 24–25, Matthew tells a series of parables to help the church make its way through the delay. The parable of the talents is one of those parables.

So, you've got a wealthy business owner who goes away on a trip. You might think of the owner as a snowbird going to Florida for the winter. About to close the trunk of the car, the owner gives control of significant assets to three slaves while he is away. I know some of the translations say "servants," but they were likely actual slaves. The owner must have paid attention in business school because he apportions talents to the slaves according to their abilities.

A talent was a sum of money. Ten talents to one. Five to another. And one talent to one slave. I remember someone saying, ruefully, "I'm just a one-talent person," meaning, "I don't have much to offer." But think about this: one talent is the equivalent of fifteen years of wages.

The slaves with ten and five talents double their money. Please. Give me their phone numbers. I would take either one as my financial manager.

But the slave with one talent buried the money. That may seem bizarre but in the ancient world people often buried money as a form of safekeeping.

---

1. Suchocki, *Fall to Violence*, 60–61, 66–71.

When armies invaded or thieves came the money would be in the ground, as safe as in a safety deposit box.

But when the owner comes home? "You wicked and lazy servant . . . You ought to have invested my money . . . [so] I would have received what was my own with interest. So, take this talent . . . give it to the one who has ten talents . . . [and] as for this worthless slave, throw [this slave] into the outer darkness where there will be weeping and gnashing of teeth."

So far, pretty familiar. But then I think about this parable in the setting for which Matthew told it. The Romans sacked Jerusalem and destroyed the temple in the year 70 CE. Judaism in crisis. Many killed. Infrastructure destroyed. Social fabric torn apart. Jewish groups competing with one another for power.

Matthew wrote a decade later in a different place. But those issues traveled and were compounded by the delay. And more than that, Matthew's church had considerable tension within itself. Someone calls Matt 18 the first manual on church conflict, "If another member of the church sins against you" (Matt 18:15). "Fightings and fears, within, without."[2]

The big questions: Where do we go? What do we do? Do you ever feel that way? I do. I feel that way a lot in our moment of history. My inclination: circle the wagons. Find a place of security. Consolidate. Take the safe route. Bury those talents.

Now the fresh perspective. In the midst of chaos, conflict, uncertainty, and delay, what should the church do? Caught in chaos, uncertainty and delay, the parable wants the congregation to step out to multiply its witness to inclusive well-being. Take its cues from the five- and ten-talent servants: multiply its witness to the Realm, increase the way in which it points to the possibility of inclusive well-being.

A point worth noting. From the perspective of the parable, God has already given the church resources for witness. Ten talents? Five talents? One talent? Different interests and abilities. Different orientations and capacities. Different resources. But we all have opportunities to invite people and communities towards the Realm.

Matthew believed that God was in control of history and that after Jesus' return, God would convene a great final judgment and would judge everyone in the church according to the degree they had multiplied their talents—used their resources—to point to the Realm of God. God would welcome the ten- and five-talent witnesses into the Realm but condemn the one-talent disciple to the outer darkness.

---

2. Elliott, "Just As I Am," 339.

I know Christians who think the language of "outer darkness . . . weeping . . . wailing of teeth is metaphorical." But as far as I can tell from first-century sources, these designations point to a place of actual suffering.

I have to say this seems a little counterintuitive. When under threat, move out. But then you get to the end and for those who did not move out, bad news.

THEOLOGICAL CONVERSATION ABOUT INVITATIONS IN THE TEXT

This part of the sermon brings some of the invitations of the text into conversation with some of the convictions of my approach to process theology. I note points of similarity and difference between then and now. This section makes use of the notions of the surface current of the text as well as the undercurrent.

So, there it is: what the parable invited people to believe and do. What do you think about these things?

One of Matthew's big points rings true to me. When the church runs up against opposition to our witness to the realm of God—qualities of well-being for everyone—the church needs to multiply its talents, to magnify its efforts. Otherwise, the agents of injustice, indignity, restriction, and forced scarcity have even more free run on the culture. One of my friends puts it this way: the more we do what we can do for the Realm of God, "the fuller our life." "The more we live it, the more of it we get."[3]

What can I do as a person? What can we do as a church?

It sounds like we are on our own. In the parable, the owner goes to Florida, and we are left by ourselves. But later in the Gospel, we hear Matthew's Jesus affirm, "Remember, I am with you always to the end of the age" (Matt 28:20). Jesus is with us as we seek to multiply our talents on behalf of the witness to the Realm of God.

But other dimensions to this parable are troubling. One is the idea that God will destroy the present age and replace it with a new one in a single, dramatic cosmic event—the second coming. I see this way of thinking as characteristic of a first-century worldview. They thought of the world as a three-story universe with God and heaven above, the earth in the middle, and an underworld below. They could account for a second coming by seeing Jesus come from the upper story (heaven) to the middle story (earth) and the condemned below (hell). Moreover, I do not believe that a God of

3. O. W. Allen, *Matthew*, 247.

unrelenting love would actively destroy the current world, unleashing the incredible pain involved.

Moreover, the world has been waiting for two thousand years, and the second has not happened. In fact, the magnitude of human suffering only gets bigger as the world population gets larger. If God has the power to end this suffering and does not do so, then God's own character comes into question.

It makes more sense for me to believe that life and history involve God, humankind, and nature interacting. God invites us to do things that contribute to the common good. God invites us to multiply our talents. And when we do, well-being happens. When we ignore or reject God's invitation, and bury our talents, then the quality of life goes down.

But here's the thing. In the parable, the slaves have one chance to say yes to the owner's invitation. One and done. Two benefit, one loses out. Game over. But in real life with God, when we make choices that subvert the Realm, God offers us another invitation that takes account of the changed circumstances. Another opportunity for well-being. It isn't the same. But it is still an opportunity to experience *some* sense of well-being in the midst of difficulty.

And yet, while the idea of God condemning people to punishment does not square with the notion of God unconditionally offering possibilities for the Realm, I believe this is what happens: when a community says "No" to the invitation to multiply our resources for good, we inadvertently set in motion values and patterns of behavior that corrode community and undermine well-being for all. God does not actively condemn.But things collapse.

For example, Matthew, like other writers of the Gospels and Letters, anticipated the collapse of the Roman Empire. It did not happen in Matthew's lifetime. Or the next lifetime, or the next. But in the end, Rome relied too much on violence to secure power and maintain peace. Graft in the government. Squalid conditions for the slaves. Internal corruption. Idolatry. It all left Rome unable to defeat invaders. No wonder the Empire in the west fell in 476 CE. When I was in high school, our literature teacher spoke poetically of the "the glory that was Rome." But a better designation would be "the deceit, exploitation and violence that was Rome."

IMPLICATIONS OF THE CONVERSATION

The sermon now tries out some implications of the theological conversation with the parable of the talents. After naming some

identifications, the sermon includes the story of Minnie Vautrin
as someone who used her talents to witness to inclusive well-being
in a season of unimaginable chaos.

I come back to the fresh thing I hear in this parable. I hear an invitation to use our resources assertively for the Realm of God, to work for the values and qualities of inclusive well-being, even when we are in chaos. Perhaps I should say *especially* when community struggles.

It looks to me like we are living in such a moment in history. So much uncertainty. So much tension. So much polarization. So much demonization. So much name-calling. So many false possibilities. So many lies. So many people making decisions to benefit themselves and to undermine others. As I write, some people refuse to take common-sense health measures in the name of freedom while being quite willing to let their freedom be the direct cause of the deaths of others.

You hear people asking, "What is going to happen to our world? What kind of world will our children have . . . and what kind of world will our grandchildren have?

And so many similar things are also happening in the church. Polarization. Name-calling. Caricature. "If they're going have those pieces of tape in the sanctuary to tell you where to sit, I'm just not going to come." And all the while the historic churches—like the Methodists, Presbyterians, Episcopalians, and Disciples—get smaller year after year. What is our future?

A powerful invitation I hear clearly in this conversation is this: God calls and empowers us to multiply how we use our resources, our talents, right now for the sake of inclusive well-being . . . especially right now in the conflict and chaos.

Do you hear the little touch of theological irony here? In the parable, when the first two servants did what the owner said—when they took the risks and used the resources—the result was something good for them. The very act of doing what they were supposed to becomes a means of grace for them.

At this time of the year, I think about Minnie Vautrin. Born in 1886, she grew up on a farm in a small town in Illinois and in the Disciples congregation. Seeing her grow up in a male-dominated small town, I imagine I would have thought of her as a one-talent person who would spend her life preparing meals, feeding chickens, watering the flowers, and hanging the laundry on the line.

But in 1912, Minnie Vautrin went to China as a missionary for our church. A teacher, she founded two schools for young women and by 1937 was President of the Ginling Girls College in Nanjing. Then, in 1937, the

Japanese invaded China and by December 1937, they reached Nanjing, a wave of destruction, violence, and killing rising in front of them

All but about a dozen foreigners fled Nanjing. But Minnie Vautrin stayed, along with several other missionaries, most of them from our church. And one German. John Rabe. A member of the Nazi party.

When the city resisted the Japanese demand to surrender, the invaders, enraged, magnified their brutality. Pulling people—including women and children—out of their homes. Burying people in the dirt, leaving only their heads above ground. Violating women. Using live human beings for bayonet practice. Beheading people. No wonder this event is sometimes called "the rape of Nanjing."

"What can we do?" "What can *we* do?" That was the question the missionaries and John Rabe asked. What can we do with our meagre talents— Bibles, a few pieces of chalk, some classrooms—in the face of the most powerfully army in Asia? The chaos . . . the danger . . . the violence . . . the fear . . . are to me unimaginable.

Minnie Vautrin and her colleagues said this: "We can consecrate our talents for God. We can create a Safety Zone around the school." It turned out to be an area of about three and a half miles. The agreement with the Japanese was that the leaders of the Safety Zone would keep Chinese soldiers out of the zone, leaving only civilians within the zone. and the invaders then agreed not to enter the zone.

Minnie Vautrin, one-time farm girl from central Illinois, heard an invitation to bring a little well-being to China. And as strange as this may sound, John Rabe, the Nazi, heard the same invitation, and served as chair of the Safety Zone committee. Who knows who will hear . . . and respond . . . to the invitation?

Eventually some 250,000 people made their way into the safety zone and survived.

TRANSITION FROM THE SERMON INTO LIFE

The transition from the sermon into life seeks to help the congregation continue thinking about how to identify and employ its talents in witness to inclusive well-being.

Minnie Vautrin was one of us. A member of the Christian Church (Disciples of Christ). And so were several of her colleagues. The same religious DNA that was in her is in . . . me . . . and you.

Our cultural setting is a long way from Nanjing in 1939. We have our issues. Our church—at least the Eurocentric part of it—gets smaller every year, but we continue in our institutional life year after year much like we did in the 1960s. How long can we go on without making major changes? Beyond the church we live in a time of caricature, polarization, name-calling, and threat of violence. On our streets right now, people of color experience Nanjing-like barbarity—some of it at the hands of the police. In the wealthiest nation of the world, 20 percent of the population is food insecure. I volunteer every week at a food bank. At first I could not believe the lines stretching clear across the parking down the driveway and into the street. And the conditions of the people who come. How do they live?

It may not be Nanjing. It may not be the world of Matthew. But I believe God gives us the imagination to see possibilities for well-being beyond these things. So do you. And we together have unimaginable imagination. I want to use the talents God has given me like the ten-talent slave . . . like the five-talent slave . . . like Minnie Vautrin.

What about you?

Afterword

God Is Omnipresent
in All Phases of the Sermon

SINCE GOD IS PRESENT and purposive in all moments of life, it follows that God is present and purposive in all phases of the sermon—preparation, embodiment, and afterglow. God does not try to dictate the sermon as that would violate the nature of the creative partnership between God and preacher. But God does invite the preacher to consider the most relevant proposals, that is, the most available intuitions, thoughts, sensitivities, discoveries, feelings, and actions that move towards optimum becoming.

However, the preacher in the process family thinks of God struggling with the complexities, ambiguities, questions, and doubts that come to the preacher in the midst of preparing the sermon, as well as when preaching it, and when responding to the congregation's responses to the sermon. God feels the preacher's questions, follows with the preacher searching for resources to help deal with those questions, ruminates with the preacher on what to say and how to say it. A preacher who senses that she or he is in tune with the divine invitation for a particular sermon may even feel inspired. Indeed, from time to time I have felt as though something elevated me off the seat of my chair in the study and that I fairly hovered above the desk. At the same time, although such moments may be clear and compelling, the preacher should examine them from the standpoints of the criteria of appropriateness to God's purposes for becoming and believability. Not all elevated feelings truly elevate the perception and activity of the self in response to proposals consistent with God's purposes. Some feelings can lead preacher and community to diminish community, and a little critical reflection along the way can often awaken the preacher and others to the dangers.

Preachers do not always respond favorably to the divine invitation, of course, and at such times, God persists in offering possibilities that can be

216

as renewing as possible for pastor and people given the other choices that they have made.

God is similarly present and purposeful when the preacher is actually speaking the sermon. God seeks to help the pastor and the congregation live into the optimum possibilities for the message in the way in which the preacher speaks it and the congregation hears it. God is at work to increase the receptivity of the listening community to the invitation of the sermon. God feels the congregation feeling the sermon. God is present in the internal relationships among preacher and congregation, attempting to help all members of the community be appropriately responsive to one another. God seeks to intensify the experience of all involved in the world of the sermon.

God continues to work in the afterglow of the sermon by nurturing the feelings generated by the sermon that contribute positively to the congregation and the larger world. Because sermons are spoken and heard by finite people God aims to limit the distortion and damage from the sermon. As implied earlier, God takes the effects of the sermon and feeds them into depths of experience out of which the community will continue to live. Indeed, Marjorie Suchocki points out that because all entities in the universe are internally related and affect one another, the effect of the sermon extends beyond the immediate congregation to the farthest atoms of the universe.[1]

Even though the preacher stops speaking, the sermon is truly not over. The contributions of the sermon are effective as long as life process continues. We might even say that God continues preaching the sermon long after pastor and listener have consciously moved to other topics.

A homily is seldom spoken *to* God. Nevertheless, the process point of view reminds us that a sermon does affect God. When a message is consistent with the divine will for all entities to experience intensity of becoming, it intensifies God's joy. When a message diminishes or distorts God's aims for the world, it grieves the divine spirit. Ministers, then, preach not just to express themselves, nor simply to affect their congregations. In the deepest sense, the preacher speaks with God. That awareness should enhance every preacher's sense of self and vocation.

1. Suchocki, *Whispered Word*, 59–60.

Bibliography

Adam, A. K. M., ed. *Handbook of Postmodern Biblical Interpretation*. St. Louis: Chalice, 2000.

Adeyamo, Tokunboh, ed. *Africa Bible Commentary: A One-Volume Commentary Written by 70 African Scholars*. Rev. ed. Grand Rapids: Zondervan Academic, 2010.

Allen, O. Wesley, Jr. *Determining the Form. Elements of Preaching*. Minneapolis: Fortress, 2009.

———. *Encounter* 78.2 (2018). Issue theme: "Is the Goal of Preaching Still to Proclaim?" 1–80.

———, ed. *The Homiletic of All Believers: A Conversational Approach to Proclamation and Preaching*. Louisville: Westminster John Knox, 2005.

———. *Reading the Synoptic Gospels: Basic Methods for Interpreting Matthew, Mark and Luke*. St. Louis: Chalice, 2000.

———, ed. *The Renewed Homiletic*. Minneapolis: Fortress, 2010.

Allen, O. Wesley, Jr., and Ronald J. Allen. *The Sermon without End: Preaching as Conversation*. Nashville: Abingdon, 2015.

Allen, O. Wesley, Jr., and Carrie La Ferle. *Preaching and the Thirty-Second Commercial: Lessons from Advertising for the Pulpit*. Louisville: Westminster John Knox, 2021.

Allen, Ronald J. "Building Bridges: Pastoral Care for the World in a Prophetic Mode." In *Preaching Prophetic Care: Building Bridges to Justice*, edited by Phillis-Isabella Sheppard et al., 47–59. Eugene, OR: Pickwick Publications, 2018.

———. *Contemporary Biblical Interpretation for Preaching*. Valley Forge, PA: Judson, 1984.

———. "Diversity Is Diverse." In *What's Right with Preaching Today?*, edited by Mike Graves and André Resner, 4–21. Eugene, OR: Cascade Books, 2021.

———. "Feeling and Form in Exegesis and Preaching: An Essay in Hermeneutics and Homiletics Based on the Philosophy of Art of Susanne K. Langer." PhD diss., Drew University, 1977.

———. *Hearing the Sermon: Relationship, Content, Feeling*. St. Louis: Chalice, 2004.

———. *The Life of Jesus for Today*. Louisville: Westminster John Knox, 2008.

———. "The Life of the Preacher as a Context for Preaching." In *Interpreting the Gospel: An Introduction to Preaching*, 54–62. St. Louis: Chalice, 1998.

———. "A Note on Mutual Critical Correlation." In *Preaching the Manifold Grace of God*, edited by Ronald J. Allen, 291–304. Eugene, OR: Cascade Books, 2022.

———. *Patterns of Preaching: A Sermon Sampler*. St. Louis: Chalice, 2018.

————. *Preaching and the Other: Studies of Postmodern Insights*. St. Louis: Chalice, 2009.

————. "Preaching as Conversation among Proposals." In *Handbook of Process Theology*, edited by Jay Bowman and Donna E. Bowman, 78–90. St. Louis: Chalice, 2006.

————. "Preaching as Invitation." In *Adventures of the Spirit: A Guide to Worship from the Perspective of Process Theology*, by Clark M. Williamson and Ronald J. Allen, 138–58. Lanham, MD: University Press of America, 1997.

————. "Preaching as Mutual Critical Correlation." In *Purposes of Preaching*, edited by Jana Childers, 1–22. St. Louis: Chalice, 2004

————. "Preaching as Theological Interpretation through Conversation." In *Interpreting the Gospel: An Introduction to Preaching*, 65–81. St. Louis: Chalice, 1998.

————. *Preaching Is Believing*. Louisville: Westminster John Knox, 2002.

————, ed. *Preaching the Manifold Grace of God*. 2 vols. Eugene, OR: Cascade Books, 2022.

————. *Preaching the Topical Sermon*. Louisville: Westminster John Knox, 1992.

————. *Sermon Treks: Trailways to Creative Preaching*. Nashville: Abingdon, 2015.

————. "Theological Criteria and Interpretive Relationships in the Preaching Conversation." In *Interpreting the Gospel: An Introduction to Preaching*, 82–96. St. Louis: Chalice, 1998.

————. "Theology Undergirding Narrative Preaching." In *What's the Shape of Narrative Preaching?*, edited by Mike Graves and David J. Schlafer, 27–40. St. Louis: Chalice, 2008.

————. *Thinking Theologically: The Preacher as Theologian*. Elements of Preaching. Minneapolis; Fortress, 2008.

————. *Wholly Scripture: Preaching Biblical Themes*. St. Louis: Chalice, 2004.

Augustine, *Confessions*. Translated by Carolyn J. B. Hammond. Loeb Classical Library. Cambridge: Harvard University Press, 2016.

Aulén, Gustaf. *Christus Victor: An Historical Study of the Three Main Types of the Idea of the Atonement*. Translated by A. G. Hebert. 1950. Reprint, Eugene, OR: Wipf & Stock, 2003.

Beardslee, William A. *A House for Hope*. Philadelphia: Westminster, 1972.

————. "Narrative Form in the New Testament and Process Theology." *Encounter* 36 (1975) 301–15.

————. "Openness to the New in Apocalyptic and in Process Theology." *Process Studies* 3 (1973) 169–78.

————. "Process." In *Handbook of Postmodern Biblical Interpretation*, edited by A. K. M. Adam, 199–205. St. Louis: Chalice, 2000.

————. "Recent Hermeneutics and Process Thought." *Process Studies* 12 (1983) 65–76.

————. "Whitehead and Hermeneutic." *Journal of the American Academy of Religion* 47 (1979) 31–37.

Beardslee, William A., and David J. Lull, eds. *New Testament Interpretation from a Process Perspective. Journal of the American Academy of Religion* 47.1 (1979).

————. *Old Testament Interpretation from a Process Perspective. Semeia* 24 (1982).

————. *Romans*. Chalice Commentaries for Today. St. Louis: Chalice, 2004.

Beardslee, William A., with David J. Lull and Barry A. Woodbridge. "Introduction: Process Thought and New Testament Exegesis." *Journal of the American Academy of Religion* 47 (1979) 21–30.

Beardslee, William A., et al. *Biblical Preaching on the Death of Jesus*. Nashville: Abingdon, 1989.

Blomberg, Craig, and Jennifer M. Markley. *Handbook of New Testament Exegesis*. Grand Rapids: Baker Academic, 2017.

Blount, Brian, et al., eds. *True to Our Native Land: An African American New Testament Commentary*. Minneapolis, Fortress, 2007.

Bond, D. Stephenson. *Interactive Preaching*. St. Louis: Chalice, 1991.

Bridgeman, Valerie, and J. Kameron Carter. "Proper 28 [33]." In *Abingdon Theological Companion to the Lectionary. Preaching Year A*, edited by Paul Scott Wilson, 295–330. Nashville: Abingdon, 2013.

Brisman, Leslie. "A Parable of Talent." *Religion and the Arts* 1 (1996) 74–99.

Brown, Delwin. *Boundaries of Our Habitations: Tradition and Theological Construction*. SUNY Series in Religious Studies. Albany: SUNY Press, 1994.

———. "Respect for Rocks." *Encounter* 50 (1989) 309–22.

Brown, Michael Joseph. "Matthew." In *True to Our Native Land: An African American New Testament Commentary*, edited by Brian K. Blount et al. Minneapolis: Fortress, 2007.

Brown, Teresa L. Fry. *Delivering the Sermon; Voice, Body, Animation, and Proclamation*. Elements of Preaching. Minneapolis: Fortress, 2008.

Brunner, Emil. *Man in Revolt: A Christian Anthropology*. Translated by Olive Wyon. Philadelphia: Westminster, 1947.

Bultmann, Rudolf. "Is Exegesis without Presuppositions Possible?" In *Existence and Faith: Shorter Writings of Rudolf Bultmann*, 289–96. Translated by Schubert M. Ogden. New York: Meridian, 1960.

———. *The New Testament and Mythology and Other Early Writings*. Translated and edited by Schubert M. Ogden. Philadelphia: Fortress, 1984.

Butler, Octavia E. *Parable of the Talents*. New York: Seven Stories, 1998.

Buttrick, David G. *Homiletic: Moves and Structures*. Philadelphia: Fortress, 1987.

Calvin, John. *Commentary on a Harmony of the Evangelists, Matthew, Mark, and Luke*. Translated by William Pringle. Grand Rapids: Baker, 2003.

Campbell, Ernest T. "Every Sermon Isn't Armageddon." In *To God Be the Glory: Sermons in Honor of George Arthur Buttrick*, edited by Theodore A. Gill, 145–51. Nashville: Abingdon, 1973.

Carrol, Jackson, et al., eds. *Handbook for Congregational Studies*. Nashville: Abingdon, 1986.

Case-Winters, Anna. *Matthew*. Belief: A Theological Commentary on the Bible. Louisville: Westminster John Knox, 2015.

Cobb, John B. "The Authority of the Bible." *Hermeneutics and the Wordliness of Faith*, edited by Charles Courtney Olin Ivy and Gordon Michalson. *The Drew Gateway* 45 (1974–75) 188–202.

———. *Beyond Dialogue: Towards a Mutual Transformation of Christianity and Buddhism*. 1982. Reprint, Eugene, OR: Wipf & Stock, 1998.

———. *A Christian Natural Theology: Based on the Thought of Alfred North Whitehead*. 2nd ed. Louisville: Westminster John Knox, 2007.

———. *The Process Perspective: Frequently Asked Questions about Process Theology*. Edited by Jeanyne B. Slettom. St. Louis: Chalice, 2003.

———. *The Process Perspective II: Frequently Asked Questions about Process Theology*. Edited by Jeanyne B. Slettom. St. Louis: Chalice, 2011.

————. "Trajectories and Historic Routes." *Semeia* 24 (1982) 89–98.

Cobb, John B., and David Ray Griffin. *Process Theology: An Introductory Exposition.* Louisville: Westminster John Knox, 1976.

Cobb, John B., and Christopher Ives, eds. *The Emptying God: A Buddhist-Christian Conversation.* Eugene, OR: Cascade Books, 2005.

Coleman, Monica. "Introduction to Process Theology." In *Creating Women's Theology: A Movement Engaging Process Thought,* edited by Monica A. Coleman et al., 12–19. Eugene, OR: Pickwick Publications, 2011.

Craddock, Fred B. *As One without Authority.* Revised and with New Sermons. St. Louis: Chalice, 2002.

————. *Preaching.* 25th ann. ed. Nashville: Abingdon, 2018.

Cross, F. L., and E. A. Livingston, eds. *The Oxford Dictionary of the Christian Church.* 3rd ed. Oxford: Oxford University Press, 2005.

Davis, H. Grady. *Design for Preaching.* Philadelphia: Fortress, 1958.

Elliott, Charlotte. "Just As I Am, without One Plea." In *Chalice Hymnal,* edited by Daniel B. Merrick, 339. St. Louis: Chalice, 1998.

Elliot, Mark Barter. *Creative Styles of Preaching.* Louisville: Westminster John Knox, 2000.

Epperly, Bruce. "Dogs and Divinity: The Presence of God in Animals." In *Replanting Ourselves in Beauty: Toward an Ecological Civilization,* edited by Jay McDaniel and Patricia Adams, 77–79. Toward an Ecological Civilization. Anoka, MN: Process Century, 2015.

————. *Process Theology: Embracing Adventure with God.* Gonzalez, FL: Energion, 2014.

————. *Process Theology: A Guide for the Perplexed.* Guides for the Perplexed. London: T. & T. Clark, 2008.

Faber, Roland. *The Becoming of God: Process Philosophy, Theology, and Multi-Religious Engagement.* Cascade Companions. Eugene, OR: Cascade Books, 2017.

————. *God as Poet of the World: Exploring Process Theologies.* Louisville: Westminster John Knox, 2008.

Farley, Edward. "Preaching the Bible and Preaching the Gospel." In *Practicing Gospel: Unconventional Thoughts on the Church's Ministry,* 71–82. Louisville: Westminster John Knox, 2003.

————. "Towards a New Paradigm for Preaching." In *Practicing Gospel: Unconventional Thoughts on the Church's Ministry,* 83–92. Louisville: Westminster John Knox, 2003.

Farmer, Patricia Adams. "The Numinosity of Rocks." In *Replanting Ourselves in Beauty: Toward an Ecological Civilization,* edited by Jay McDaniel and Patricia Adams, 80–87. Anoka, MN: Process Century, 2015.

Farmer, Ronald. *Beyond the Impasse: The Promise of a Process Hermeneutic.* Macon, GA: Mercer University Press, 1977.

————. *Process Theology and Biblical Interpretation.* Topical Line Drives. Gonzalez: Energion, 2021.

————. *Revelation.* Chalice Commentaries for Today. St. Louis: Chalice, 2005.

Farris, Stephen. *Preaching That Matters: The Bible and Our Lives.* Louisville: Westminster John Knox, 1998.

Fee, Gordon. *New Testament Exegesis: A Handbook for Students and Pastors.* 3rd ed. Louisville: Westminster John Knox, 2002.

Florence, Anna Carter. *Preaching as Testimony.* Louisville: Westminster John Knox, 2007.

Ford, Lewis. *The Lure of God: A Biblical Background for Process Theism.* Philadelphia: Fortress, 1978.

Foskett, Mary, and Jeffrey Kuan, eds. *Ways of Being, Ways of Reading: Asian American Biblical Interpretation.* St. Louis: Chalice, 2006.

Frank, Thomas Edward. *The Soul of the Congregation: An Invitation to Congregational Reflection.* Nashville: Abingdon, 2000.

Franklin, Stephen T. *Speaking from the Depths: Alfred North Whitehead's Hermeneutical Metaphysics of Propositions, Experience, Symbolism, Language, and Religion.* Grand Rapids: Eerdmans, 1990.

Fretheim, Terence E. "Genesis." In *The New Interpreter's Bible,* edited by Leander Keck et al., 1:19–374. Nashville: Abingdon, 1994.

———. *God and World in the Old Testament: A Relational Theology of Creation.* Nashville: Abingdon, 2010.

———. *God So Enters into Relationships: A Biblical View.* Word and World Book 8. Minneapolis: Fortress, 2020.

———. *The Suffering of God: An Old Testament Perspective.* Overtures to Biblical Theology. Philadelphia: Fortress, 1984.

Gaarden, Marianne. *The Third Room of Preaching: A New Empirical Approach.* Eugene, OR: Pickwick Publications, 2021.

Gadamer, Hans. *Truth and Method.* Translated by Joel Weinsheimer and Donald J. Marshall. Bloomsbury Revelations Series. New York: Bloomsbury, 2013.

George, Timothy, ed. *Reformation Commentary on Scripture.* 20 vols. Downers Grove, IL: IVP Academic, 2011–.

Gilkey, Langdon. "God." In *Christian Theology: An Introduction to Its Traditions and Tasks,* edited by Peter C. Hodgson and Robert B. King, 88–119. 2nd ed. Philadelphia: Fortress, 1985.

Gnuse, Robert K. *The Old Testament and Process Theology.* St. Louis: Chalice, 2000.

Gorman, Michael J. *Elements of Biblical Exegesis: A Basic Guide for Students and Ministers.* Revised and expanded edition. Grand Rapids: Baker Academic, 2020.

Gossai, Hemchand, ed. *Postcolonial Commentary on the Old Testament.* New York: T. & T. Clark, 2019.

Green, Joel B., ed. *Hearing the New Testament: Strategies for Interpretation.* 2nd ed. Grand Rapids: Eerdmans, 2010.

Griffin, David R. "Religious Pluralism." In *Handbook of Process Theology,* edited by Jay McDaniel and Donna Bowman, 49–58. St. Louis: Chalice, 2006.

———. *Varieties of Postmodern Theology.* SUNY Series in Constructive Postmodern Thought. Albany: State University of New York Press, 1989.

Guest, Deryn, et al. *The Queer Bible Commentary.* London: SCM, 2015.

Gunter, Stephen W., et al. *Wesley and the Quadrilateral: Renewing the Conversation.* Nashville: Abingdon, 1997.

Hamilton, Neill Q. *Jesus for a No-God World.* Philadelphia: Westminster, 1969.

Hartshorne, Charles. "The Logic of Ultimate Contrasts." In *Creative Synthesis and Philosophic Methods,* 99–110. LaSalle, IL: Open Court, 1970.

Hartshorne, Charles, and William L. Reese, eds. *Philosophers Speak of God.* Chicago: University of Chicago Press, 1953.

Hayes, John H., and Carl R. Holliday. *Biblical Exegesis: A Beginner's Handbook.* 3rd ed. Nashville: Abingdon, 2007.

Henley, William Ernest. "Invictus." https://poets.org/poem/invictus?gclid= CjoKCQjwqfz6BRD8ARIsAIXQCf2HwfSohPdTu_BBV6E_ Q7iQjkxgffl54wXs2Kmoh2jQ8oUdszmkajUaAqN8EALw_wcB.

Heraclitus. "You Never Step into the Same River Twice." In *Heraclitus*, by Philip Wheelwright, 29. Princeton: Princeton University Press, 1959.

Herzog, William R., II. *Parables as Subversive Speech: Jesus as Pedagogue of the Oppressed.* Louisville: Westminster John Knox, 1994.

Hogan, Lucy Lind. *Graceful Speech: An Invitation to Preaching.* Louisville: Westminster John Knox, 2006.

Holbert, John C., and Ronald J. Allen. *Holy Root, Holy Branches: Christian Preaching from the Old Testament.* Nashville: Abingdon, 1995.

Hollander, John. *Powers of Thirteen: Poems.* New York: Atheneum, 1983.

Hosinski, Thomas E. *Stubborn Fact and Creative Advance: An Introduction to the Metaphysics of Alfred North Whitehead.* Lanham: Rowman & Littlefield, 1993.

Janzen, J. Gerald. *Abraham and All the Families of the Earth: A Commentary on the Book of Genesis 12–50.* International Theological Commentary. Grand Rapids: Eerdmans, 1993.

———. *Exodus.* Westminster Bible Companion. Louisville: Westminster John Knox, 1997.

———. *Job.* Interpretation. Atlanta: John Knox, 1985.

———. "Modes of Power and the Divine Relativity." *Encounter* 36 (1975) 379–406.

———. "The Old Testament in 'Process' Perspective: Proposal for a Way Forward in Biblical Theology." In *Magnalia Dei: The Mighty Acts of God*, edited by Frank Moore Cross et al., 480–509. Garden City, NY: Doubleday, 1976.

Jordan, Clarence, and Bill Lane Doulos. *Cotton Patch Parables of Liberation.* Scottdale, PA: Herald, 1976.

Junior, Nyasha. *An Introduction to Womanist Biblical Interpretation.* Louisville: Westminster John Knox, 2015.

Karia, Akash. *TED Talks Storytelling: 23 Storytelling Techniques from the Best TED Talks.* Charleston, SC: CreateSpace, 2015.

Keller, Catherine. *Apocalypse Now and Then: A Feminist Guide to the End of the World.* Boston: Beacon, 1996.

———. *On the Mystery: Discerning God in Process.* Minneapolis: Fortress, 2008.

Kelsey, David. "Human Being." In *Christian Theology: An Introduction to Its Traditions and Tasks*, edited by Peter C. Hodgson and Robert H. King, 167–93. Rev. ed. Philadelphia: Fortress, 1985.

———. "The Theological Use of Scripture in Process Hermeneutics." *Process Studies* 13.3 (1983) 181–88.

———. "The Theological Uses of Scripture in Process Hermeneutics." *Process Studies* 13 (1983) 181–88.

———. *The Uses of Scripture in Recent Theology.* Philadelphia: Fortress, 1975.

Kennel-Shank, Celeste. "At Gilead Church in Chicago, Storytelling Is Central to Worship." https://www.christiancentury.org/article/features/gilead-church-chicago-storytelling-central-worship.

Klein, William W., et al. *Introduction to Biblical Interpretation.* 3rd ed. Grand Rapids: Zondervan, 2017.

Knight, Douglas A. *Methods of Biblical Interpretation*. Nashville: Abingdon, 2004.

Langer, Susanne K. *Feeling and Form: A Theory of Art*. New York: Scribner's, 1955.

————. *Philosophical Sketches*. Baltimore: Johns Hopkins University Press, 1962.

————. *Philosophy in a New Key: A Study in the Symbolism of Reason, Rite, and Art*. 3rd ed. Cambridge: Harvard University Press, 1957.

Levine, Amy-Jill, and Marc Zvi Brettler, eds. *The Jewish Annotated New Testament: Revised Standard Version Translation*. New York: Oxford University Press, 2011.

Locke, John. *An Essay Concerning Human Understanding*. Edited by K. P. Winkler. Indianapolis: Hackett, 1996.

Long, Jeffery D. "A Whiteheadian Vedanta: Outline of a Hindu Process Theology." In *Handbook of Process Theology*, edited by Jay McDaniel and Donna Bowman, 262–73. St. Louis: Chalice, 2006.

Long, Thomas G. *Preaching and the Literary Forms of the Bible*. Philadelphia: Fortress, 1988.

————. *Testimony: Talking Ourselves into Being Christian*. San Francisco: Jossey-Bass, 2004.

————. *The Witness of Preaching*. 3rd ed. Louisville: Westminster John Knox, 2016.

Long, Thomas G., and Cornelius Plantinga, eds. *A Chorus of Witnesses: Model Sermons for Today's Preacher*. Louisville: Westminster John Knox, 1994.

Lose, David J. "Preaching as Conversation." In *Under the Oak Tree: The Church as Community of Conversation in a Conflicted and Pluralistic World*, edited by Ronald J. Allen et al., 71–92. Eugene, OR: Cascade Books, 2013.

Lowe, Victor. *Alfred North Whitehead: The Man and His Work*. 2 vols. Baltimore: Johns Hopkins University Press, 1985.

Lowry, Eugene L. *The Homiletical Plot: The Sermon as Narrative Art Form*. Expanded edition. Louisville: Westminster John Knox, 2000.

————. *How to Preach a Parable: Designs for Narrative Sermons*. Nashville: Abingdon, 1989.

Lozada, Francisco, Jr., and Fernando F. Segovia. *Latino/a Theology and the Bible: Ethnic-Racial Reflections on Interpretation*. Minneapolis: Fortress Academic, 2021.

Lubarsky, Sandra B. "Covenant and Responsible Creativity: Towards a Jewish Process Theology." In *Handbook of Process Theology*, edited by Jan McDaniel and Donna Bowman, 274–85. St. Louis: Chalice, 2006.

Lull, David. "The Spirit and the Creative Transformation of Human Existence." *Journal of the American Academy of Religion* 47 (1979), 39–55.

————. *The Spirit in Galatia: Paul's Interpretation of PNEUMA as Divine Power*. Society of Biblical Literature Dissertation Series 49. Eugene, OR: Wipf & Stock, 2006.

————. "What Is 'Process Hermeneutics'?" *Process Studies* 13 (1983) 189–201.

Lull, David J., and William A. Beardslee. *First Corinthians*. Chalice Commentaries for Today. Revised and expanded edition. St. Louis: Chalice, 2007.

Lundeen, Lyman. "The Authority of the Word in a Process Perspective." *Encounter* 36 (1975) 281–301.

————. *Risk and Rhetoric in Religion: Whitehead's Theory of Language and the Discourse of Faith*. Philadelphia: Fortress, 1972.

Luther, Martin. *Festival Sermons of Martin Luther: The Church Postils: Sermons for the Main Festivals and Saints Days of the Church Year: Winter and Summer Seasons*. Translated by Joel R. Baseley. Dearborn: Mark V, 2005.

Luther, Martin. *Luther's Works*. Vol. 54, *Table Talk*. Translated by Theodore G. Tappert. Edited by Helmut T. Lehman. Philadelphia: Fortress Press, 1959.

Malherbe, Abraham. "The Task and Methods of Exegesis." In *Light from the Gentiles: Hellenistic Philosophy and Early Christianity*, edited by Carl R. Holladay et al., 27–40. Supplements to Vetus Testamentum 150. Leiden: Brill, 2014.

McClure, John S., et. al. *Listening to Listeners: Homiletical Case Studies*. Channels of Listening. St. Louis: Chalice, 2004.

———. *The Roundtable Pulpit: Where Leadership and Preaching Meet*. Nashville: Abingdon, 1995.

McDaniel, Jay E. *Earth, Sky, Gods, and Mortals: Developing an Ecological Spirituality*. 1990. Reprint, Eugene, OR: Wipf & Stock, 2008.

———. *Ghandi's Truth: Learning from the World's Religions as a Path Toward Peace*. New York: Orbis, 2005.

———. *Of God and Pelicans: A Theology of Reverence for Life*. Louisville: Westminster John Knox, 1989.

———. *What Is Process Thought? Seven Answers to Seven Questions*. Anoka, MN: Process Century, 2021.

McDaniel, Jay E., and Donna Bowman, eds. *Handbook of Process Theology*. St. Louis: Chalice, 2006.

McDaniel, Jay E., and Patricia Adams Farmer, eds. *Replanting Ourselves in Beauty: Toward an Ecological Civilization*. Anoka, MN: Process Century, 2015.

McFarland, Ian, ed. *The Cambridge Dictionary of Christian Theology*. Cambridge: Cambridge University Press, 2014.

McKenzie, Alyce M. *Novel Preaching: Tips from Top Writers Crafting Creative Sermons*. Louisville: Westminster John Knox, 2010.

McKenzie, Stephen L., and Stephen R. Haynes, eds. *To Each Its Own Meaning: An Introduction to Biblical Criticisms and Their Applications*. Revised and expanded edition. Louisville: Westminster John Knox, 1999.

McKenzie, Stephen L., and John Kaltner, eds. *New Meanings for Ancient Texts: Recent Approaches to Biblical Criticisms and Their Applications*. Louisville: Westminster John Knox, 2013.

McKim, Donald, ed. *The Westminster Dictionary of Theological Terms*. 2nd ed. Louisville: Westminster John Knox, 2014.

Meland, Bernard E. *Fallible Forms and Symbols: Discourses on Method in a Theology of Culture*. Philadelphia: Fortress, 1976.

Mesle, C. Robert. *Process-Relational Philosophy: An Introduction to Alfred North Whitehead*. West Conshohocken, PA: Templeton, 2008.

———. *Process Theology: A Basic Introduction*. St. Louis: Chalice, 1993.

Milton, John. *The Complete Poems of John Milton: With Introduction and Notes*. New York: Collier, 1909.

Mitchell, Henry. *Black Preaching: The Recovery of a Powerful Art*. Nashville: Abingdon, 1990.

Moth, The. "About the Moth." https://themoth.org/about.

———. "The Moth on Tumblr." https://moth-stories.tumblr.com/post/28431369982/telling-a-story-tonight-the-rules-and-guidelines/amp.

Network of Biblical Storytellers. "Resources." https://www.nbsint.org/resources/.

Newsome, Carol A., et al., eds. *The Women's Bible Commentary*, Louisville: Westminster John Knox, 2012.

Niebuhr, H. Richard. *The Meaning of Revelation*. 1941. Reprint, Louisville: Westminster John Knox, 2006.

Niebuhr, Reinhold. *An Interpretation of Christian Ethics*. New York: Meridian, 1956.

———. *The Nature and Destiny of Man*. 2 vols. New York: Scribner, 1964.

Nieman, James. *Knowing the Context: Frames, Tools, and Signs for Preaching*. Elements of Preaching. Minneapolis: Fortress, 2008.

Nieman, James R., and Thomas G. Rogers. *Preaching to Every Pew: Cross-Cultural Strategies*. Minneapolis: Fortress, 2001.

O'Day, Gail R., and David L. Peterson, eds. *Theological Biblical Commentary*. Louisville: Westminster John Knox, 2009.

Oden, Thomas C., ed. *Ancient Christian Commentary on Scripture*. 29 vols. Downers Grove, IL: InterVarsity, 1998–2006.

Oden, Thomas C., et al., eds. *Ancient Christian Texts*. Downers Grove, IL: IVP Academic, 2009–.

Okey, Stephen. *A Theology of Conversation: An Introduction to David Tracy*. Collegeville, MN: Liturgical, 2018.

Ong, Walter. *Orality and Literacy: The Technologizing of the Word*. 30th anniversary ed. New York: Routledge, 2002.

———. *The Presence of the Word: Some Prolegomena for Cultural and Religious History*. New Haven: Yale University Press, 1967.

Page, Hugh, Jr., ed. *The Africana Bible: Reading Israel's Scriptures from Africa and from the Africa Diaspora*. Minneapolis: Fortress, 2010.

Pagitt, Doug. *Preaching in the Inventive Age*. Minneapolis: Sparkhouse, 2011. Originally published as *Preaching Re-Imagined: The Role of the Sermon in Communities of Faith*. Grand Rapids: Zondervan, 2005.

Park, Richard Hee-Chun. *Organic Homiletic: Samuel T. Coleridge, Henry G. Davis, and the New Homiletic*. American University Studies 251. New York: Lang, 2006.

Patte, Daniel, ed. *The Global Bible Commentary*. Nashville: Abingdon, 2004.

Pauw, Amy Plantinga, and William C. Placher, eds. *Belief: A Theological Commentary on the Bible*. Louisville: Westminster John Knox, 2010–.

Pittenger, Norman. *Picturing God*. London: SCM, 1982.

———. *Preaching the Gospel*. Wilton, CT: Morehouse-Barlow, 1984.

———. *Proclaiming Christ Today*. Greenwich, CT: Seabury, 1962.

Pixley, Jorge. *Jeremiah*. Chalice Commentaries for Today. St. Louis: Chalice, 2004.

Pollard, Adelaide A. "Have Thine Own Way, Lord!" In *Chalice Hymnal*, edited by Daniel Merrick, 588. St. Louis: Chalice, 1995.

Powery, Emerson. "Matthew." In *True to Our Native Land: An African American New Testament Commentary*, edited by Brian Blount, 85–120. Minneapolis, Fortress, 2007.

Pregeant, Russell. *Christology beyond Dogma: Matthew's Christ in Process Hermeneutic*. Society of Biblical Literature Semeia Supplements. Philadelphia: Fortress, 1978.

———. *Engaging the New Testament: An Interdisciplinary Introduction*. Minneapolis: Fortress, 1997.

———. *Matthew*. Chalice Commentaries for Today. St. Louis: Chalice, 2004.

———. *Mystery without Magic*. Oak Park, IL: Meyer-Stone, 1988.

———. *Reading the Bible for All the Wrong Reasons*. Minneapolis: Fortress, 2011.

———. "Scripture and Revelation." In *Handbook of Process Theology*, edited by Jay McDaniel and Donna Bowman, 67–77. St. Louis: Chalice, 2006.

———. "Where Is the Meaning? Metaphysical Criticism and the Problem of Indeterminancy." *Journal of Religion* 63 (1983) 107–24.

Proctor, Samuel D. *The Certain Sound of the Trumpet: Crafting a Sermon of Authority.* Valley Forge, PA: Judson, 1994.

Reid, Robert S., et al. "Preaching as the Creation of Experience: The Not-so-Rational Revolution of the New Homiletic." *Journal of Communication and Religion* 18 (1995) 19.

Rhoads, David. "What Is Performance Criticism?" In *The Bible in Ancient and Modern Media: Story and Performance,* edited by Holly E. Hearon and Philip Ruge-Jones, 83–100. Biblical Performance Criticism Series 1. Eugene, OR: Cascade Books, 2009.

Robinson, Haddon W. *Biblical Preaching: The Development and Delivery of Expository Messages.* 3rd ed. Grand Rapids: Baker Academic, 2014.

Rose, Lucy Atkinson. *Sharing the Word: Preaching in the Roundtable Church.* Louisville: Westminster John Knox, 1997.

Rossiter, Phyllis. "I'm from Missouri—You'll Have to Show Me." *Rural Missouri* 42.3 (1989) 16.

Roy, David E. "The Creative Adventure of Pastoral Counseling: Process Assurances and Illuminations." In *Handbook of Process Theology,* edited by Jay Bowman and Donna E. Bowman, 103–16. St. Louis: Chalice, 2006.

Ruge-Jones. Phil. "Preparing to Perform." https://www.biblicalperformancecriticism. org/index.php/49-news/announcements/sbl-2012-chicago/77-preparing-to-perform.

Rzepka, Jane, and Kenneth Sawyer. *Thematic Preaching: An Introduction.* St. Louis: Chalice, 2001.

Saiving, Valerie. "The Human Situation: A Feminine View." *Journal of Religion* 40 (1960) 100–112.

Sanders, James A. *Canon and Community: A Guide to Canonical Criticism.* Guides to Biblical Scholarship. 1984. Reprint, Eugene, OR: Wipf & Stock, 2000.

———. *Torah and Canon.* 2nd ed. Eugene, OR: Cascade Books, 2005.

Sangster, W. E. *The Craft of Preaching.* Philadelphia: Westminster, 1951.

Schlafer, David. *Your Way with God's Word: Discovering Your Distinctive Preaching Voice.* Boston: Cowley, 1995.

Schottroff, Luise. *The Parables of Jesus.* Translated by Linda M. Maloney. Minneapolis: Fortress, 2006.

Schüssler Fiorenza, Elizabeth, ed. *Searching the Scriptures: A Feminist Commentary.* 2 vols. New York: Crossroad, 2004.

Schweitzer, Albert. *The Quest of the Historical Jesus.* Translated by W. Montgomery et al. First Complete Edition. Fortress Classics in Biblical Studies. Edited by John Bowden. Minneapolis: Fortress, 2001.

Seeberg, Reinhold. *The History of Doctrines.* 2 vols. Translated by Charles E. Hay. Grand Rapids: Baker, 1977.

Segovia, Fernando F., and R. S. Sugirtharajah, eds. *A Postcolonial Commentary on the New Testament Writings.* New York: T. & T. Clark, 2009.

Senokoane, B. B. Tumi. "A Black Reading of the Parable of the Talents." *Black Theology* 18 (2020) 288–98.

Sheppard, Phillis-Isabella, et al., eds. *Preaching Prophetic Care: Building Bridges to Justice.* Eugene, OR: Pickwick Publications, 2018.

Sherburne, Donald W. *A Key to Whitehead's Process and Reality.* Chicago: University of Chicago Press, 1966.

Sigmon, Casey Thornburgh. "Engaging the Gadfly: A Process Homilecclesiology for a Digital Age." PhD diss., Vanderbilt University, 2017.

———. "Preaching from the Perspective of the Process Theology Family." In *Preaching the Manifold Grace of God,* edited by Ronald J. Allen, 000–000[X-REF]. Eugene, OR: Cascade Books, 2021.

Simonetti, Manilo. *Matthew 14–28.* Ancient Christian Commentary on Scripture. Downers Grove, IL: InterVarsity, 2002.

Snodgrass, Klyne R. *Stories with Intent: A Comprehensive Guide to the Parables of Jesus.* Grand Rapids: Eerdmans, 2008.

Soulen, Kendall. *Handbook of Biblical Criticism.* 4th ed. Louisville: Westminster John Knox, 2011.

Steimle, Edmund A., et al. *Preaching the Story.* Philadelphia: Fortress, 1980.

Steussy, Marti J. *Psalms.* Chalice Commentaries for Today. St. Louis; Chalice, 2004.

Stone, Howard W., and James O. Duke. *How to Think Theologically.* 3rd ed. Minneapolis: Fortress, 2013.

Stuart, Douglas. *Old Testament Exegesis: A Handbook for Students and Pastors.* 4th ed. Louisville: Westminster John Knox, 2009.

Suchocki, Marjorie. *Divinity and Diversity: A Christian Affirmation of Religious Pluralism.* Nashville: Abingdon, 2003.

———. *The End of Evil: Eschatology in Historical Context.* Eugene, OR: Wipf & Stock, 2005.

———. *The Fall to Violence.* New Edition. New York: Continuum, 1995.

———. *God, Christ, Church: A Practical Guide to Process Theology.* Rev. ed. New York: Crossroad, 1999.

———. *In God's Presence: Theological Reflections on Prayer.* St. Louis: Chalice, 2004.

———. *The Whispered Word: A Theology of Preaching.* St. Louis: Chalice, 1999.

Tate, W. Randolph. *Biblical Interpretation: An Integrated Approach.* Grand Rapids: Baker Academic, 2014.

———. *Interpreting the Bible: A Handbook of Terms and Methods.* Grand Rapids: Baker Academic, 2006.

"TED Talks." https://www.ted.com/about/programs-initiatives/ted-talks.

Thomas, Frank A. *Introduction to the Practice of African American Preaching.* Nashville: Abingdon, 2016.

———. *They Like To Never Quit Praisin' God.* Rev. ed. Cleveland: Pilgrim, 2013.

Tiffany, Frederick C., and Sharon L. Ringe. *Biblical Interpretation: A Roadmap.* Nashville: Abingdon, 1996.

Tillich, Paul. *Systematic Theology.* 3 vols. in 1. Chicago: University of Chicago Press, 1967.

———. "You Are Accepted." In *The Shaking of the Foundations,* 153–63. New York: Scribner's, 1948.

Tisdale, Leonora Tubbs. *Preaching as Local Theology and Folk Art.* Fortress Resources for Preaching. Minneapolis: Fortress, 1997.

———. *Prophetic Preaching: A Pastoral Approach.* Louisville: Westminster John Knox, 2010.

Tönsing, J. Gertrude. "Scolding the 'Wicked, Lazy' Servant: Is the Master God? A Redaction-Critical Study of Matthew 25:14–30 and Luke 19:11–27. *Neotesta-menica.* 53 (2019) 123–47.

Tracy, David. *The Analogical Imagination: Christian Theology and the Culture of Pluralism.* New York: Crossroad, 1981.

———. *Blessed Rage for Order: The New Pluralism in Theology.* New York: Seabury, 1975.

———. "Hermeneutical Reflections on the New Paradigm." In *Paradigm Change in Theology*, edited by Hans Küng and David Tracy, 334–62. Translated by Margaret Kohl. Edinburgh: T. & T. Clark, 1989.

———. *Plurality and Ambiguity: Hermeneutics, Religion, and Hope.* San Francisco: Harper & Row, 1987.

———. "Theological Method." In *Christian Theology: An Introduction*, edited by Peter C. Hodgson and Robert H. King, 35–60. Philadelphia: Fortress, 1985.

Troeger, Thomas H. *Imagining a Sermon.* Nashville: Abingdon, 1990.

Upong, Justin. "The Parable of the Talents (Matt 25:14–30): Commendation or Critique of Exploitation? A Social-Historical and Theological Reading." *Neotestamenica* 46 (2012) 190–207.

Ward, Richard F., and David Trobisch. *Bringing the Word to Life: Engaging the New Testament through Performing It.* Grand Rapids: Eerdmans, 2013.

———. *Speaking of the Holy: The Art of Communication in Preaching.* Nashville: Abingdon, 2001.

Weaver, J. Denny. *The Nonviolent Atonement.* 2nd ed. Grand Rapids: Eerdmans, 2011.

Weeden, Theodore J. "The Potential and Promise of a Process Hermeneutic." *Encounter* 36 (1975) 316–30.

Welchel, Hugh. "Five Lessons for Our Lives from the Parable of the Talents." https://tifwe.org/five-lessons-for-our-lives-from-the-parable-of-the-talents/.

Wesley, Charles. "Love Divine, All Loves Excelling." In *Chalice Hymnal*, edited by Daniel Merrick, 517. St. Louis: Chalice, 1995.

Wheelwright, Philip. *The Burning Fountain: A Study in the Language of Symbolism.* 1954. Reprint, Bloomington: University of Indiana Press, 1968.

———. *Heraclitus.* Princeton: Princeton University Press, 1959.

———. *Metaphor and Reality.* Bloomington: Indiana University Press, 1962.

Whitehead, Alfred North. *Adventures of Ideas.* 1933. Reprint, New York: Free Press, 1961.

———. *The Aims of Education and Other Essays.* 1919. Reprint, New York: Free Press, 1967.

———. *Modes of Thought.* 1938. Reprint, New York: Free Press, 1966.

———. *Process and Reality.* Corrected Edition. Edited by David Ray Griffin and Donald W. Sherburne. 1929. Reprint, New York: Free Press, 1978.

———. *Religion in the Making.* New York: Macmillan, 1930.

———. *Science and the Modern World.* 1925. Reprint, New York: Free Press, 1967.

———. *Symbolism: Its Meaning and Effect.* 1927. Reprint, New York: Capricorn, 1959.

Williams, Daniel Day. *God's Grace and Man's Hope: An Interpretation of Christian Life in History.* 1949. Reprint, New York: Harper & Row, 1965.

———. *The Spirit and the Forms of Love.* New York: Harper & Row, 1968.

Williamson, Clark M. "The Dialogue between Christians and Jews." In *Handbook of Process Theology*, edited by Jay McDaniel and Donna Bowman, 59–66. St. Louis: Chalice, 2006.

———. *God Is Never Absent*. St. Louis: Chalice, 1977.

———. "Preaching as Conversation." *Encounter* 78 (2018) 71–76.

———. "Process Hermeneutics and Christianity's Post-Holocaust Reinterpretation of Itself." *Process Studies* 12 (1982) 77–93.

———. *Way of Blessing/Way of Life: A Christian Theology*. St. Louis; Chalice, 1998.

Williamson, Clark M., and Ronald J. Allen. *Adventures of the Spirit: A Guide to Worship from the Perspective of Process Theology*. Lanham, MD: University Press of America, 1997.

———. *A Credible and Timely Word: Process Theology and Preaching*. St. Louis: Chalice, 1999.

Wilson, Paul Scott, ed. *Abingdon Theological Commentary on the Lectionary*. 3 vols. Nashville: Abingdon, 2012–14.

———. *Abingdon Theological Companion to the Lectionary*. Nashville: Abingdon, Year A: 2013. Year B: 2014. Year C: 2012.

———. *The Four Pages of the Sermon: A Guide to Biblical Preaching*. Rev. ed. Nashville: Abingdon, 2018.

———. *The Practice of Preaching*. Rev. ed. Abingdon, Nashville, 2007.

———. "Preaching, Performance, and the Life and Death of 'Now.'" In *Performance in Preaching: Bringing the Sermon to Life*, edited by Jana Childers and Clayton J. Schmit, 37–52. Grand Rapids: Baker Academic, 2008.

Winston, Bruce E. *Biblical Principles of Being an Employee in Contemporary Organizations*. New York: Palgrave Macmillan, 2019.

———. *Biblical Principles of Hiring and Developing Employees*. New York: Macmillan, 2018.

Wintle, Brian, et al., eds. *South Asia Bible Commentary: A One-Volume Commentary on the Whole Bible*. Grand Rapids: Zondervan Academic, 2015

Woodbridge, Barry. "An Assessment and a Prospectus for a Process Hermeneutic." *Journal of the American Academy of Religion* 47 (1979) 212–28.

———. "Process Hermeneutics: An Approach to Biblical Texts." In *Society of Biblical Literature Seminar Papers*, edited by Paul J. Achtemeier, 79–87. Missoula: Scholars, 1977.

"World Café (Conversation)." https://en.wikipedia.org/wiki/World_caf%C3%A9_(conversation).